NAVAL POWER AND TRADE
IN THE MEDITERRANEAN
A.D. 500 TO 1100

PRINCETON STUDIES IN HISTORY

Naval Power
and Trade
in the Mediterranean
A.D. 500-1100

BY ARCHIBALD R. LEWIS

Princeton University Press, Princeton, New Jersey

1951

Printed in the United States of America by
Princeton University Press at Princeton, New Jersey

To

D. H. L.

Companion, Friend, and More

Preface

Fifty years ago Mahan introduced to the scholarly world the concept of the importance of sea power in history. Since that time many talented historians of the ancient, late medieval, and modern periods have examined the influence that the control of the seas has had on their fields of historical study. Yet sea power during the period from 500 to 1100 A.D., with the exception of certain modest fragmentary contributions, has been almost totally neglected. Pirenne, it is true, in his *Mahomet et Charlemagne* pointed out the importance that control of the sea had in the formation of a Western European nexus feudalized and separate from the Byzantine and Moslem worlds nearby. He had earlier emphasized in his *Medieval Cities* the crucial part played by the reopening of the Mediterranean to Western commerce sometime in the eleventh century. Though there has been much disagreement about certain aspects of his theories, none has denied the importance of his conceptions to a proper understanding of those six confused and disturbed centuries in Mediterranean history. Unfortunately Pirenne, having emphasized the importance of sea power, never really examined it, except as he conceived it to have affected Western Europe and more particularly that portion of Southern Europe along the coasts of Northwestern Italy and Southern France. More careful examination is necessary to make clear, first, how sea power operated in the early medieval period, and also just what was its influence on Mediterranean trade and history.

The greatest barrier, however, to a full appreciation and study of this subject comes from another source. The Arab invasions of the seventh and eighth centuries and the Iconoclast heresy that followed on their heels did more than divide the Mediterranean world into three rather distinct culture areas, Western European, Byzantine and Moslem. They have, since those times, divided historians in a similar way. This has made it difficult for scholars to view the Mediterranean Sea as a unit, which of course it is from the standpoint of sea power. Seas do not divide. They join. They are not barriers, but highways to those who have the means to cross them. Particularly was this so before the coming of the modern railroad, highway and airplane. Today North and South America resemble Western Europe, though thousands of miles of water separate them from it, far more than the latter resembles Eastern Europe nearby. This is the effect of the sea-connection made possible by control of the seas.

Yet most medievalists seem to gaze on the Mediterranean from Rome or some part of Italy, from France or Germany or even England. Most Byzantine scholars seem firmly ensconced in the mighty city of Constantinople as they look north to the Black Sea or south through the island-studded Aegean to the Middle Sea beyond. Most Arabists appear from their writings to be seated in Damascus, Bagdad, Cairo, Kairouan, Palermo or Cordova. Even the Slavists look out from the Balkans or the steppes of South Russia. Few indeed are those who, like Lopez and Vasiliev, have the wider view. The result, from the standpoint of the Mediterranean and its sea power, has been the loss of the whole in the sum of its parts and an outstanding failure in perspective.

This study is an endeavor to avoid such pitfalls. It attempts to view the Mediterranean as a whole, with the Black Sea as an integral part of it, from the year A.D. 500 to the year A.D. 1100. The former date saw the collapse of the Roman Empire in the West. It marked the end of an era in Mediterranean history that had lasted approximately six hundred years—a period when all of the shores of this inland sea were controlled by a single imperial destiny. The latter date witnessed the beginning of a new era, for by that time the Mediterranean had fallen into the hands of mariners from Western Europe. In their hands it has remained, with the exception of a brief Ottoman interlude in the sixteenth century, until the present day.

The problems of such a study are staggering. They concern largely the sources available. Pertinent source material is scattered and for certain crucial periods extremely scanty. It is, for instance, difficult to ascertain many facts about the very important late sixth, seventh and eighth centuries. Wide acquaintanceship with Byzantine annalists, Arab geographers and historians, monkish Syriac, Coptic, Armenian and Russian scriveners and Western European chroniclers and records is essential before it is possible to piece together even the barest outline of events for certain periods. The unreliability of the figures given by Arabic historians and annalists is also a problem. Thus the historian must interpret often with far too little to guide him, and must make use of later sources to throw light on earlier events. Happily, he can rely most heavily

on the fine scholarship contributed in the last eighty years in the
three major fields in which his inquiry must lead him. Without
the keen intellect and labors of Boak, Bury, Charanis, Diehl,
Grégoire, Runciman, Schlumberger and Vasiliev in the Byzantine
field; without Bloch, Dopsch, Gay, Halphen, Lopez and Pirenne
in Western European history; without Hitti and Mez in the general Arabic field and Dozy and Lévi-Provençal on Spain, Amari
on Sicily, Gautier and Marçais on North Africa and Lane-Poole
and Wiet on Egypt—to mention only a few, this work would not
be possible. The classic studies on trade by Heyd and Schaube
have also been invaluable in establishing a broad perspective.

Another problem presented is that of dating specific events.
Frequently Arabic, Byzantine, and Western authorities differ
widely in the date they assign to the same happening. Partly this
lies in the fact that their calendar systems are so different. Since
this work is intended for the general as well as the scholarly
reader, the liberty has been taken in many cases of choosing arbi-
trarily a certain date and eliminating other possibilities. It can
only be hoped that the choices made have generally been in ac-
cordance with the best informed opinion in the field. If not, the
author must bear all responsibility for over-simplification. In the
same spirit all references in footnotes are given as far as possible
from translated sources. Partly this is due to the author's own lack
of familiarity with the original Coptic, Syriac, Arabic and Medieval
Greek. Partly it is a desire to make it easier for the reader to follow
footnote references. In eliminating as far as possible multiple footnote references a similar policy has been followed in the interest
of simplicity and readability. It is hoped that the scholarly reader
will forgive these presumptions.

In addition, it should be emphasized that not all the problems
raised in these pages are answered satisfactorily. Some, perhaps,
are unanswerable in any definitive way. Others may be clarified
by further work in provincial Byzantine sources, scant though
they are, in the vast still-unedited collections of Egyptian papyri,
and in the labor that is proceeding apace in the economic aspects
of Islamic culture and civilization. The author must regret his own
limited knowledge and lack of omniscience. He hopes, however,
that it may be considered more important at this stage to ask the
right questions than to get all the right answers. It is in that spirit
that he has proceeded with this study.

It should be noted, as well, that this volume contains no general bibliographical section. Partially this is because an exhaustive bibliography in this vast field would require almost as many pages as the text itself. But mainly it is because an excellent and complete bibliography is already available, that compiled by Dr. R. S. Lopez in his article on Medieval Mediterranean trade and commerce in *The Cambridge Economic History*, Vol. II, soon to appear.

The author wishes to thank many friends and colleagues for their assistance. First he wishes to thank the University of South Carolina and the American Council of Learned Societies whose generous financial aid made both the research for and writing of this work possible. He wishes also to thank Dr. R. S. Lopez of Yale University for invaluable help in the primary stages in bibliography and general orientation and many suggestions of great value; Dr. J. R. Strayer of Princeton University, the late Mr. J. R. Watkins of Princeton, Mr. Burdette G. Lewis, Jr., of East Aurora, New York, and Mr. and Mrs. Irving Van Zandt, Jr., of Princeton for help and suggestions in the preparation of the manuscript for publication. He also wishes to thank Dr. Gray C. Boyce of Northwestern University for help in revisions and bibliographical assistance.

ARCHIBALD R. LEWIS

Columbia, S.C.
January 1950

Contents

List of Maps

NAVAL POWER AND TRADE
IN THE MEDITERRANEAN
A.D. 500 TO 1100

1. The Mediterranean World

About A.D. 500 the Mediterranean world was at peace for the first time in about a century. The Germans who had overturned the Empire in the West from 378 on, had settled down into organized kingdoms. In the East the Roman Empire survived unshaken in the Balkans, Asia Minor, Syria, Egypt, and Cyrene. On the throne of the Caesars sat shrewd old Anasthasius, giving the people he ruled the benefit of his wisdom and prudence in administration and piling up the treasure that Justinian was to use to such advantage several decades later. Triumphant over the mercenary Isaurians to whom Zeno had given such free rein and inclining enough toward Monophysitism to keep Syria and Egypt in line, he ruled a rich, prosperous, and peaceful domain.

In the West, weak successors of the terrible Gaeseric the Vandal controlled a sea empire consisting of North Africa, Sardinia, the Balearics, and perhaps Corsica. Enervated by the riches this fruitful domain provided and forgetful of the piratical skill that had made the Vandals so feared fifty years before, they were scarcely able to protect their African lands from encroachments by the wild Berber tribes of the hills. Their holdings had thus shrunk to some coastal cities and the old Roman province of Africa proper.

In Spain and Southern France lay the kingdom of the Visigoths under an able ruler, Alaric. The domains of the Visigoths were rich, but the turbulence of their independent nobility made it difficult for their kings to rule effectively. Furthermore, the Franks were driving them out of their holdings in the valleys of the Loire and Garonne and threatening to reach the Mediterranean itself at their expense.

In Italy the great Theodoric the Ostrogoth reigned. Most able of the German monarchs in the West, he showed a surprising skill in ruling both Goth and Roman. He used such talented Latin officials as Boethius and Cassiodorus in his administration and succeeded in making Italy more prosperous than it had been in centuries. He held the grain-rich island of Sicily as well as Italy and protected the Alpine passes to the north and northeast with a firm hold on Rhaetia, Noricum, Pannonia, and Dalmatia. By arriage he allied himself with the Vandal, Visigothic, Frankish, d Burgundian royal families. He also set up a balance of power by supporting his weaker Visigothic relatives against the aggressiveness of the booty-hungry Frankish Clovis, who, after overwhelming the Visigothic Rhone and Garonne provinces in Gaul and seeping into Burgundy, was proceeding toward the Mediterranean. In 508 Theodoric's army inflicted a defeat on the Franks and annexed Provence. Languedoc remained Visigothic.[1] From this time on, in spite of the fact that Clovis gained sympathy by his and his people's conversion to Orthodox Christianity and despite the intrigues of the august ruler of Constantinople who named him Patrician, the greedy Frankish king turned away from the Mediterranean. He proceeded instead to murder his Riparian Frankish kinsmen, add their domains to his, and expand at the expense of the Alemanni in Germany. It was almost a half century before the Franks became a Mediterranean power and then only with the disappearance of Ostrogothic Italy.

Different though Ostrogothic, Visigothic, and Vandal kingdoms were in many ways, they had much in common. They were all German in origin and represented a small German military minority ruling over large Latin-speaking populations. They were further separated from their subjects by religion. The Ostrogoths, Visigoths and Vandals were Arian heretics, while their non-German subjects were Orthodox Catholics looking to Papal Rome and beyond that to Constantinople for religious leadership. This religious differentiation, however, seems to have accentuated difficulties between rulers and ruled only in North Africa, where the Vandals had in the late fifth century fiercely persecuted the Orthodox bishops and church. Elsewhere religious and other relationships were on the whole harmonious.

The reason for this lies in the fact that the German kings kept intact and tried to preserve the Roman civilization they found about them. Theodoric in Italy is an excellent example of this. He received, after some friction and delay, a recognition of his status as a sort of viceroy from the Emperor at Constantinople. He continued in force Roman officialdom, consuls and public games, bureaucracy, language, law, coinage, and custom. He even pre-

---

[1] This prevented the Franks from becoming a Mediterranean power for half a century. Hodgkin, T. *Theodoric the Goth* (New York 1891), p. 197-206. J. B. Bury *The Invasion of Europe by the Barbarians* (London 1928), p. 205.

served the free distribution of grain, which had so long nourished the lower classes in Rome. He interfered little with the church, and until his last days felt the Roman officials who served him were as important and as trustworthy as his Gothic warrior followers.[2]

The same is true of Visigothic Spain. There not only were Roman administration and traditions respected, but Roman law was codified about 500 in the famous *Breviary* of Alaric for the benefit of the Roman population.[3] To a lesser degree the Vandal kingdom and even that of the more barbarous Franks represented a similar state of affairs.

Thus these kingdoms represented no violent break with the past for the mass of the population of the West, but rather a temporary occupation of Roman land by German auxiliaries. And, since the army had been German for the most part since the third century, this represented no essential change. It was an empire without an immediate Western emperor. But even this was, in theory at least, of little consequence. All rights that had been held by the Emperor of the West had simply passed to the Augustus who still held sway as the legitimate heir of the Caesars in Constantinople. The Empire was still one, and both German rulers and the Imperial despot at Constantinople hastened to assist this view of affairs. The latter did so by investing monarchs like Clovis the Frank and Theodoric the Ostrogoth with a legitimate right over the lands they held. The former continued to date their state documents as of the reigns of the rulers of the East, to place their effigies on the coinage they issued, and, in the case of Theodoric, even to submit their consuls for approval by Constantinople. The universal Catholic church which similarly looked to the Emperor at Byzantium as its head, emphasized the reality of these claims in every Orthodox church in the West.[4]

There was also a growing fusion, though a slow one, of the upper classes of Romans in the West with the noble Germans in

[2] Hodgkin *op. cit.*, p. 134-74. Bury *op. cit.*, p. 186-204.

[3] Pirenne, H. *Mohammed and Charlemagne* (New York 1939), p. 1-62. Pirenne here exaggerates the Romanic nature of the Merovingian state, though not of the other barbarian kingdoms which bordered on the Mediterranean. See D. C. Dennett, Jr. "Pirenne and Mohammed" in *Speculum* (1948) xxiii, 181-85.

[4] An example is the case of Boethius's famous treason which apparently consisted of too fervent a loyalty to Constantinople. Coster, C. H. "Procopius and Boethius" in *Speculum* (1948) xxiii, 284-85. See also Von Simson *Sacred Fortress* (Chicago 1948) on importance Constantinople attached to its religious connections with Italy.

almost every area. And the eagerness with which such men as King Alaric of the Visigoths, that friend of Appollinaris Sidonius,[5] and Theodoric the Ostrogoth patronized and admired Latin letters and culture made the bonds even closer. Orthodox Christianity, Latin culture and language, Roman administration and law, a preservation of the social groupings of society, and a recognition of the theoretical overlordship of the Emperor of Constantinople—all these combined to give the West a sense of still belonging to a vast Mediterranean Roman world whose center was the great city on the Bosphorus.

The Eastern portion of the Middle Sea was, of course, still firmly in the hands of its Roman rulers. The year 500 saw it untouched by the forces that had disturbed the West. Only its Greek and Balkan provinces, the least important area economically speaking, had been troubled by the German barbarian invasions. Elsewhere it had known only peace and prosperity. One reason for this lay in the fact that for over a century peace had reigned on its Eastern borders between Constantinople and Persia. The time of the terrible third century, when Sassanian Persian conqueror and Palmyran opportunist had all but torn the rich lands of Syria, Palestine and Egypt from the weak grasp of Rome was but a faint memory. Aurelian had humbled Palmyra's proud Zenobia, and Constantine's successors had fought the last battles against Persia in the late fourth century. Since that time Persia, attacked by the terrible White Huns to the northeast and disturbed by civil disorders within, had been glad to keep peace with its Western Roman antagonist. Asia Minor, Syria, and Egypt had profited by the lull to repair the damages of the third century and become more prosperous than ever.[6]

Only the religious controversy engendered by Chalcedon between Monophysite Egypt, Syria, and Armenia on the one hand and Orthodox Constantinople on the other endangered the harmony that prevailed. And here Zeno and Anasthasius, in favoring the Monophysite Bishops over the protests of their Orthodox capital, kept a balanced peace between the two parties.

    [5] Sidonius *Letters* trans. W. B. Anderson (London 1936) i, 335-45.

    [6] West, L. C., and Johnson, A. C. *Currency in Roman and Byzantine Egypt* (Princeton 1945). For a diametrically opposed point of view see G. Michwitz "The Problem of Gold in Antiquity" in *Annales d'Histoire Economique et Sociale* (1934) vi, 246-47. See particularly West, L. C. and Johnson, A. C. *Byzantine Egypt, Economic Studies* (Princeton 1949).

By the reign of Anasthasius, however, the long peace seemed to be drawing to a close as ambitious and able Persian shah-in-shahs triumphed over foreign enemies and domestic unrest. It was thought wise to begin to strengthen the vast series of border fortifications that protected the Syrian-Armenian frontier, and a test of Persian military prowess in a short border war revealed surprising strength in the Sassanian adversary.[7] The fear of a renewal of Persian pressure toward the West was thus a cloud on the otherwise peaceful and prosperous horizon in the East.

War, however, held less terror for the Eastern Emperors than it might have, had their military forces been less dependable. The Eastern Emperors began to avoid employing those German mercenaries who had proved dangerous in the armies of their Western colleagues. Anasthasius had further dismissed and broken the power of the Isaurian warriors who had proved such a menace in the capitol in Zeno's time.[8] His troops and commanders were in the main native to the Empire, either recruited from the Latin population of the Balkans, like Justin, who was to succeed him, or from loyal hill peoples of Asia Minor. There was thus in the East no alien Stilicho or Aëtius on whom the Eastern Emperor had to depend, and the attempts of Vitalian to play such a role with Hunnish and Slavic support were thwarted without too much difficulty by the diplomacy and prudence of his Imperial Master. Vitalian died a pitiful failure, a victim to the ambition which had succeeded all too frequently in the previous century at Ravenna and elsewhere in the West.

The real strength of the Empire in the East, however, was not military but economic. Industry, agriculture and trade were flourishing. This prosperity was centered in three areas, Asia Minor, Syria, and Egypt. Each of these areas boasted a large cosmopolitan metropolis—Constantinople for Asia Minor, Alexandria for Egypt, and Antioch for Syria. In addition there was a host of other cities in both Syria and Asia Minor which shared the general level of riches of the larger centers.

The prosperity of these areas seems to have been due to a number of factors besides the long peace enjoyed for more than a century. In the first place, agriculture was prosperous and vital. Egypt's agricultural riches had long been proverbial, thanks to

[7] Procopius *History of the Wars* ed. Dewing (New York 1914-1940) i, 49-83.

[8] W. G. Holmes *The Age of Justinian and Theodora* (London 1912) i, 175-76.

the fertility annually brought to its fields by the overflowing of the Nile. High productivity continued under late Roman rule, and Egypt produced a large surplus of grain. Some of this was sent as part of her Imperial tribute to nourish the great cosmopolitan city of Constantinople where, as in Rome, free grain was provided for the lower classes by the government. The collection and transport of this grain was the first charge on the Roman Imperial Governor of Egypt with his headquarters in Alexandria, and a special *collegium* of *navicularii* was maintained, charged with the responsibility of seeing that it arrived at the capital.[9] We hear no more of Egyptian grain going to Rome after the establishment of Ostrogothic Italy, which apparently drew its supplies from Sicily and Sardinia and Africa. Perhaps it was diverted from Rome in this period, but it seems more likely that the change in destination dates back to the time of Constantine's move of the capital to his new city on the Golden Horn. At any rate, there was additional grain for export by private means after the grain tribute had been sent.

In addition, Egypt produced other agricultural goods of exportable value. Syria exported wine, timber, and perhaps some olive oil; Asia Minor horses, iron, marble, and a variety of other products.

Furthermore, the status of the agricultural population in the East does not seem to have approached that of the West. Though the decrees of Diocletian and Constantine appear to have bound the peasants to the soil in the East as in the West (the Egyptian fellaheen had been in that state since before the Ptolemys), there may well have been fewer huge estates such as dotted Africa, Spain, Sicily, and Gaul in the West. There were many small prosperous middle-class farmers and estate owners—even in Egypt,[10] and the strong, independent peasant communities, so noticeable in Asia Minor in Isaurian times, were not lacking in the fourth and fifth centuries.[11] Less is known about Syria and Palestine, but from what we know of these areas in Islamic times

[9] *Codex Just.* xi, 6, 6.

[10] Johnson, A. C. *Roman Egypt* (Baltimore 1936), p. 27. West, L. C., and Johnson, A. C. *Byzantine Egypt* (Princeton 1949) has excellent new data on this point.

[11] Charanis, P. "The Social Structure of the Later Roman Empire" in *Byzantion* (1942) xvii, 41-47. Ostrogorsky, G. "Agrarian Conditions in the Byzantine Empire in the Middle Ages" in *Cambridge Economic History* I.

there is little reason to believe that they differed markedly from Egypt or Asia Minor. Thus a prosperous countryside was the first important ingredient in the prosperity of the Eastern provinces.

The second factor lies in the industrial development of these regions. The cities and towns in Syria, Asia Minor, and even Egypt were in the fourth and fifth centuries by no means parasitical on the countryside. They were not the mere abodes of a rentier aristocracy drawing their wealth from governmental exactions or an exploited peasantry. They were the workshops of the entire Mediterranean world. Of greatest importance was the textile industry. Alexandria, Constantinople, Ephesus, Tarsus, and Syrian centers like Beirut, Gaza, Caesarea, Tripoli, Antioch, and Damascus produced fine articles of linen, silk and wool, not only for themselves, but for a wide export market.[12] Other specialties were papyrus, glass, and metalware of steel, bronze, and copper. These specialties were most frequently luxury articles, and the Tyrian purple of Syria, the linen, hangings, and brocades of Egypt, and the silks of Constantinople and Syria were particularly important. The population of these centers shows their economic vigor. Only Rome in the West could match the teeming thousands who dwelt in Alexandria, Constantinople, and Antioch.

In the third place, the East was a great exporting area. Partly these exports represented a middleman's procedure of reexporting the silk and spices that reached these regions from China, India, and the East Indies. But in addition, they exported their own industrial and agricultural surplus as well and reworked raw silk into the finished product.

The routes whereby Eastern wares reached the trade marts of the Near East are well known to us. One route was a northern one starting in Turkestan and going by way of the Caspian and the Black Sea to the Crimea. In the late fifth century the White Huns, having defeated the Persians and holding Sogdiana, controlled the middleman's position in this silk route to China and kept it open.[13] It was important enough to that in 488 the Byzantine government felt it was worth while to repair and reestablish its control over the Crimean city of Cherson (Sevastopol),[14] important also as a center

[12] Lombard, M. "L'or Mussulman du VIIe au XIe Siècle" in *Annales* (1947) II, 143. *Procopius* VI, 297.

[13] *Agathias* (ed. Bonn), p. 266. *Procopius* I, 13-31. *Theophanes* I, 188-190.

[14] Vasiliev, A. A. *The Goths in the Crimea* (Cambridge, Mass. 1936), p. 43-47.

for the fur trade with Russia.[15] In general, however, throughout most of the fourth and fifth centuries this northern route was disturbed by those great Nomadic hordes, from Huns through Avars, who swept across South Russia. Its terminus was, of course, Constantinople.

Another route was a southern one, discovered by the Ptolemys and used by their Roman successors. It was a sea route starting in Ceylon and Southern India and reaching the land of Egypt by way of the Red Sea. Its Red Sea termini were Clisma and Jotabe, not far from modern Suez.[16] Bernice, further down the Red Sea coast was also used at times.[17] From these ports the imported products found their way to Alexandria.

Most Eastern wares, however, prior to the sixth century, followed the central route through Sassanian territory. Some went by water from Ceylon and India through the Arabian Sea, up the Persian Gulf, and on through Mesopotamia to the borders of Syria. Others followed a land route from Turkestan through northern Persia to the borders of Armenia and Syria. Here they passed through a series of Roman frontier cities; Dara, Artaxata, Callinicum, and Nisibis.[18] From these centers the imported wares continued to the Syrian seaports or Constantinople. Thus each of the major economic areas in the Eastern Empire was a terminus of an important Far Eastern trade route—Egypt of the Red Sea route, Syria of the Persian Gulf and Persian land routes, and Constantinople of the Armenian and Black Sea routes. Each shared in the prosperity gained in the reexport of these products.

The whole Mediterranean area was the field for the export of Near Eastern wares, both those produced and processed there and those brought from the far Orient. From the second century on, as a matter of fact, the Syrians, Greeks, Jews and Egyptians (these latter of Greek or Jewish origin) had had what amounted to a monopoly of this rich and valuable international trade. Colonies of Easterners drawn West by this lucrative commerce had long before the late Roman period spread into Gaul, Spain, Italy, North

[15] Mierow, C. C. *The Gothic History of Jordanes* (Princeton 1915), p. 60. Vernadsky *Ancient Russia* (New Haven 1942), p. 146.

[16] Heyd *Histoire du Commerce du Levant* (Leipsig 1885) i, 10-11. *Codex Just.* xi, 2, 40, 41, 63, 4. *Digest* 39, 4.

[17] *ibid.*

[18] Lopez, R. S. "The Silk Industry of Byzantium" in *Speculum* (1945) xx, 25-28.

Africa, and even Britain.[19] The Tiber had been inundated by the Orontes. In close touch with their native lands, they were the merchant importers of the luxury goods, the spices, fine wines, silks and expensive textiles used by the upper classes in the West.[20] Probably more mundane articles such as pottery, papyrus, grain, and metal products were also in their province of trade. The spread of Christianity into the Western portion of the Empire up to the third century was in no small measure due to their presence there— for, knowing Greek and Hebrew, they had immediate access to the early Gospels. It is interesting to note that the earliest Western centers of Christianity were just those where international trade with the East was most active. The pursuit of trade advantage had carried the *Syri* and the others far into the interior beyond the seaport cities. Before the end of the fourth century they were to be found in most of the major cities of the West. St. Jerome at about that time commented on their ubiquitousness and their zeal for profit.[21]

The problem of what the Western portions of the Empire exported to pay for these Eastern imports is a thorny one and one on which not all authorities are agreed. Agricultural and natural products, like the olive oil of North Africa, iron and other metals from Spain and Gaul, and large supplies of timber needed in the deforested and desiccated East certainly helped to balance the account. But by the fourth century A.D. the West had ceased to be an important industrial area. Its losses in the terrible third-century disorders seem never to have been made good. Those areas of Gaul and Italy which were flourishing manufacturing areas in the last century of the Republic and the first two centuries of the Empire were so no more. Founded originally on capital in no small measure based on booty and tribute wrenched from the East in the last century of Republican exploitation of the Mediterranean world, they had no source of capital after the third century wiped the original investment away. They probably could not meet the competition of the better capitalized and technologically more advanced Eastern manufacturers anyway.[22]

[19] Charlesworth, P. *Trade Routes and Commerce of the Roman Empire* 2nd Ed. (Cambridge 1926), pp. 178, 202, 238.

[20] Heyd *op. cit.*, p. 20-21. Pirenne *op. cit.*, p. 62.

[21] *Hieronymus* ed ad Demetriedei et Maurin IV, 2, p. 788.

[22] D. C. Dennett, Jr. *op. cit.*, p. 178-80. Grenier, A. "La Gaule Romaine" in *An Economic Survey of Rome* III, 567, 573, 599-603, 617-20, 632.

In addition, much of the town life in the West had a fatal weakness. Towns in large parts of Gaul, Britain, Spain and even North Africa—though not so much in Italy—were artificial creations. They were administrative centers created by the Roman state for governing purposes and housed not so much a natural industrial and commercial population as an upper-class rentier aristocracy living on the dues from the peasants on their estates.[23] Non-productive except in a purely local sense, they produced, after the third century, few commodities of an industrial nature that the Eastern traders wanted. Hence the West was hard put to it to pay for its imports. Its only recourse was a large-scale export of gold to meet the unfavorable balance of payments necessitated by its purchases from the East.[24] Thus were Pydna, Cynocephylae, Magnesia and a whole series of plunderings of the East by Rome being avenged in the late Empire.

Regimentation imposed by the Imperial government from the time of Diocletian and Constantine hid the seriousness of this situation. Towns in the West nevertheless declined steadily in size and wealth. Large estates, the curse of the Roman world, grew steadily. But as long as the Empire was a single governmental unit, it is possible that a rough balance was maintained in the following way: the Imperial Government simply raised taxes in the East and spent them in the West. In some areas like Northern France and Belgium and along the Danube frontier the government's stimulus to trade and industry because of the need of supplying its frontier troops with food, clothing, weapons, and other such materials even caused a false boom in urban and industrial life. Fourth-century Treves is a good case in point.[25]

But after the end of the fourth century all this changed. The separation into Eastern and Western Empires meant that the West had to raise its own revenues locally. There was no governmental balance of Eastern taxes spent in the West. The East, relieved of this burden, prospered as a result. But the drain of gold eastward continued. Finally, unable to support itself, the Roman Western government collapsed and the barbarians marched in.

This does not mean that town life disappeared in the West in

[23] Rostovtzeff *History of Rome* (Oxford 1927), p. 249-51.

[24] Lombard *op. cit.*, p. 143-44.

[25] Lot, F. *The End of the Ancient World* (London 1931) gives a different interpretation and does not mention any rally in 4th century Gaul.

the course of the fifth century. It certainly did not. Not only did many cities, particularly those in Italy, Spain, Southern France and North Africa remain important centers of trade and industry—the last of a somewhat local nature—but the riches of Ostrogothic Italy, Vandal North Africa,[26] Visigothic Spain[27] and Frankish Gaul,[28] as shown in their courts and the gold coinage they issued, suggest a real prosperity. Ostrogothic Italy under Theodoric is a particularly good example of this.[29] But there is little evidence of any town growth or much reversal of the trend that had started in the third century.

Perhaps four things even helped to arrest the downward economic spiral and give some measure of recovery to the West in the late fifth century. In the first place, there was a reestablishment of relatively peaceful conditions. Theodoric's diplomacy and balance of power had much to do with this. Second, the Vandal fleet, which must have interfered with Mediterranean trade during the days of the terrible Gaeseric, ceased under his successors to threaten the major trade routes from its North African lair. Third, the simpler administrations of the German kings and armies were less expensive to maintain than the last Roman ones were. This boon both Italians and North Africans were to realize with bitterness when Justinian's tax gatherers followed his generals in the course of the next century.[30] And last of all, the troubled times resulted in one product in the West of high price and in great demand in the East. This product was slaves. From this time on, the seaports of Southern France and Italy did a brisk trade in these human chattels destined for the East.[31] These factors may have lessened the drain of gold eastward by the year 500.

Nevertheless the end of the fifth century and the opening of the sixth saw little change in the Eastern monopoly of international Mediterranean trade and commerce. Important colonies of Eastern merchants were still found in all important Western cities. Greeks, Syrians, and Jews were in large numbers at Narbonne, Marseille and Arles—termini of the vital Rhone trade.[32] Sidonius reports

[26] Pirenne *op. cit.*, p. 79-117. Dopsch, A. *Economic and Social Foundations of European Civilization* (New York 1937), p. 339-57.

[27] *ibid.*   [28] *ibid.*

[29] Hodgkin *op. cit.*, p. 139-43.   [30] *Procopius* II, 278-79; IV, 159-61.

[31] Pirenne *op. cit.*, p. 96-100.

[32] *Acta Concil. Narbon.* a 589 con. 4 in Mansi *Coll. Concil.* IX, 1015. Gregory of Tours *Hist. of the Franks* VII, 31; VIII, 1; IX, 26.

many Syrians at Ravenna in the late fifth century.[33] Spain was filled with Jews who inhabited its larger cities like Seville, Cadiz, Toledo, and Cordova. A flourishing Jewish community at Naples, protected by Theodoric, traded with the East.[34] The gold *nomismata* of Constantinople of the standard set up by Constantine was still the medium of international exchange, and the barbarian rulers were careful to coin it in the name and with the image of the Imperial Augustus of the East.[35] East and West were still tied together economically to the benefit of the Eastern traders, who continued to man the ships that plied the Middle Sea, collecting carrying charges on the goods they brought with them and even selling the products themselves in the West. With the possible exception of parts of Italy like the Venetian shore, which may have carried on some trade in its own ships with the East,[36] the West remained passive from an economic and industrial standpoint—a colonial area exploited for the benefit of Syria, Alexandria, and Constantinople as it had been for several centuries previously.

The economic relationships established between the Eastern Empire and the Sassanian Empire to the East differed markedly in many ways from those with the Mediterranean West. There were several reasons for this. In the first place, Sassanian Persia could not be considered as part of the Roman Empire, as the barbarian kingdoms undoubtedly were considered. Therefore, trade with it was alien trade outside the borders of the *Pax Romana*, actual or theoretical, which had so long existed in the Mediterranean and Black Sea areas. In the second place, the Far Eastern trade was not so profitable as the Western. Spices and silk, arriving, mostly, through trade routes controlled by the Persians, had to be paid for in gold[37] —though the possibility that this Eastern trade was not such a drain upon the gold resources of the Empire as generally supposed is one that cannot be dismissed. At any rate, the Persians, as middlemen, controlled products which the Eastern Empire vitally needed and wanted, while the West did not.

Political and military considerations in dealing with Persia (an actual or potential enemy), and the important economic nature

---

[33] Sidonius *op. cit.*, p. 383.   [34] Dopsch *op. cit.*, p. 342.

[35] Gasquet, A. *L'Empire Byzantin et la Monarchie Franque* (Paris 1888), p. 171-78.

[36] This was probably largely a local trade. Diehl, C. *Venise: Une République Patricienne* (Paris 1928), p. 7.

[37] Lombard *op. cit.*, p. 146-48.

of the transactions, had long caused the Roman government to supervise carefully this Eastern trade. Nisibis, Artaxata, Callinicum, and Dara, the border cities which were the termini of the silk and spice trade passing through Persian territory, were the only ports of entry allowed for these imports. They were carefully controlled by the Imperial Government, and a law of the early fifth century forbade Roman citizens to go further than these cities or to receive foreign merchants without the knowledge of the Count of Commerce *per Orientem*.[38] Lopez believes similar outposts existed on the Northern border under the Counts of Commerce for Moesia, Scythia, the Black Sea, Illyricum, and Pannonia.[39] For the Red Sea trade, Clisma and Jotabe were similar establishments.[40] Foreign merchants arriving at these special trade outposts were carefully examined and had to have special passports, and lists of their merchandise and of the products they desired to buy in the Empire.[41] There were laws against the export of gold, and as early as the year 287 Persia recognized by treaty these specially established, specially controlled trade portals as the only way in which trade could pass between the two Empires.[42] Thus the danger of export of gold was minimized, and the danger of spies and alien merchants penetrating into the Empire was reduced to a minimum. It is possible that this system was an old one, and that it had long been in force along the entire borders of the Roman state. If so, such centers as Cologne, Ratisbon, and Vienna in the West owed their growth in the Roman Period in part to the fact that they were similarly controlled trade portals for exchanges with the German barbarians beyond the frontiers.

In addition to controlling this Eastern trade, the Roman Emperors in the East had long made sure that their gold coinage met no competitors there either. Pacts with the Persian monarchs ensured that the latter stuck to silver coinage, while gold was reserved for coins bearing the image of the Emperor or Basileus of Constantinople.[43] As a matter of fact, from the time of Theodosius up to the middle of the sixth century Persia remained on a silver standard, while the Mediterranean world was on a gold standard in its trade.[44] Such continued to be the case until the ninth century,

[38] Lopez *op. cit.*, p. 26.　　　　[39] *ibid.*

[40] Heyd *op. cit.*, p. 15-18.　　　　[41] Lopez *op. cit.*, p. 27.

[42] *ibid.*, p. 26-27.

[43] Fr. Lenormat *La Monnaie dans L'Antiquité* ii, 387.

[44] Lombard *op. cit.*, p. 146-47.

even after the Moslem conquest. For the silver dirhem modelled on the Sassanian silver coinage up to that time continued to be the standard coinage of Mesopotamia and Persia;[45] yet Cosmas Indopleustes found the gold *nomismata* the master of Indian international exchanges in the sixth century.[46] How long this had been true cannot be ascertained, but it probably was no new development.

This leads to an interesting speculation. Most economic historians have assumed an unfavorable balance of trade between the Eastern Mediterranean world and the East—Persia, India, and China. They assume a constant drain of gold to the East to pay for the spices and silk imported for local Near Eastern consumption and the Mediterranean trade.[47] They base this on a first-century statement by Pliny as to the cost in gold of the spice trade of the Empire,[48] on the hordes of Roman gold coins found in India and Ceylon, and on the restrictions imposed by the Roman Emperors on the export of gold from their domains. But though there might have been such a drain in the second and third centuries A.D., there is little basis for assuming it in the fourth and fifth. In fact the silver standard of the Persians seems to point to quite another conclusion; that the Roman Near East actually enjoyed a favorable balance of trade with the Persians, in spite of their control of the valuable spice and silk trade; that this favorable balance of trade drained the Sassanian Empire of gold and forced them to adopt a silver standard, just as Europe from the eighth to the thirteenth centuries found itself compelled to do. There are obvious reasons for adopting this point of view. Save in Mesopotamia, Persian urban life was not nearly so well developed as that of Syria, Egypt, and Asia Minor. The same advantages possessed by the industrial Near East over the West were equally valid for its economic relationships with the Persians.[49] True, there

---

[45] *ibid.*

[46] Diehl, C. *Justinien et la Civilization Byzantine du VIᵉ Siècle* (Paris 1901), p. 544-45.

[47] Hudson, G. T. *Europe and China* (London 1931), p. 99-100.

[48] *ibid.*

[49] For a diametrically opposed view see Lombard *op. cit.*, p. 145-46. Yet his reasons for the Sassanian retention of silver coinage seem rather unconvincing. *ibid.*, p. 146-47. Interestingly enough, to have the Mediterranean world on a gold standard and Persia on a silver one reversed the picture of the Hellenic period prior to Alexander's conquest of the East when Greece used silver money and the Persian Empire gold. On Persia's agrarian type of civilization in this period see Sykes *A History of Persia* I, p. 180ff.

was the valuable silk and spice transit trade, but it is doubtful if this could balance the value of the manufactured and other articles Persia imported from Syria, Egypt, and Asia Minor. Regulations by the Roman Government merely ensured that this trade stay even more unfavorable for the Sassanians. Viewed in this fashion, the wealth in gold of the Eastern Roman Empire becomes more understandable. So do certain undeniable changes that took place in the Eastern Empire in the late fifth century.

First, there is the abolition by Anasthasius of the *chrysargyron* or gold tax on all handicrafts and possessions in the Empire. Its abolition was greeted with enthusiasm by the population,[50] and its importance as a source of revenue can be gauged by the fact that from it in the border city of Edessa alone the Imperial Government in the late fifth century raised 120 pounds of gold a year.[51] This, incidentally, is an important indication of the value of the Persian trade, for Edessa's location must have made it an important participant in exchange of commodities across the border. Second was the step of abolishing Constantine's and Diocletian's regulations holding town corporations responsible for taxes to the Imperial treasury. New officials or *vindices* were charged with the raising of these revenues.[52] This, too, is a reflection of prosperity. And finally, we have the fact that upon Anasthasius's death he left a huge horde saved up in his treasury—320,000 lbs. of gold.[53]

All in all, in viewing the Mediterranean world about 500 we can thus see an extremely prosperous Near East controlling through Syrian, Egyptian, Jewish, and Greek traders the vital international export trade and dominating the marts of both East and West. We see an Empire still existing—in theory at least—and held together even in the barbarian West by a common gold coinage, a common religious loyalty, a common recognition of Constantinople's overlordship of all the old territory once Roman, save far-off Britain. We notice a continuation of this Empire's Roman institutions in East and West, of its town life—though less so in the West—of its earlier reason for being in an economic sense. We see its superiority to the Sassanian kingdom to the east with its silver coinage and lack of urbanization, and its influence felt as far as

---

[50] Evagrius *Historia Ecclesiastica* (ed. Bidez-Parmentier) III, 39, p. 137.
[51] *Chronicle of Joshua the Sylite* trans. by W. Wright (Cambridge 1884), p. 22.
[52] Vasiliev, A. *A History of the Byzantine Empire* (Madison, Wis. 1925), I, 142-43.
[53] *ibid.*

China and India. The Empire in the West may have fallen, but Mediterranean "Romania" was a fact. It was to be Justinian's destiny to clothe this fact in concrete political forms.

But what of naval power in this Mediterranean dominated economically, institutionally and even to a large degree politically by the Eastern Empire? Here we have a definite paradox. The Eastern Roman state seems to have had, prior to the reign of Anasthasius, little understanding, appreciation, or even interest in organized naval power. We can understand the reasons for this fact only by looking at past Roman naval history.

The Romans had little use for the sea. In startling contrast to the Greeks, they were always essentially a land people. We know no names of intrepid Roman navigators, sailors or explorers. They excelled as builders of roads, of fortifications, of cities. It is the Roman soldier, rather than sailor, who springs immediately to mind as an emblem and symbol of Rome's imperial might.

Nevertheless, from the period of the Punic Wars up through Actium, the Romans were acquainted with and understood the importance of naval power.[54] After Actium they ceased to think in naval terms—and for an excellent reason. The entire Mediterranean was theirs. They had no naval rivals. Their efforts were military, along the Rhine-Danube, Persian, and Saharan frontiers. They had no need of naval defenses, except in faraway Britain, where the Count of the Saxon Shore found it necessary to hold the plundering Saxon pirates in check. Such naval power as they kept was purely police in nature—to keep down pirates and protect the annual grain shipments from Egypt and North Africa to Rome and Constantinople. This explains their helplessness, when, in the third century, the Goths in the Crimea and South Russia took to the sea, passed through the Dardanelles and plundered through the Aegean and beyond.[55]

It also explains why the Vandals met so little opposition in the late fifth century when their pirate fleets, based on North Africa, were the terror of the Western Mediterranean. Under Gaeseric they set up a naval kingdom including the Balearics, Sardinia,

[54] Clark, F. W. *The Influence of Sea Power on the History of the Roman Republic* (Menasha, Wis. 1915). On the decay of this fleet under the Empire see Starr, C. G. *The Roman Imperial Navy* (Cornell 1941), p. 167-98.

[55] Zosimus *Historia Nova* ed. Mendelssohn (Bonn 1881), p. 31-42. Starr *op. cit.*, p. 194-96.

and Corsica and sacked Rome in 455. The Romans could muster only two naval expeditions against them. One, from the West, under Majorian was an utter failure.[56] The other, sent from Constantinople by Leo I under Marcellinus, had some initial success, but after reconquering Sardinia in 468, dared not attack the main Vandal North African fleet. This expedition, too, thus ended in failure. The Vandals soon recovered Sardinia.[57]

Just how these fifth-century expeditions were organized is difficult to say. Probably they were simply levies of commercial vessels and captains pressed into service for a single expedition—which explains their ineffectiveness. After Gaeseric, the Vandal fleet ceased to be a menace, and, following his death in 477, we hear no more of its piratical expeditions. Perhaps Theodoric maintained a skeleton fleet of ships at Ostia and Ravenna (Classis) in the old Roman manner, and undoubtedly there were Italian mariners who could be forced into service in impressed ships for specific purposes as Totila was to prove in the sixth century. But organized naval power did not exist in the West by 500 A.D.

With Anasthasius the first steps appear to have been taken toward setting up an established standing naval force in the Mediterranean. Whether he was responsible for the naval arsenals at Alexandria and Tyre and Constantinople is difficult to say, but in 508 he sent out one of the first well-organized naval expeditions —a force of 100 armed ships and as many small ones under Romanus, Count of the Domestics and Rusticus, Count of the Scholarii, carrying 5,000 soldiers. This expedition was directed against Ostrogothic Italy, whose pretensions in the Balkans worried Anasthasius. It ravaged the Italian coast as far as Tarentum.[58] Again, the difficulty with Vitalian, who had 200 ships manned by Danubian Slavs, showed the need for a definite naval force. In 515 Anasthasius, lacking ships to oppose Vitalian, gave in.[59] In 516, however, he mustered a fleet under Marinus, using a chemical compound invented by Proclus the Athenian (which appears to be very much like the later famous Greek Fire), set the enemy

---

[56] *Procopius* II, 65-69.   [57] *ibid.*, p. 55-63.

[58] Hodgkin *op. cit.*, p. 219. Baynes exaggerates the role of Vandal sea power and its effects. The Vandals were never strong enough to take and hold Sicily, the vital link in Mediterranean naval control. N. Baynes *The Byzantine Empire* (New York 1926), p. 144.

[59] *Theophanes*, p. 161.

ships on fire and saved the city.[60] A definite naval force had been set up, and the nucleus of what was to be the great Byzantine squadrons of the future lay in the harbor of the Golden Horn. A new naval era had begun for Byzantium and the Mediterranean.

[60] *Malalas,* p. 405. Constantine Porphyrogenitus *Excepta Historica* ed. DeBoor (Berlin 1906), p. 169.

2. The Return to Romania

In 518 Anasthasius died. His successor on the throne of the Caesars in Constantinople was Justin, his chief military assistant. Justin, however, bluff able old soldier that he was, was not the real ruler of the Empire. It was Justinian, his slender, intellectual nephew, who exercised the real power during his uncle's lifetime. In 527 he succeeded him as Emperor. All in all, Justinian controlled the Empire for almost a half century. He was ably assisted in this task by his wife, Theodora. She remained throughout her lifetime his indispensable partner and helper. We are fully informed on both Justinian's and Theodora's abilities and characters, thanks to the full, scandalous, and unfair portraits of them given by Procopius in his *Secret History*. In this work he vented his spleen upon the imperial pair. But not even Procopius's vindictiveness can obscure the ability with which they guided the destinies of the Eastern Roman world, nor destroy our understanding of the real successes that they gained. The sixth century in the Mediterranean was in a real sense the Age of Justinian. His accomplishments and those of his consort are enshrined for all time in the Justinian Code, in the soaring beauty of Hagia Sophia and in a revived and revitalized Roman Mediterranean Empire which lasted eighty years after his passing.

Justinian, with Theodora's able assistance, bent his energies throughout his reign upon one main object, the return of the Mediterranean world to Roman unity. This meant the recovery of the Western provinces occupied by the Ostrogoths, Vandals, Visigoths, and Franks, and their return to the direct rule of Constantinople. To this dream of a restored Romania, Justinian sometimes sacrificed, perhaps unwisely, the interests of his domains in Syria, Egypt, and Asia Minor, subjecting them to heavy taxation to pay for his Western campaigns and leaving them open to Persian aggression. To this object he also sacrificed the religious balance between Orthodox and Monophysite parties so precariously maintained by his predecessors, Zeno and Anasthasius. By his savage persecutions of the Monophysite party, particularly later in his reign when the restraining influence of Theodora had been removed, he widened the religious cleavage between Syria and Egypt and the rest of the Empire. He thus laid the ground-work for later Persian and Islamic successes. But his achievements were more impressive than his failures, and the Empire that sur-vived intact up to late in Heraclius's reign was in a real sense his personal creation.[1]

Upon coming to power, Justinian found conditions ideal for realizing his dream of a restored Romania. Anasthasius had main-tained the Empire in prosperous and healthy condition. He had left to his successors a well-filled treasury, the nucleus of a good fleet and in Belisarius a general tested in Persian border wars. The situation in the West was propitious for Justinian's plans as well. The Vandals and Visigoths were in decline, and with the death of the great Theodoric the Ostrogothic state was in the hands of incompetents.

Justinian made his preparations with care. He signed a "per-petual" peace with Persia, and to assure the maintenance of this treaty poured out a large yearly gold subsidy to the Sassanian monarch.[2] He weakened his Western victims by diplomatic ma-neuvers. Then he gathered a large expeditionary force. It consisted of five hundred transports and ninety-two war vessels. The ships were manned by 30,000 sailors and carried 15,000 troops—10,000 of them infantry, 5,000 to 6,000 of them cavalry. The naval convoy of ninety-two vessels carried, in addition, 2,000 rowers who manned the oars.[3] The expedition's objective was Vandal North Africa, and in 533 it set sail from Constantinople.

To make certain that it was successful, Justinian added one further stratagem. With gold and a small advance naval force he stirred up a revolt in Sardinia, hoping to lure the Vandal fleet there and out of the way of his armada. The Vandal monarch rose to the bait. He sent his war fleet and 5,000 men to Cagliari to recover the island.[4] Justinian's expedition thus reached the African shore

---

[1] The best account of Justinian's reign is to be found in Diehl, C. *Justinien et la Civilization Byzantine du VI*e *Siècle* (Paris 1901). Also excellent, but too much influenced by Procopius' *Anecdota* is Holmes, W. G. *The Age of Justinian and Theodora* 2 vols. (London 1905-07).

[2] Lombard *op. cit.*, p. 145.

[3] *Procopius* (ed. Dewing) ii, 105-07. Diehl, C. *L'Afrique Byzantine*, p. 360.

[4] *Procopius* ii, 107-09. This naval force, which made up the entire Vandal navy, amounted to only 120 ships, an indication of how the once powerful Vandal fleet had decayed by the early 6th century.

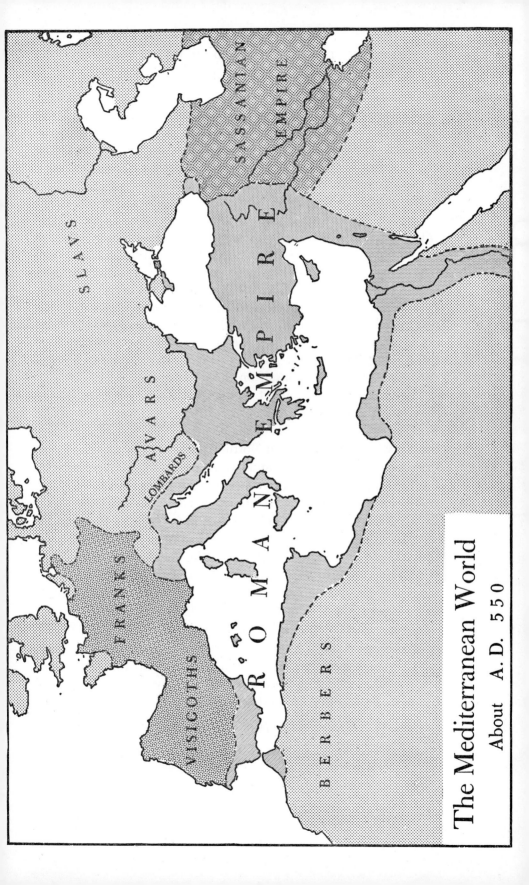

The Mediterranean World
About A.D. 550

unopposed, and the army commanded by Belisarius was landed without incident. The campaign that followed was swift and easy. Two victories decided the war. Carthage was taken, and North Africa fell into Justinian's hands. With it went Sardinia, the Balearics, and Corsica all of which were occupied without difficulty by Justinian's naval squadrons when news of the Byzantine African successes reached those outposts.[5]

The next step was Italy. Here, again, in 535 the initial stages were easy. Belisarius, supported by the fleet, occupied Sicily, and with a force of 10,000 men was soon master of Southern Italy and Rome. But at this point Ostrogothic resistance stiffened. The chief reason seems to lie in Belisarius's lack of troops. Justinian, jealous of his victorious general, refused his pleas for reenforcements. Perhaps another cause of his failure to support adequately the war in Italy was the need of diverting military forces to the Eastern frontiers where Persia, despite her perpetual peace treaty, was threatening invasion. At any rate, Belisarius's forward progress ended, and he found himself on the defensive.[6]

The Ostrogoths took heart. Under Totila's inspired leadership they took the offensive. Not only did they recapture most of the Northern and Central parts of the peninsula, but they also took to the sea with flotillas built in Northern Italy. In 551 this fleet captured Corsica and Sardinia, and Byzantine sea communication with the East was put in jeopardy.[7] Belisarius was recalled in disgrace, and it remained for the aged eunuch Narses to complete his work. In 553 Narses led by land from Dalmatia into the Po River valley the first adequately large army that Justinian had provided for Italy. There he crushed Totila in battle. By the end of the next year Italy was Justinian's after eighteen years of conflict. In the same year Corsica and Sardinia were recovered, and Ostrogothic naval power, like that of the Vandals, disappeared from history.[8]

There remained one further conquest by Justinian in the West— Southern Spain. In 554, taking advantage of Visigothic weakness, a Byzantine expedition was landed in Spain and took over most of Andalusia, including Cadiz, Seville, Cordova, and Malaga, and Ceuta on the North African shore opposite.[9] In the Western Medi-

---

[5] *Procopius* II, 247-49. Carta-Raspi, R. *La Sardegna nell'alto Mediaevo* (Cagliari 1935), p. 38-46.

[6] *Procopius* III, 167.　　　　　　[7] *Procopius* V, 283, 313-14.

[8] *ibid.*, p. 347-419.　　　　　　[9] Vasiliev *Byzantine Empire*, p. 170-71.

terranean only the Northeastern Spanish coast and the shores of Southern France, where the Franks were now ensconced from the Rhone to Italy, were in other than Roman hands. Romania had been recreated by the persistence and genius of Justinian.

One thing is worth noting about these wars in the West. It is that they were not decided on the land but on the sea. It was naval command of the sea which gave Justinian his victories. The sure instinct with which he chose the Vandals, the only considerable naval power, as his first adversary shows that the great Byzantine ruler fully understood the importance of this factor. With Vandal sea power gone he could proceed unimpeded with Italy and Spain.

Totila, Justinian's only worthy Western opponent came to understand this too. The latter built a fleet and took to the sea, and thus furnished Justinian his only real opposition. He came close to destroying Byzantine plans when he made communications between the western coast of Italy and the East impossible to maintain. With his overthrow this naval menace ceased, and Justinian not only completed his conquest of Italy but was able to add the rich cities of Spain to his Empire.

The importance of control of the seas is shown by another fact, the small number of troops used by the Byzantines in these wars. Contrasted with the large armies of the earlier Roman period, Justinian's expeditionary forces seem very small indeed. Fifteen thousand men conquered Vandal North Africa.[10] Italy was invaded by an army of only ten or eleven thousand men.[11] Various reinforcements sent in numbered only fifteen thousand.[12] Thus it took only twenty-five to thirty thousand men to overthrow the strong state Theodoric had founded fifty years before. There are no figures available on the size of the expedition sent to Spain which recovered Andalusia for the Empire, but it cannot have been large.

It is obvious that many non-military factors assisted Justinian in his reconquests of Western lands. The large colonies of Easterners—Syrians, Greeks, and Jews—in the major commercial centers of the West must have provided a fifth column upon which the Byzantines could rely.[13] The support of the Western Church,

[10] *Procopius* II, 103.   [11] *ibid.*, p. 43.
[12] *Procopius* III, 43; V, 329-35.
[13] For two examples of Eastern merchants so minded see *Procopius* II, 171 in Africa and III, 75 in Italy.

already loyal to Justinian as its recognized head and wooed by his abandonment of Anasthasius's pro-Monophysite position for a stern orthodoxy, was invaluable. There is little doubt that churchmen welcomed the chance to throw off the yoke of the heretical Arian Germans, particularly in North Africa. Their churches provided centers of pro-Byzantine propaganda. In addition, the natural lure of Roman rule to a Latin population, who had not forgotten the centuries of Romania preceding their German masters' brief sway over them, must have assisted.

Yet this is not enough to explain victories with such small forces. It is naval power which provides the clue. Justinian could take North Africa, Italy, part of Spain and the islands of the Western Mediterranean so easily because his fleet controlled these waters and kept communications open to ample supplies of money and reinforcements. At the same time this same naval control could deny similar advantages to Byzantium's enemies. Byzantine troops, on the other hand, had difficulties when they were inland far from the sea. The interior of Northern Italy proved a hard nut to crack, and the Franks had to be called on for assistance before Ostrogothic resistance could be crushed there.[14] Again, not the Vandals but the revolts and opposition of the Berber tribes of the interior in the hills and mountains of North Africa were the real problem to Justinian's commanders there.[15] Successes in the interior were more difficult to gain.

It is this dependence on sea power which accounts for the nature of the Empire from Justinian through Heraclius. It explains not merely the pattern, scope, and difficulties of Justinian's wars in the West, but also the way in which the territory of the rulers of Constantinople was held and defended up to A.D. 641. It was because of this dependence on sea power that Byzantine Africa was much smaller in territorial extent than Roman Africa and remained so throughout the sixth and seventh centuries—though all the main ports and fertile plains areas were fully occupied.[16] It explains the picture presented by Byzantine Sardinia in which only fertile lowlands and mining areas were firmly held, while

[14] *Procopius* III, 379-425, IV and V.

[15] *Procopius* II, 285-459.

[16] Gautier, E. F. *Les Siècles Obscurs du Magreb* (Paris 1927), p. 185-218. Caropino, J. "Le limes de Numidie et sa garde syrienne" in *Syrie* (1925). Geforer's views that Justinian neglected the fleet also seem unjustified. Geforer *Byz. Geschichte* II, 401-08.

the interior was left to the primitive Barbaricini.[17] The same pattern is apparent in the Crimea. Justinian and his successors established firm control in the coastal cities and plains. The interior remained in the hands of the Goths and others.[18] If we knew more about Byzantine Spain we might be able to say with some assurance that the same thing was true there. In startling comparison to earlier Roman experience, with Justinian and his successors there appears a naval empire in the Mediterranean, held together and made possible by efficient use of supreme naval power. This explains why little effort was made to tie the Empire together by land connections. Roads linked the provinces of Augustus, Trajan, Constantine, and even Theodosius. Ships performed this function for Justinian, Maurice, and Heraclius. Sea power assured firm control by Constantinople of all the territory governed by the Empire in Mediterranean and Black Sea areas. In this sense Justinian's age marks a break with the Roman past and a beginning of a new era.

Naval power, however, had limitations from a military standpoint. It could not secure the interior from raids by barbarians and other peoples hostile to the Empire. Here, too, this period marks a break in some respects with earlier Roman precedents, though not so sharp a one as in the new dependence upon the sea and its control. The defense of Byzantine territory from the land side was based by the sixth and seventh century rulers of Constantinople on huge fortifications and strongpoints established along the frontiers and far back into territory held by Byzantium. This is, of course, a copy of the second and third century *limes* system of Rome, but the scope and number of these fortresses were immensely increased in the course of the sixth and early seventh centuries by Byzantium's rulers. Those of Byzantine Africa were particularly extensive; so were those constructed in Sardinia, Italy, the Crimea, and the Balkans, where few had existed previously. So, too, were those along the explosive and vitally important Persian frontier. The Byzantine rulers garrisoned the more important ones with levies of their professional standing army. Most, however, were held by local militia or *foederati* settled in the surrounding countryside. Some fortresses seem to have been established primarily as places of refuge for the local population of

[17] *Procopius* II, 327; VII, 391. Carta-Raspi *op. cit.*, p. 60-64.
[18] Vasiliev *Goths in the Crimea*, p. 70-71.

an area in times of invasion and were large enough to accommodate their flocks, herds, and belongings as well as themselves. We know from Procopius's *Buildings* just how extensive these defensive works were and what vast sums were expended upon them by Justinian and his successors.[19]

Many historians have seen in this extensive fortification program an example of weakness, of panic on the part of the Byzantine state in this period. They cite it as a useless waste of money and effort. To do so is to misunderstand the problems faced by the Empire and its rulers. It was not money that was lacking to Justinian and his successors half so much as it was trustworthy manpower. The heavily-armed, professional Byzantine *cataphracti*, who were the élite troops in the armies of Belisarius, Narses, Maurice, and Heraclius, were generally unbeatable in the field, but in other ways were unsatisfactory. They were expensive to maintain, often mutinous—as Maurice was to discover to his sorrow—and particularly cruel and overbearing to the civilian population in the areas in which they operated. The long Ostrogothic war in Italy proved this over and over again.[20] So did engagements with the Berbers in North Africa, wars along the Danube frontier, and campaigns against the Sassanians in the East. To make matters worse, they were, in the hands of victorious generals, a positive danger to the Emperor himself, if ambition for the throne pervaded the minds of military commanders.

The policy of Justinian and his successors was thus to limit the size of the standing army drastically, far from the figures of the earlier Roman state, both in the interests of economy and of safety for themselves. Here lies the value of the extensive border defenses coupled with an efficient naval force. A local militia manning these fortifications could be depended upon to defend themselves and their homes against all but a major threat. They, with a few professional troops, could hold out with these defenses until the Imperial Government could rush larger professional forces by land and sea to the danger points. Sea power thus allowed a concentration of troops quickly where most needed.

Such was the defense system of the Mediterranean world under Justinian and his successors up to the time of the Moslem invasions. In general, it worked rather well. It was only in areas far

[19] *Procopius* VII, 97-177; 187-219; 223-393.
[20] *Procopius* IV, 157-59.

from the sea—in Northern Italy, along the Danube, and in the East—that it failed to defend adequately the Empire. Here, and particularly in the East, where Persian opposition was organized and strong, it failed to achieve its object and finally broke down completely under the impact of Islam. But until the seventh century the effectiveness and economy of this system of naval control, fortifications, and a small professional striking army was very real.

The defense system of Byzantium in the sixth and seventh centuries thus marks a break with that established by the land-based Roman world from Augustus through Theodosius with large forces established along the Rhine and Danube, Saharan Desert, and Persian frontiers. But it does have a remarkable similarity to a successful modern empire, that of Great Britain in the eighteenth and nineteenth centuries. Like Britain, the Byzantines had no effective naval rivals in the seas they dominated. Like Britain, they needed to maintain only a small professional army to supplement local defense forces in threatened areas. Like Britain, they avoided holding vast interior areas at high cost in men and money and concentrated on those spots worth the effort. Like Britain, they controlled areas which would enable their ships based on them to dominate, not just the seas, but the principal trade routes. Byzantine power in the sixth and early seventh centuries over Ceuta and Southern Spain, over North Africa, over Sicily, Sardinia, the Balkans, Corsica, Crete, and Cyprus, over Genoa, Naples, and Ravenna in Italy, over the Crimea, the Dardanelles, and Alexandria all made certain that this control remained effective. So, too, Britain controlled the seas in the eighteenth and nineteenth centuries from similar spots—Gibraltar, Malta, Cyprus, Suez, Aden, Singapore, Hongkong, Ceylon, Capetown, Newfoundland, the Falkland Islands, and the British West Indies. So, in conjunction with Britain, does the United States control the oceans today. In each case a sea empire proved cheap and relatively easy to maintain.

To understand this fact is to realize how relatively unimportant were the losses in territory suffered by Byzantium up to the Persian and Islamic invasions of the seventh century. Parts of the interior of Northern and Central Italy were lost by Byzantium in the late sixth and seventh centuries when the Lombards seeped into Italy. But as long as the Empire could hold the Venetian shore, Ravenna, and the Pentapolis in the Adriatic and Genoa, Rome, and Southern Italy on the other side, Lombard power was annoying but relatively ineffective. The importance of the Lombard invasions has probably been somewhat overrated. Similar is the case of the Avar-Slav advance south of the Danube into the Balkans and Greece. Here the damage done by the invaders seems more considerable than that in Italy. Many Greeks of the Peloponnesus, for instance, fled in the late sixth century to Sicily and Southern Italy,[21] just as many Italians left Lombardy to seek refuge in Venetia, Genoa, and the Pentapolis.[22] But neither invasion touched areas sufficiently important economically to the Empire to justify attempts to hold them, though attempts were made to do so. And more important, neither invasion seriously threatened the sea Empire which Byzantium had established in the Mediterranean world. Not until the seventh century, when Persians and Arabs entered the rich and vital provinces of Syria and Egypt, was Justinian's foundation seriously menaced.

There remains one important question. Just how did the Byzantine state in this period organize and control its naval power? Did it operate a large standing Imperial navy, or did it depend upon levies of ships used for commercial purposes to supplement its fleet in times of need? Unfortunately, only tentative answers can be given to such questions.

There seems no doubt that from the time of Justinian on, Byzantium maintained a respectable Imperial professional navy. In the seventh century we know the state maintained naval bases and shipyards at Carthage,[23] Acre,[24] Alexandria,[25] and Constantinople,[26] where many of the swift dromons, the armed naval vessels of the period, were built. Other naval stations appear to have been

[21] Charanis, P. "The Hellenization of Sicily" in *The American Historical Review* (1946) LVI, 80-81.

[22] Paul the Deacon *History of the Langobards* trans. W. Foulke (Phila. 1907), p. 79. Diehl, C. *Etudes sur l'Administration Byzantine dans l'Exarchat de Ravenne (568-71)* (Paris 1888), p. 351.

[23] *Procopius* II, 339.

[24] Hitti, P. K. *History of the Arabs* (New York 1940), p. 193.

[25] Butler *The Arab Conquest of Egypt* (Oxford 1902), p. 112-15. In Justinian's invasion of Vandal North Africa the admiral in charge and many of the sailors were Egyptians. *Procopius* II, 105.

[26] *Procopius* VII, 93-95. In the late eighth century Constantinople fitted out a fleet for Justinian II. Runciman *Byzantine Civilization* (London 1933), p. 153.

operated at Syracuse in Sicily[27] and Ravenna,[28] where were based those ships which patrolled the Tyrrhenian and Adriatic Seas respectively. Possibly another naval station was maintained in the Ceuta-Spanish Balearic area as well.[29] But there also seems to be a possibility that there were in existence, as early as the sixth century, provincial fleets not unlike the squadrons of the later Byzantine period. Thus we find in 536 that Scythia, Moesia, Caria, the Cyclades, and Cyprus were grouped by Justinian under a *Quaestor Iustianus exercitus*.[30] This must have been a naval command. There is also the possibility that the Crimea was depended upon for some naval service as is revealed in a *novella* by Tiberius in 575. This provided that the lands of Lazi, Bosporos, and Cherson were to be exempted from the previously imposed duty of building naval vessels.[31]

In addition to these Imperial and possibly provincial naval forces, in time of war the government could certainly impress commercial vessels into the fleet—particularly for use in transporting soldiers and supplies. But there is little evidence of just how this was accomplished in this period.

One thing is certain. Up to the time of the Islamic invasions, Byzantine naval might was not challenged in any serious fashion. Both Lombards and Slavs did take to the sea in the late sixth century. There is evidence that a Lombard squadron, probably from Southern Italy, attacked and failed to take Cagliari in 599.[32] It is also true that in 602, after a Byzantine fleet on the Danube had destroyed his rafts and forced abandonment of a contemplated attack on Constantinople, the Kagan of the Avars imported experienced boatbuilders from Lombard Italy to assist in the construction of a Slav fleet in Dalmatia.[33] But none of these efforts was more than local and, apparently, temporary. In 626 the Avars possessed only light boats for their attack on the Byzantine capital, and they were easily scattered by the fleet of Heraclius.[34]

But the Byzantine Empire of this period resembled the British

[27] *Liber Pontificalis* ed. Duchesne, p. 137. Diehl *Exarchat*, p. 197.

[28] Angelliqui et Andreas *Lib. Pont. Eccl. Ravennatis* in *Script. Rer. Lang. et Ital. Saec.* III. Diehl, *Exarchat*, p. 372.

[29] Carta-Raspi *op. cit.*, p. 88-98.

[30] Hill *History of Cyprus* (Cambridge 1940) I, 258.

[31] Zachariae von Lingenthal *Jus Graeco-Romanum* III, 23.

[32] Carta-Raspi *op. cit.*, p. 85-86.   [33] Vernadsky *Ancient Russia*, p. 196.

[34] Vasiliev *Byzantine Empire*, p. 235-41.

Empire of recent years in more than its use of naval power. It resembled it in being based on commerce and trade as well. Perhaps the economic basis of Justinian's creation was, as a matter of fact, even more important than its naval and military side. And in this, too, it marked a departure from the earlier Roman state which was much less sensitive to commercial and trading interests and much more agrarian in its basic economy and thinking.

A glance at the map of the Empire up to 641 shows its economic basis clearly. In the first place, every important industrial and commercial area of Mediterranean and Black Sea was directly or indirectly under the control of Constantinople's ruler. In the East, Syria, Egypt, Asia Minor, and the Crimean coast were firmly held; and in the West, North Africa, Southern Spain, the seaport cities of Italy and Dalmatia likewise were part of it. Only the Rhone River area of Southern France belonged to another power, the Franks. And here the nearby islands of Corsica, Sardinia, and the Balearics in Byzantine hands made minute surveillance and indirect control possible. How effective such control could be the Franks learned at the time of Maurice in the late sixth century. The expedition of Gonawald into Provence, backed by Byzantium, was a warning of just how intervention could take place.[35] It is not surprising that the Franks, possessing the strongest Germanic state in the West, found it wiser in this period to cooperate with the policies of the Eastern Roman Emperor. The same is true of the Visigoths in Spain.[36]

In addition to this control over the important economic areas of the Middle Sea, the Byzantines at this time controlled its exits also. Constantinople, Egypt, and Ceuta in Byzantine hands made it impossible for outside trade and commerce to enter this sea without permission of Byzantium. The western exit past Ceuta and Gibraltar incidentally, may have been more important in the sixth and seventh centuries—when the route between the Mediterranean world and the northern islands of Ireland and Britain was in some use—than is generally supposed.[37]

To the East the same commercial basis of Byzantium is also apparent in this period. For here were trade routes even more

[35] *Chronicle of Fredegarius* (Historiens de France) v, ii, 6. Gregory of Tours *op. cit.* iii, 53; vi, 26; vii, 36. Paul the Deacon *op. cit.*, p. 126.

[36] Gregory of Tours *op. cit.*, v, 39; vi, 40, 43. Gregory the Great *Epistolae* xiii, ep. xlvii. Paul the Deacon *op. cit.*, p. 125-26.

[37] Leonitus *Vita S. Johannis Eleemosynarii* ed. Gelzer (Leipsig 1883), x.

vital to Egypt, Syria and Asia Minor than those to the West. From the Far East came the valuable silks and spices so highly prized in the Mediterranean world and beyond. Byzantium's naval power could not extend beyond the shores of the Middle Sea, but her commercial interests could and did. Justinian and his successors made every effort to dominate economically this Far Eastern trade to the advantage of their Empire. In this effort these rulers ran into opposition from Sassanian Persia which fattened on its middleman's position between China, India, and the East Indies and the Mediterranean-Black Sea areas. The attempts of these Eastern Roman rulers to break Sassanian economic power took various forms. They probably explain much of the hostility between Ctesiphon and Constantinople up to 629.

First an attempt was made to by-pass Persia to the north and open up a northern trade route to Chinese products, principally silk. This led to Byzantine occupation and development of Crimean ports and to efforts to bring Armenia and the Caucasus area under the influence of Constantinople.[38] Commercial and political negotiations were entered into with the Turkish-Kazar state in the South Russian-Volga area which had direct connections with China through Turkestan. What success this policy achieved it is difficult to say, but Turkish ambassadors visited Byzantium in 563[39] and 568,[40] and at least one Byzantine embassy was sent to the Turkish capital late in the century. Cherson was firmly held against Turkish pressure in 581.[41] By 590 a firm policy of friendship was established with the Turkish-Kazar state.[42] This remained one of the cornerstones of Byzantine diplomacy for the next three centuries, and the kingdom of the Kazars remained a thorn in the side of Persian and later Arab attempts to dominate the land silk route to the Far East.

Equally active were sixth-century attempts to by-pass Persia to the south and reach Ceylon, the East Indies, and China by sea. Here the intermediary was the Christian Abyssinian kingdom on the lower Red Sea. Justinian and his successors supported diplomatically the use of Abyssinian shipping in the Indian Ocean,

---

[38] Vernadsky op. cit., pp. 155, 192-93. Vasiliev Goths in the Crimea, p. 70-71. Diehl Justinien, p. 378-86.

[39] Theophanes (ed. Bonn), p. 239.

[40] Menander Fragmenta (ed. Bonn), p. 47-56.

[41] Vernadsky op. cit., p. 41.   [42] Menander op. cit., p. 404.

hoping the Abyssinians would develop a Ceylon-Red Sea trade to the detriment of the Sassanians and the profit of the Byzantines.[43] It was also largely due to them that Abyssinia embarked in this period on a career of conquest on the Arabian side of the Red Sea.[44] Neither policy was a great success. By 532 Cosmas Indopleustes reveals that Abyssinian attempts to break Persian sea monopoly of the Ceylon-South Indian trade had ended in failure.[45] And in 570 Persian intervention in Hijaz thwarted Axsum's Arabian plans at the very moment when, with the Yemen conquered, an Ethiopian army was marching on the caravan city of Mecca.[46] Abyssinian troops were soon driven back across the Red Sea. Thus the Red Sea route was, at best, only partially opened up, though commerce arriving in Egypt by this route appears to have been not inconsiderable up to the seventh century.

Only partially successful to the north and south, Byzantium tried in still another way to deal economically with Persia and cut her profits in the important spice and silk trade. This involved the introduction of silk worms into the Empire itself. In 552 Nestorian monks smuggled some silk worms across Asia,[47] and within a few years the raising of them had spread into Syria[48] and perhaps even Cyprus. Justin II showed raw silk, domestically produced, to inquiring Turkish ambassadors in 568.[49] This may have lessened Byzantine dependence on the imported product, but it is doubtful if the Empire ever became more than partially self-sufficient in silk. Justinian also tried one more form of pressure on his Sassanian rivals. He set up at the frontier a state monopoly on purchase of Persian silk and attempted to set the price he was willing to pay for the imported product. The Persians refused to sell, apparently, at his figure, and the system eventually was abandoned.[50]

But this mercantilistic concern with the Eastern trade of the Empire continued. The old border system of import and export controls at Dara, Artaxata, Nisibis, and Callinicum remained in force throughout this period. A commercial treaty negotiated with the Persians in 562 contained a recognition of this system.[51] Economic control of foreign trade and commerce seems to have con-

[43] Diehl *Justinien*, pp. 392-400, 488. *Procopius* i, 192.

[44] *Procopius* i, 191-92. Hitti *op. cit.*, p. 63-65.

[45] Diehl *op. cit.*, p. 544-45.   [46] Hitti *op. cit.*, p. 64-66.

[47] *Procopius* v, 229-31. *Excerpta e Theophanes Historia* (ed. Bonn), p. 484.

[48] *ibid.*   [49] *ibid.*

[50] Lopez "Silk Industry," p. 12-13.   [51] Menander *op. cit.*, p. 361.

cerned Byzantine rulers, from Justinian on, far more than it ever did their Roman predecessors.

Along the same line is concern over gold coinage, both from the domestic and foreign standpoint. Export of gold outside the Empire had been forbidden since the late Empire, and the coinage of gold remained a most important regalian right. All coins within the state bore the image of the Emperor of Constantinople. Partly for economic reasons and partly for reasons of prestige, the Imperial government extended this system beyond its borders. Franks and Visigoths, beyond the direct political control of Byzantium, were careful not to infringe on these regulations. All gold coins that they struck up to 641, with the exception of a short period when Theodobert of the Franks was at war with Justinian, bore the image of Constantinople's ruler.[52] They were also careful to keep such gold coins as they struck at the same standard of weight and purity as the golden *nomismata* of the Emperors. Persian kings were equally careful not to infringe on the Byzantine gold monopoly. The only coins they issued with their own effigies upon them were of silver.[53] And in 562 they recognized, in a treaty negotiated between the two realms, that gold coinage was Byzantium's monopoly.[54] And Cosmas Indopleustes informs us that this gold coinage was the international trade medium of the Indian Ocean as well in the middle of the sixth century.[55] The Byzantine *nomismata*, like the almighty dollar in the modern world, was the international money par excellence and one protected and controlled at home and abroad by the rulers who issued it.

A similar mercantilistic concern over economic matters was manifested by the Byzantine government in internal as well as foreign trade and industry. One important regalian right which the Roman government had reserved to itself from the time of the late Empire was the manufacture of certain luxury items such as purple-dyed silk cloth and gold cloth. State monopolies since the late fourth century A.D., they remained so throughout this period. These textiles were manufactured in Imperial workshops employing state guilds of weavers and dyers. They alone had the right

[52] Prou *Catalogue des Monnaies Merovingiennes de la Bibliothèque Nationale* (Paris 1892). Lopez, R. S. "Mohammed and Charlemagne, A Revision" in *Speculum* (1943) xviii, p. 16-21.

[53] Lombard *op. cit.*, p. 146-47.   [54] Lopez "Silk Industry," p. 23-25.

[55] Cosmas Indicopleustes *Top. Christ (Pat Graeca* ed. Migne lxxxviii), pp. 115 and 447.

to make the Imperial purple, and only Emperors could decide how the products of these workshops would be disposed of.[56] In Justinian's time this was apparently a most prosperous activity, since there were more candidates for the Imperial silk makers' guild than there were places to fill.[57] By Heraclius's reign it was found necessary to restrict the right to join such guilds on an hereditary basis.[58]

Justinian, however, was not satisfied with monopoly over the manufacture of these fine special luxury products. He went even further. He set up a monopoly over the entire silk trade. Possibly this was an attempt to lower the high prices charged by Persians for raw silk at the Empire's border trade stations, but more probably it represented an attempt to gain revenue for the Imperial treasury. Only the Imperial *commerkiarioi* at the frontiers were allowed to buy imported raw silk. They were to sell it only to Imperial workshops. This policy was so drastic that it ruined many private silk manufacturers, particularly in Syria, and the Persians simply refused to sell at Justinian's price.[59] Some manufacturers even appear to have fled the Empire for Persian domains, taking with them their know-how in silk making.[60] At any rate, a portion of the Justinian monopoly was abandoned late in the sixth century. *Commerkiarioi* still bought the silk from the Persians at the frontiers, but at a price which apparently was sufficiently high to encourage sales, and they sold a portion of it to private silk merchants and others.[61] The manufacture of the special luxury silks and textiles, however, remained in control of the state.

There were other regalian rights possessed by the Imperial government in this period as well. Papyrus by the time of Justinian was processed and sold by the state in Egypt, and most probably arms production, the mining and sale of iron, and timber for naval purposes were under close state supervision.[62]

This paternalistic interest of the Eastern Roman Emperors in internal and foreign industry and trade, far beyond that possessed by the earlier Roman state, was more than justified. For trade and industry brought in money, and money was more indispensable

[56] Lopez "Moh. and Charlemagne," p. 16-21.
[57] *Nov. Just.* xxxviii, 6.   [58] *Basil* liv, 16.
[59] *Procopius* vi, 297-301.   [60] *ibid.*
[61] Lopez "Silk Industry," p. 12-13.
[62] Lopez "Moh. and Charlemagne," p. 16-21.

to them and their control of their Mediterranean Empire than it was to their predecessors. To understand this is to appreciate why coinage and economic matters were so much a concern of Justinian and his successors through Heraclius.

Money was needed at Byzantium for more than normal governmental purposes—the payment of professional army, navy, and bureaucracy. It was indispensable in diplomacy as well. And diplomacy was in this period as important as army or navy in tying together and protecting the scattered lands of the Mediterranean and Black Sea over whom the Basileus of Constantinople ruled. Gold was an invaluable adjunct to naval power and military force.

Large subsidies of 20,000 to 30,000 pieces of gold a year were poured out to Persia by Constantinople in times of peace.[63] This probably made Sassanian rulers less willing to attack Constantinople than might otherwise have been the case. Similar subsidies were paid at regular intervals to the Avars and were scattered among the barbarian tribes along the Northern, African, and Syrian frontiers. With this gold went honorary Byzantine titles and special gifts of priceless purple Imperial silk cloth. Used properly, such gold and presents were a great protection to the Empire. They were used to incite one people or faction against another which might be a threat to Byzantium. They transformed most border peoples into clients who looked to Constantinople's golden palace for support. They heightened the prestige of the Imperial Caesars. At one time or another Ghassanids in Syria, Abyssinian monarchs, Avars and Slavs in Eastern Europe, Franks, Lombards, and Visigoths in the West, and Berber tribes in North Africa were all recipients of Byzantine bounty. As a system of control it was probably as effective as and much less costly than full-scale war. The earlier Roman state had previously used this policy along its borders. Justinian was not the originator of it. But with him the scope and extent of the system increased immensely.[64] Down to the end of the Byzantine period it was to remain an almost instinctive ingredient of Constantinople's foreign policy.

This system of subsidies has been much criticized by historians since the time of Procopius.[65] It has been viewed as a bad substitute for real military force properly applied and as a terrible drain on the gold resources of the Mediterranean world. While it is

[63] Lombard *op. cit.*, p. 144-46.   [64] Diehl *Justinian*, p. 367-77.
[65] *ibid.*, p. 409-13. Vasiliev *Byzantine Empire*, p. 174.

possible that Justinian in his later years relied on it too exclusively, criticisms of the system seem greatly to exaggerate its weaknesses.

In the first place, a large part of the gold scattered among client states along Byzantium's frontiers finally returned to the Empire in trade and commercial dealings. Subsidies then not only protected the Empire and heightened its prestige, but also served to expand its commercial and trade interests, particularly in the Western portion of the Mediterranean world. Such gold helped stimulate international trade. It may actually have helped to settle the unfavorable trade balance of the agricultural West and possibly Persia in relation to the more advanced industrial and commercial areas of Syria, Egypt, and Asia Minor. As a policy it bears a startling resemblance to Imperial Britain's eighteenth- and nineteenth-century practice of loans and subsidies to allies and clients all over the world. It seems even more like the loans, Lend-Lease and Marshall Plan of the United States of our own day. Its success must have been considerable, for all Byzantine rulers used it as an adjunct to military and naval force. It could not take the place of such force, but it could assist in the defense of Imperial frontiers and interests.

Supplies of gold and the Byzantine Empire itself, however, depended on the maintenance of a high level of prosperity within the Empire. Byzantine governmental economic interests show the awareness of this fact by the Emperors during this period. The problem is to judge the extent of their success. In what measure did prosperity in the Mediterranean areas they controlled keep a constant golden lifeblood flowing into the coffers of their treasury?

At the time of Anasthasius in the early sixth century there can be little doubt that the realms of the Eastern Emperor were prosperous. The abolition of the *chrysargyron*, the ending of the enforced fiscal accountability of local town officials in the collection of taxes, the Imperial treasure horde of 320,000 pounds of gold—all these point to a flourishing state of affairs in the East. In the West, as has been noted, Ostrogothic Italy enjoyed a real prosperity in this period. So, too, did Vandal Africa and Visigothic Spain. But what of the world after the expanded and restored Romania of Justinian and his successors?

Here many historians have followed Procopius and his criticisms far too blindly. He, critic of Justinian in all things, is nowhere more biting than in his review of the latter's fiscal and financial policies. He shows us a gloomy Mediterranean world by the time of Justinian's death. We are given a picture of an exhausted treasury, wasted in fruitless wars and foolish subsidies to Persians and other enemies of the Empire.[66] We are told of the terrible weight of Imperial taxation placed upon the people by venal tax-gatherers led by John of Cappadocia in the East[67] and the fiscal jackals who, in the West, followed Belisarius into North Africa[68] and Narses into Italy.[69] We get a view of an unpaid soldiery, of fortresses left undefended on the borders, of a state exhausted, decadent and on point of collapse.[70] Now can this really be an accurate picture? The evidence up to the time of Phocas and the invasions of Syria and Egypt by the Persians needs to be examined before any definite conclusion can be reached.

In the first place, it must be admitted that many of Procopius's criticisms are just. Justinian did use immense amounts of money, did use a venal and corrupt bureaucracy to gather it, and did tax his Empire heavily. So, too, did his immediate successors. There is ample evidence from sources other than Procopius to prove this Byzantine fiscal tyranny. The letters of Gregory the Great at the close of the sixth century condemning the venality and rapacity of Byzantine officials in Corsica, Sicily, and elsewhere bear out his contentions.[71] So does evidence from independent Coptic sources in Egypt.[72] So, too, do Justinian's own decrees, which attempted to undo with one hand what his fiscal policies were doing with the other.[73] There is further ample evidence of constant interference of the Byzantine state in the economic lives of its subjects.

But what is not proved is that this taxation and governmental interference with economic life were such as to result in financial exhaustion and ruination of the Mediterranean world that Byzantium controlled. Heavy taxation does not necessarily result in economic stagnation, as the United States at the present time seems to show clearly. Neither does light taxation necessarily make for prosperity, as eighth- and tenth-century France prove with equal vehemence. A corrupt and venal taxgathering system does not necessarily mean an impoverished state, though it does infuriate

---

[66] *Procopius* VI, 131-35, 227-33. [67] *ibid.*, p. 233-55.
[68] *Procopius* II, 277-79. [69] *Procopius* IV, 159-61; VI, 313.
[70] *Procopius*, VI, 179-81, 279-91, 351-53.
[71] Gregory the Great *Epistolae.*
[72] Butler *Arab Conquest of Egypt*, p. 175-83.
[73] Holmes *Age of Justinian and Theodora* II, 440-55, 472-88.

its victims. It may be coexistent with real prosperity. Fatimid Egypt, early fourteenth-century or eighteenth-century France, and China throughout most of its history, warn one to beware of that generalization. Nor is state direction of a large measure of a realm's economy necessarily fatal to its economic life. Venice, Tudor and eighteenth-century England, Inca Peru, and nineteenth-century Germany give the lie to such a contention. What is important is that the industrial, commercial, and productive potentialities of an area be fully operative. Let us examine the Byzantine Mediterranean world of the sixth century to see if this was so.

In the first place, governmental revenues did not seriously decrease under Justinian and his successors up to the time of Heraclius. Rather the evidence is to the contrary. When Justinian died, Procopius admits that a large portion of the gold stored up by Anasthasius was still in the treasury.[74] Fiscal policies adopted by him were continued by his successors until the early seventh century. Not until the time of Heraclius is there found much evidence of fiscal difficulties, and in this case, as will be noted, special conditions were the cause. The Slav invasions of the Balkans and the Lombard penetrations of Italy touched regions that were not fiscally important to the treasury or contributors in any important way to the Mediterranean's economic life. Elsewhere comparative peace prevailed. But most important of all, Justin II, Tiberius, and Maurice all followed the same type of governmental policy as Justinian—a policy based on ample supplies of golden nomismata. The same expensive fortification system, the same wide use of subsidies to client states, East and West, the same professional army and navy and bureaucracy were apparently used. If the state was exhausted financially there is little evidence of it here.

Such modifications of state regimentation as we do find in this century are an evidence of the state's financial prosperity rather than the reverse. In this class is the abandonment of the Imperial monopoly of the silk trade. So, too, is a real relaxation in shipping regulations on the tribute grain delivered to Constantinople. Justinian increased tenfold the compensation of the navicularii who transported this grain from Egypt,[75] and Maurice went even further. He lightened the statutory responsibilities of the captains in charge of the grain ships by providing that the State Treasury,

74 Procopius VI, 229-31.
75 Charanis "Soc. Struct. of the Later Roman Empire," p. 49.

rather than these latter, would pay for losses incurred by ship-wrecks.[76]

Other evidence of wealth is to be found in the vast *limes* and fortifications that Justinian and his successors constructed and maintained. In Africa, Italy, the Crimea, the Balkans, and the East, these constructions stand even today as remarkable tribute to the economic strength of a state that could construct them. So, too, does Justinian's rebuilding of much of Antioch destroyed by earth-quake,[77] and his reconstruction of cities and irrigation systems in North Africa. Perhaps even more impressive is the evidence pro-vided by the vast church of Hagia Sophia, the basilicas of St. Vitale and St. Apollinare-in-Classe in Ravenna and the rich and opulent churches and monasteries of sixth-century Coptic Egypt.

The tenor and extent of the artistic and intellectual life of the sixth-century Mediterranean world exhibit the same feeling of vigor and prosperity. It was Justinian's Constantinople that devel-oped, or rather perfected, the great Byzantine style in architecture and mosaic art. The richness of ivories, silks and smaller objects of this period and style is equally impressive.[78] In Egypt the time is that of the greatest development of Coptic textiles and artistic creations.[79] Even a smaller center like Cyprus was able in this century to make real artistic contributions.

In addition, intellectual life was impressive. Not only did Con-stantinople produce Procopius, but other writers like Agathias, Menander, and John Malalas. The intellectual achievement of the great Code Justinian showed the acuteness of such legal minds as Tribonian and others. Syrian centers like Beirut show clearly that this legal intellect was not confined to the capital.[80] Alexandria, too, made its contribution in its revived interest in the Greek phi-losophy and science. We are just beginning to realize the debt that later Moslem intellectual life owes to Alexandria's sixth-century renaissance in these subjects.[81] Even the West saw in this period such figures as Gregory the Great and Isadore of Seville. Can a world which shows such developments be thought of as exhausted and decadent?

A closer examination of the economic life of various sections

[76] John of Nikiu *Chronicle* trans. R. H. Charles (London 1916), p. 165.
[77] Holmes *op. cit.*, II, 539-43.   [78] *ibid.*, p. 529-39, 749-53.
[79] Butler *op. cit.*, p. 103.
[80] Dawson, C. *The Making of Europe* (London 1932), p. 117-21.
[81] *ibid.*, p. 115-16.

of the Mediterranean world make this even clearer. In the East, Constantinople continued to be the greatest city of the sixth- and seventh-century Empire. It had outgrown its late Roman fortifications, and its suburbs were extensive. Diehl estimates its population at the time of Justinian at about a million.[82] Its commerce was world-wide in extent, fed by many trade streams from both Mediterranean and Black Sea areas. The seat of the great imperial luxury textile production, its industrial life was extensive.

To the north was the Crimea with cities like Cherson and Bosporos. Both Justinian and those who succeeded him took care to fortify these and other centers and hold them against Kazar pressure.[83] Termini of the Russian fur trade[84] and of the northern silk routes, they were important and prosperous centers.

Of Asia Minor and its many cities there is little known in this period except that it continued to make important economic contributions to the Empire's trade and prosperity. Across the Aegean the Balkans were certainly in large part not prosperous at this time. Convulsed by Avar and Slavic invasions in the late sixth century, this area was particularly unfortunate. The Slavic penetrations went as far as the Peloponnesus in Greece, and large numbers of harassed Peloponnesian Greeks in this period fled the land to find safer homes in Sicily and Southern Italy. It should be emphasized, however, that this area had not even in the second century been of much economic importance to the Roman Empire. However, the lack of prosperity of this unfortunate area may be overstressed, for the Avar treasure, gathered in no small measure in the form of booty from this land and seized later by Charlemagne, was so considerable as to show indications that wealth was not unknown even just south of the Danube.[85]

Syria was, along with Asia Minor, another very prosperous section of the Empire. Though adversely affected in certain areas by earthquakes and Persian invasions it remained enormously wealthy up to the early seventh century. Procopius attests to its flourishing condition.[86] The introduction of sericulture in the late sixth century must have added to its agricultural prosperity, as well as providing its important silk manufacturing centers like Tyre and Beirut with

[82] Diehl *Justinien*, p. 540-50.   [83] *Procopius* VII, 215-17.
[84] Mierow *The Gothic History of Jordanes*, p. 60.
[85] Russell *Charlemagne* (New York 1930), p. 175-76.
[86] *Procopius* VI, 297.

a portion of their indispensable raw material. Its coastal cities, in particular, seem to have been wealthy in no small measure owing to the enterprise of their merchants in trading with the entire Mediterranean world.

Perhaps even more prosperous was Egypt and its great city of Alexandria in particular. Alexandria was, after Constantinople in this period, the most important metropolis in the Mediterranean world and perhaps even more important than the former as a commercial center. Trading with the East, it was the terminus of the Red Sea spice and silk trade route. It exported these goods, Egypt's agricultural surplus and the products of its own industrial workshops throughout the Mediterranean. It had thus a vast Mediterranean commerce. Its grain went to Constantinople, its ships to Italy filled with grain and luxury manufactures which it exchanged for timber.[87] It sent its merchants to Spain and to Marseilles and other cities of Southern France.[88] It traded extensively with North Africa.[89] It seems probable, also, that its great ships sailed through the Pillars of Hercules and carried on an extensive trade in tin with distant Britain.[90] If so, this would explain the source of Eastern and Greek elements in Irish Iconography and the Celtic Church and the surprising knowledge of Greek possessed by Irish scholars.

Some index of Alexandria's wealth is to be found in the riches possessed by the Church. John the Almsgiver, Patriarch of Alexandria in the late sixth century, fell heir to 8,000 pounds of gold in the Episcopal palace upon his accession.[91] He possessed a fleet of thirteen large trading vessels engaged in commerce with the Pentapolis and the Adriatic regions of Italy alone.[92] He engaged between 596 and 603 in a long series of negotiations with Gregory the Great on procuring from Italy ship timbers suitable for naval construction.[93] When Jerusalem, taken and devastated by the Persians in the early seventh century, needed relief, he was wealthy enough to send 1,000 *nomismata*, 1,000 sacks of grain, 1,000 measures of dried beans, 1,000 pounds of iron, 1,000 ropes of dried fish, 1,000 jugs of wine, and 1,000 Coptic Egyptian workmen to aid in

[87] Diehl *L'Egypte Chrétienne et Byzantine* (Paris 1937), p. 486.
[88] Leonitus *Vita S. Johannis Eleemosynarii* xiii. *Registrum* vi, 4.
[89] Diehl *op. cit.*, p. 486.   [90] Diehl *L'Afrique Byzantine*, p. 406-07.
[91] Leonitus *op. cit.*, xlv.   [92] *ibid.*, xxv, iii. Diehl *Egypte*, p. 486.
[93] *Registrum* vi, 58; vii, 37; viii, 38, 29; ix, 175; xiii, 45.

its restoration.[94] Since the wine, iron, and possibly the fish were not indigenous to Egypt, this reflects the scope of Alexandria's foreign trade. The close connection between church and commerce in Egypt is emphasized in several other instances. The Patriarch Apollinaris gave fifty pounds of gold to the youthful son of a bankrupt merchant to set him up again in business.[95] John the Almsgiver also once gave three ships in succession to a certain captain. The first two were wrecked in the treacherous waters of the Syrtis Gulfs. The third, a "great" ship, capable of carrying 20,000 measures of grain, he navigated more successfully.[96]

Alexandria was, like Constantinople where bankers accepted deposits at interest, also an important financial center in this period. Money was loaned at 12 per cent interest, the legal rate under the Justinian code.[97] Alexandrian bankers may have had branches in Constantinople as well. In 541, for example, an Alexandrian priest in Constantinople borrowed twenty *solidi* for four months. He repaid it in Alexandria at 8 per cent interest and 4 per cent supplementary charges—12 per cent in all, the legal rate.[98] The *argentarius* employed by Pope Gregory the Great at the end of the century seems to have served as a banker on a similar international scale,[99] showing that the West was linked to the East in international finance.

Examination of the Western provinces of the Empire shows a similar pattern of prosperity. North Africa may have suffered from revolts and the rapacity of Byzantine taxgatherers in the period immediately after it was conquered by Belisarius, but if so, it soon became very prosperous. It remained largely agricultural. Its rich soil provided an exportable surplus of grain and olive oil. Some grain was exported to Constantinople,[100] perhaps to supplement Egypt's tribute contributions. Its olive oil drawn from the vast groves established by Carthaginians was a more important source of wealth. When, in 647, the Arab raiders who defeated Gregory, the Patrician of Africa, asked whence came the immense richness and gold they found in his treasure, it was answered that this came from the olive whose oil the Greeks

---

[94] Leonitus *op. cit.*, xx.

[95] Moscus *Pratum Spirituale* cxciii.

[96] Leonitus *op. cit.*, x, xiii.

[97] *Codex Just.* iv, 32.

[98] Caire, P. *Masp.*, 67, 126.

[99] Gregory the Great *Epist.* xi, 16.

[100] In 608, Heraclius, Exarch of Africa, kept in North Africa the ships that carried grain to Constantinople. *Theophanes*, p. 296.

bought in large amounts for gold.[101] Carthage was in this period an important international trading city.

The same is true of Italy. The Lombard invasion may have caused economic difficulties in the interior, but large areas around Rome, Ravenna, Genoa, Naples and Sicily remained prosperous. The letters of Pope Gregory reveal an Italy almost as wealthy as that of Theodoric.[102] There seems little doubt that the losses resulting from the long Ostrogothic Wars were soon made good. An especially active commerce with the East was maintained at Ravenna and the Pentapolis,[103] a forerunner of Venice's later great trade and prosperity in the same general area.

About Spain in this period there is little information other than the fact that Greek and eastern merchants were found in the interior far beyond the limits of Byzantine territory.[104] The Arab conquest of 711, however, found Spain with flourishing cities containing large Jewish colonies, and the treasure of the Visigothic kings captured by Tarik and Musa was so great that it assumed legendary proportions in Arab folklore.[105] The source of this wealth seems to have been largely agricultural and natural products.

There is more available information about France in these early Merovingian times, thanks to Gregory of Tours. Though outside of direct Byzantine control, France shared in the general prosperity of the West. Its great Mediterranean port of Marseilles and the smaller centers of Fos and Arles were entrepôts that tapped a rich trade to the interior by way of the Rhone valley route. Gold coins were in current use[106] and the court of the Merovingians was luxurious with its wines and spices imported from the East.[107] France, too, seems to have been mainly agricultural in this period, with slaves shipped from Marseilles and other ports in Provence serving as one of its most important exports.[108]

The international trade that linked the agricultural West with the East was in this period, as earlier, almost entirely in the hands

101 Ibn Idhari Bayano 'l Magreb trans. E. Fagnan (Algiers 1901) I, 7.
102 See Gregory the Great Epistolae.   103 Registrum VI, 58; VII, 37; IX, 175.
104 Paul Diac. Emerit. De Vita Patr. Emerit in España Sagrada ed. Florez, XIII, 348.
105 Marçais La Berbérie Musulmane et L'Orient au Moyen Age (Paris 1947), p. 24. C. Sánchez-Albornoz y Menduina Ruina y extinctión del municipio Romano en España (Buenos Aires 1943) gives a less sanguine view of urban survival.
106 Bloch, M. "Le Problème de l'Or au Moyen Age" in Ann. d'Hist. Econ. et Soc. (1933) V, 8-11.
107 Pirenne op. cit., p. 88-91.   108 ibid., p. 96-100.

of Eastern entrepreneurs, Syrians, Greeks, and Jews. In France the
Syrians in the sixth and early seventh centuries imported spices,
wines, and papyrus not only to Marseilles, but as far inland as
Paris and Tours.[109] Colonies of them were settled in almost every
important commercial center.[110] The same is true of the Jews, who
were particularly active in the slave trade in the cities of Southern
France.[111] Greeks seem to have been less active in the trade of this
region, though there were some in the area in this period.[112]

In Italy, colonies of Easterners were particularly active and important. Ravenna had a sizable Greek population[113] and even an
Armenian quarter.[114] Rome had Greeks,[115] Alexandrians[116] and
Syrians[117] whose number included many merchants. Jews were
found in Ravenna,[118] Naples[119] and elsewhere. Many of these
Easterners, particularly the Greeks, seem to have been brought to
Italy in official capacity as members of the Byzantine governmental service or to have held positions in the Church. Others
settled in the peninsula for trading reasons. Rome in this period
was, like Ravenna, half Greek.[120]

North Africa, Sicily, and Sardinia present a similar picture. As
late as the ninth century the Arab geographer Yaqubi found many
Greeks (Roum) settled in the cities of North Africa.[121] These
Greeks seem to have been descendants of those brought to this
province in the Byzantine period by trade or governmental service. The activity of Greek merchants in the trade in olive oil has
already been noted. Similarly Syrians and Egyptians were active
in the commerce between the East and this rich area.[122] Spain
provides less information except that Alexandrian merchants
traded thither regularly, and its foreign commerce, like that of
other Western areas, seems to have been largely Eastern controlled.

[109] *ibid.*, p. 80-81.   [110] *ibid.*, p. 82-85.   [111] *ibid.*, p. 99.
[112] *Acta Concil. Narbon.* in Mansi *Coll. Concil.*, IX. Heyd *op. cit.*, p. 22. Pirenne
op. cit., p. 80-81.
[113] Diehl *Exarchat*, p. 279.   [114] *ibid.*
[115] Gregarovius *Geschichte der Stat Rum in Mittelalter* 3rd ed. (Stuttgart 1876)
II, 382.
[116] Rossi *Inscriptiones Christianae* (Rome 1857) II, 454-55.
[117] Gregory the Great *Epist.* x, 39. *Liber Pont.* pp. 15, 125.
[118] *Procopius* III, 99.
[119] Heyd *op. cit.*, p. 125-28. Dopsch *Foundations of Western Civilization*, p. 342.
[120] *Procopius* III, 74.   [121] Marçais *Berbérie*, p. 70-73.
[122] Diehl *L'Afrique Byzantine*, p. 406-07.

It cannot be denied that there was some commerce in the hands of native Western merchants as well as these Easterners. Some Italians from the Adriatic area traded with the East[123] and North African merchants sent their wares to Spain and Southern France.[124] But except for strictly local trade and the exceptions noted above, the pattern of commerce is similar everywhere in the Mediterranean-Black Sea area and not basically different from that of earlier centuries. Greeks, Syrians, and Jews were the great international traders who linked a relatively prosperous agricultural West and a prosperous industrial East. It is possible that the conditions of peace established for almost a century by Byzantium in the Middle Sea increased both the amount of trade and Eastern dominance of it. From an economic standpoint, then, the Byzantine Empire was simply a recognition of this Eastern dominance in political terms. Imperial gold *nomismata* and Eastern merchants were as important as symbols of this dominance as the Byzantine fleet. The Franks, Visigoths, and others outside immediate Imperial control paid the former two even more tribute than they did the latter.

Yet there is one difficult point that needs clarification—that is, whether or not the agricultural West was drained of gold during the period by Eastern commercial dominance of Mediterranean trade. Perhaps the best that can be said is that there is little evidence of such a drain. Urban life did not increase in large areas of the West in the sixth and early seventh centuries, but neither is there any evidence of decline.[125] The gold coinage that the Franks continued to strike in the sixth and early seventh centuries is still of Byzantine design and shows little evidence of lowering of purity and standard.[126] The evidences of prosperity in the West, the fact that in Italy and North Africa and perhaps even Southern France some native merchants entered into international trade themselves, seems to point to other conclusions.[127]

The grain of Sicily, olive oil and wheat of North Africa, the

---

[123] Angelliqui et Andreas *Lib. Pont. Eccl. Rav.*, 30, p. 294. Diehl *Exarchat*, p. 279-80.

[124] Pirenne *op. cit.*, p. 86.

[125] For an opposing view that these centuries saw a steady and progressive economic decline, see Lombard *op. cit.*, p. 143-44. Both Dopsch and Pirenne, however, take a less extreme position.

[126] See opposite view in Lombard *op. cit.*, p. 144. But Lombard is talking here mainly about the late seventh and the eighth centuries.

[127] See notes 123 and 124.

timber and salt of the Adriatic, the iron and metals of Spain and Gaul, and the exportable surplus of slaves, as well as many other natural products, were in high demand in the East, just as the spices, papyrus, wines, silks, and textiles and other industrial and luxury products of Alexandria, Syria, and Constantinople were prized in the West. If the East had the edge in these transactions, selling highly priced goods and controlling shipping and distribution profits as well and buying in return lower priced natural products, the West did not lose too much. It, too, gained in the exchange. Procopius's picture of an exhausted and wasted Empire seems far from reality.

Equally difficult is the problem of the Mediterranean world's relationship, from an economic standpoint, with the Eastern lands of Persia, India, and China. Did the same prosperity prevail in this trade in this period, and was the balance of trade in favor of Syria, Egypt, and Constantinople on that side as it was to the West? Or did gold drain even further eastward? These are difficult problems to answer. As has been noted, the Byzantine government's efforts to develop northern and southern routes by passing the Sassanians were only partially successful. So, too, were attempts to relieve dependence on imported silk by growing a native variety and efforts to force Persian exporters to accept a buyer's price for silk. By and large, Byzantine dependence on the Persian middleman remained, and most Far Eastern wares reached the Mediterranean world through the central Sassanian-dominated routes. In addition, for many years large subsidies of 20,000 to 30,000 pieces of gold a year were sent by Byzantium to the Persian monarchs. But did these two drain gold East, or did the industrial efficiency of Syria, Egypt, and Constantinople permit a trade balance with Persia to be maintained in spite of the purchases of Eastern wares and gold subsidies? Two facts seem to indicate that the latter is a possible solution. First the Byzantine *nomismata* was still in the middle of the sixth century the international money par excellence in an area in the Indian Ocean controlled by Persian merchants. Secondly, the Sassanians never coined the more valuable gold, but only silver. Both these facts seem to point to an economic dominance, however indirect, as effective in the East as the West on the part of the Byzantine monarchs.[128]

[128] Again Lombard holds opposing views in *op. cit.*, p. 146-47. His explanations,

From a naval and economic standpoint the Byzantine Mediterranean Empire was up to the early seventh century a strong and vital state, but it had two major weaknesses. The first of these weaknesses lay in the religious sphere. For Syria and Egypt, though prosperous, hated the Orthodoxy that Constantinople and the rest of the Empire insisted upon. Justinian, expanding West into Spain, Italy and North Africa, abandoned the pro-Monophysite position of Zeno and Anasthasius. His orthodoxy was popular in Constantinople, Asia Minor and the West, but not in the East. While Theodora lived she favored the Monophysite party, and thus the imperial pair managed to carry water on both shoulders.[129] But with her death Justinian turned to a fierce persecution of Syrian and Coptic national churches. To make matters worse he developed in his old age certain heretical opinions unacceptable to the Orthodox party as well.[130]

The result was a serious breach in Imperial unity. Justinian's successors continued his policies in the religious sphere. As a result Syria and Egypt became steadily more estranged from Constantinople and the rest of the Empire. This cleavage was, of course, more than religious. It represented a socio-cultural split between Graeco-Roman thinking and culture on the one hand and Eastern-dominated Syriac-Coptic culture on the other. It was possibly sharpened by an economic struggle between Alexandria and Constantinople for Mediterranean markets as well. The close connection between Church and commerce in Egypt bears out this possibility. Far from diminishing, the cleavage grew throughout the sixth and early seventh centuries. The policy of saddling the Syrian and Egyptian Churches with Orthodox Melchite bishops, hated by their Monophysite suffragans, did not help. Neither did the heavy taxation levied on these areas by a rapacious alien Greek bureaucracy. Syria and Egypt, prosperous though they were, became more and more restless and unwilling to bear the yoke of the Imperial rulers of Byzantium.

The second weakness was a military one. Byzantium's navy, coupled with extensive fortifications, local militia forces and a small professional army was an inexpensive and generally adequate system for protecting most of the Empire's borders. It was

---

however, seem somewhat unconvincing, particularly as to the disposition of gold supposedly drained East by the Sassanian rulers.

[129] Holmes *op. cit.*, II, 668-72. [130] *ibid.*, p. 702-05.

not so satisfactory for holding any long interior frontier against a well-organized opponent. The Avars with their Slavic allies proved this in the Balkans, as the Lombards did in some respects in Italy. Yet neither of these areas was important enough for this to matter very much. It was quite different with Persia. Across this border lay Syria and Egypt, the Empire's richest provinces. Their loss would represent a tragedy to the Empire.

Until the death of Maurice, murdered in 602 by his own troops in the midst of a satisfactory campaign against the Avars on the Danube frontiers,[131] Persian offensive efforts were largely thwarted by Byzantine gold and her armed forces. The army, though small, was, as Maurice's *Tactikon* clearly shows, still excellently equipped, organized, paid, and commanded.[132] But with his death its discipline vanished. The brutal and incompetent Phocas seized power. Soon the administration was paralyzed, the provinces left without leadership. Disaster struck the Byzantine world.

The Avars pushed across the Danube frontiers. Still worse, able Sassanian monarchs realized their opportunity had come. They proclaimed their interest in the Monophysite churches and swarmed across the frontiers into Syria and Egypt.[133] The disaffected local Syrian and Egyptian militia were both unwilling and unable to defend themselves. In 611[134] Antioch fell, and in 614 Jerusalem followed suit.[135] By 619 all Egypt, including the rich city of Alexandria was in the hands of Chosroes II, the Sassanian monarch.[136] Constantinople paid the price for its long religious persecutions in Syria and Egypt. Then the Persians closed in for the kill. Persian armies moved into Asia Minor and in 626 appeared at Asiatic Chalcedon opposite the Golden Horn. An Avar army, allied to the Sassanians, appeared on the European side and cut off the capital by land.[137] The last days of Byzantium seemed at hand.

Two things saved the Empire in its moment of peril—leadership and sea power. In 616 the incompetent Phocas was deposed, and power was seized by Heraclius, governor of North Africa, who had sailed with a fleet from Africa to the rescue of his Empire.

---

[131] Paul the Deacon *op. cit.*, p. 168.

[132] Maurice *Strategicon* ed. Scheffer. Runciman *Byzantine Civilization*, p. 139-40.

[133] Vasiliev *Byzantine Empire*, p. 237-38.

[134] Conybeare, F. C. "Antiochus Strategos" "Account of the Sack of Jerusalem" in *English Historical Review* xxv (1910).

[135] Vasiliev *op. cit.*, p. 238.   [136] *ibid.*

[137] Butler *Arab Conquest of Egypt*, p. 120. Runciman *op. cit.*, p. 40.

He found affairs in a deplorable state—the treasury empty, since revenues of Syria and Egypt and other revolted and disorganized provinces could not be collected, the army unpaid and mutinous, and the capital city all but undefended.[138]

His first task was the reestablishment of order. Next he stripped the churches of their treasure in gold and used this to pay and equip the army and the fleet. He then made careful preparations, and from 622 to 628 waged a series of brilliant campaigns. It was control of the sea maintained by his fleet that enabled him to do so. This naval control enabled him to transport and supply his army in Armenia on the borders of Persia itself. It also enabled Constantinople to resist an attack launched in 626. Byzantine naval forces easily scattered the Avar flotilla of small boats that was its enemies' only sea threat,[139] and by keeping the water approaches to the Golden Horn open were able to provision and supply the besieged capital. Unable to take Byzantium by assault, first the Avar and then the Persian forces melted away.[140]

Meanwhile Heraclius from his Armenian position menaced communications between Mesopotamia and Persian armies in Syria, Egypt, and Asia Minor. Unable to dislodge Heraclius, and beaten by his generalship several times in the open field, the Sassanians, so near to victory, began to draw back. Whereupon Heraclius carried the war into the enemy camp. He marched on Ctesiphon, the Persian capital, and destroyed the last enemy army that barred his way. The capital city and immense booty fell into his hands. By 629 the war was over. The Persians murdered their king, and his successor sued for peace. Heraclius's price was the abandonment of the Persians' Syrian and Egyptian conquests and the payment of a heavy indemnity. Byzantium was the unconditional victor over its ancient foe. Heraclius carrying the Cross rescued from Persian hands, was greeted on his triumphant return to Constantinople with a Te Deum by a deliriously happy population. Romania had been restored. Order was soon reestablished in all the provinces.[141] Only Spain did not return entirely to its Byzantine allegiance. Here the Visigoths had used Byzantium's crisis to

[138] The best account of this reign is Pernice, A. *L'Imperatore Eraclio* (Florence 1905).

[139] Vasiliev *op. cit.*, p. 239-40.   [140] *ibid.*

[141] Pernice, A. *op. cit.*, for fullest account.

retake in 616[142] and 625[143] most of the area taken from them by Justinian in 554. Some measure of Byzantine control was probably maintained or reestablished, however, over Ceuta and some areas nearby, for the Imperial government kept a foothold in Spain as late as the end of the seventh century.[144]

But reestablishment of Romania was not greeted in Syria and Egypt with any of Constantinople's joy. Heraclius was in large measure responsible for this fact. He repeated all his predecessors' mistakes. He reestablished a fiscal tyranny and Greek taxgatherers.[145] Worse, he persecuted the Coptic and Syrian Monophysites cruelly, perhaps because of their support of Persia in the recent decades.[146] When this persecution failed to bring religious unity or break down the opposition to Orthodoxy on the part of these areas, he went one step further. He attempted a religious compromise, his own doctrine of Monothelitism. This was even worse. Orthodoxy enforced from Constantinople had alienated most of Egypt and Syria. Monothelitism alienated practically everyone. The Orthodox West refused to accept it.[147] So, too, did the Orthodox Greek population of the Syrian coastal towns and Egypt.[148] Heraclius then persecuted both groups and tried to enforce his doctrines on a resisting East and West. In vain. He merely weakened his Empire, already exhausted by the two decades of war with Persia. The wounds were not bound up, and religious hatred bubbled and boiled.

It was thus in 634 a weakened and divided Mediterranean world which witnessed the first bands of Arab raiders, following the monotheistic teachings of an unknown Meccan prophet, appear out of the desert on the Syrian border. They were beaten off, and little attention was paid to the incident.[149] This indifference was a costly error. Two years later Yarmak had been fought, and Syria lay open to its Arab conquerors. In 640 Egypt was gone as well, and by 641 Alexandria lost. Heraclius, the heroic restorer of the Empire, lived to see all his efforts vain and to die a ghastly failure in the same year that Alexandria fell. His work had been undone.

---

[142] Isadore of Seville *Chronicle* ed. Mommsen, p. 479. Isadore *Hist. Reg. Goth*, pp. 291, 295.

[143] Isadore of Seville *Chron.*, p. 48 and *Hist. Reg. Goth*, p. 785.

[144] Diehl *L'Afrique Byzantine*, p. 531.   [145] Hitti *Hist. of the Arabs*, p. 166.

[146] Butler *Arab Conquest of Egypt*, p. 183-93.

[147] *ibid.*, p. 134-37.   [148] *ibid.*, p. 180.

[149] Hitti *op. cit.*, p. 147.

The unity of Romania in the Mediterranean was shattered for all time. Not only was Justinian's creation destroyed, but more as well. The verdict of Alexander over Darius, of Rome over Hannibal, of Aurelian over Zenobia was reversed. The East had rejected and turned against an alien Western civilization forced upon it. The age of Islam in the Mediterranean was at hand.

3. The Arab Assault

In 641 the fall of Alexandria to the Arab invaders and the death of the aged hero Heraclius mark the beginning of a new Mediterranean era. Islam made its appearance by the waters of the Middle Sea. This represented no temporary phenomenon like the coming of the Sassanians to Syria and Egypt a few years earlier. It was to become a permanent situation, a basic change in the orientation and culture of the mass of the population of Syria, Palestine, Egypt, and North Africa. Today the impact of this change is still the basic fact of that part of the world.

One of the most interesting aspects of this Arab conquest lies in the ease with which it was accomplished. Partly this was due to the Byzantine Empire's exhaustion in its century-long struggle with Persia which had just ended as the Arabs began their attacks. In part it was due to the difficulty that a sea-based Byzantine state had in coping with any large-scale land assault. To some extent it was caused by the religious zeal that Islam gave to its invading warriors. But there can be little doubt that the chief reason for Arab success lay in none of these. It was due to the refusal of most of the Syrians and Egyptians to resist. Angered by Heraclius's persecution of their Monophysite faith and his fiscal exactions, they opened their gates to the Arab armies. One battle, Yarmak, decided the fate of Syria. One at Babylon that of Egypt. Few indeed were the cities that offered more than a token resistance, and most of these, except on the coast, did not hold out for long. The good terms that the Arabs offered those who submitted may have helped, and so did the tolerance they accorded Christians and Jews in Syria and Egypt. Conquest to the inhabitants of these areas seems to have appeared much like liberation.[1]

When the Arab conquerors reached the sea at Alexandria and along the Syrian coast, however, they found a somewhat different situation. Here the population was more Greek, more Orthodox in its faith and less opposed to Byzantium. More important, the Arabs were landsmen, desert bedouins of inland areas. The sea was an element with which they were at first neither ready nor

[1] Hitti *op. cit.*, p. 153.

willing to cope.[2] This fear of the sea is perhaps best shown in the centers of government and administration which they set up for rule of these conquered territories. During ten centuries of Graeco-Roman control, Egypt had been governed from Alexandria and Syria from Antioch. The Arabs established Al-Fustat (Old Cairo) as their Egyptian capital and Damascus as their Syrian administrative center—both far inland from the sea.

But if instinct and lack of familiarity warned the Arabs away from the dark-blue water, wise statesmanship counseled them to accept the challenge. In the first place, geography made both Egypt and coastal Syria essentially Mediterranean lands. A glance at the map shows how each looks seaward rather than landward toward its desert interior. More important, in taking over these areas the Arabs annexed, of necessity, their commerce and commercial interests as well. The source of much of Egypt's and most of Syria's wealth came from their commerce and trade connections throughout the Mediterranean world. To turn one's back and eliminate the economic connections the Mediterranean provided would be to shut off much of the gold which made these provinces so attractive to their new rulers. Whether they willed it or not, the Arabs in Syria and Egypt were involved almost immediately with the Mediterranean.

Most important, however, in urging them seaward was the necessity of defending their newly won domains. They held the land, but the sea still belonged to Byzantium. How great a potential menace this was may not have been appreciated fully until 645. In that year a large Byzantine naval expedition landed an army in Egypt and retook Alexandria. It required a difficult campaign to dislodge this force.[3] When it had been accomplished, Amr, Moslem governor of Egypt, pulled down Alexandria's fortifications to ensure that no future expedition of this kind would be able to hold out against his land-based forces.[4] This, however, was obviously only a temporary solution of the problem.

In Syria a somewhat similar situation prevailed. Here Moawiyah, the Arab governor, soon came to realize how weak his control of the Syrian coast was with Byzantine naval power offshore. The

[2] Arabic words for the sea and nautical terms, for instance, are either borrowings from the Greek, or are land words given a new nautical meaning.

[3] Lane-Poole A History of Egypt in the Middle Ages (New York 1901), p. 21.

[4] ibid. Wiet, G. L'Egypte Arabe (Paris 1937), p. 28.

large Greek Orthodox population of the seaport cities would continue to look seaward for deliverance unless he took measures to still such hopes. One city, Aratus, supplied from the sea, even continued to hold out against him long after the rest of Syria submitted.[5] It was he, then, who organized the first Arab navy and the first Arab expedition on the waters of the Mediterranean.

This expedition took the form of a naval attack in 648 against the nearby Byzantine-held island of Cyprus. It was partly a simple raid or razzia. In part it was a defensive naval operation. Moawiyah collected large numbers of vessels from the coastal towns of Syria, including an Egyptian contingent. This naval force was probably not, in the main, made up of Arabs. Since the Byzantine shipyards of Alexandria and Syria had fallen intact into Arab hands, warships were either available or easily constructed. So, too, were commercial ships belonging to native Syrians and Egyptians which could be pressed into service along with ample numbers of experienced seamen from these same ports. It is interesting to note, also, that Arab tradition has preserved the opposition of the Caliph Omar to this naval project. He, representing the Meccan land bedouin tradition, was fearful of the innovation of an Arab expedition upon the sea.[6] It was, nevertheless, a success. The large armada of 1,700 ships, according to Arab annalists, easily overran Cyprus, took much booty, and imposed upon the Cypriots a tribute of 7,200 gold pieces to be paid annually to Damascus. In addition, these latter were to inform the Arabs in advance of any Byzantine expedition being organized to sail against them.[7] This last shows best of all Moawiyah's concern over Byzantine sea power. In the next year Aratus, last Byzantine stronghold on the Syrian coast, fell to an Arab joint land and sea assault.

The successful Cyprus operation opened a period of Arab sea activity. For the next seven years the Moslems launched a series of sea raids from Egyptian and Syrian bases. In 652 an expedition from Syria, consisting of 200 ships, raided the distant island of Sicily and carried off a rich booty.[8] In the same year another was

[5] Hitti *op. cit.*, p. 167.

[6] Al Baladuri *The Origins of the Islamic State* trans. P. K. Hitti (New York 1919) I, 431-32.

[7] *Theophanes*, p. 525. Paul the Deacon *Hist. Misc.* (*Pat. Lat.* ed. Migne xcv), 1049.

[8] Amari *Storia dei Musulmani di Sicilia* new ed. (Catania 1933) I, 195-96. Marçais *Berbérie*, p. 64.

directed against Rhodes, in which the raiders carried off the copper remains of its fallen Colossus.[9] Cyprus apparently had not lived up to its treaty of 648, for in 654 it was raided again. This time its port of Constantia was destroyed, and an actual occupation of the island took place, with 12,000 Moslem troops being established at Lepithos on its north coast. Its tribute remained at the same level as before.[10]

These raids and the occupation of Cyprus apparently spurred on the Byzantine government, quiescent on the sea since its failure at Alexandria in 645, to take naval action. For in 655, Constans II, successor to Heraclius, gathered a large fleet of 700 to 1,000 sail. In this year it met a smaller Arab-Egyptian force of 200 vessels off the Syrian coast of Asia Minor near a place called Phoenix. This engagement was the famous "Battle of the Masts." It resulted in the first victory in naval contest for the Arabs. Their success seems to have been the result of some unusual tactics. The Arabs linked their ships with heavy chains and thus made it impossible for their opponents to pierce their battle line. They also used long hooks to cut the rigging and sails of opposing vessels. The result was a Byzantine disaster. The Emperor Constans was lucky to escape from the battle with his life, thanks to a fast ship.[11] Also interesting is the area in which the battle took place. The coast of Anatolia at this point was heavily forested with cypress used for ships' masts. It thus seems possible that the engagement was caused by Byzantine determination to prevent this needed ship timber from falling into Arab hands. If so, this is the first important indication of the importance of timber in the naval contests between the Arabs and Byzantium.

This great Arab naval victory was, however, the last naval action which took place between the two antagonists for more than a decade. The Moslems did not follow up their success on the sea. Nor did Byzantium, apparently, attempt to regain the naval initiative. The reasons lie in domestic difficulties on both sides which made at least a tacit naval truce between the antagonists advisable. On the Moslem side Moawiyah was distracted by his struggle with

[9] *Al Baladuri*, p. 236.

[10] *ibid.*, p. 253-55. Michael the Syrian *Chronicle* (ed. Chabot) II, 441 f.

[11] Lane-Poole *op. cit.*, p. 23. *Theophanes*, p. 528. Canard, M. "Les Expeditions des Arabes contre Constantinople dans l'histoire et dans la legende" in *Journal Asiatique* new ser. (1925-26) CCVII, 63-67. Al-Kindi *The Governors and Judges of Egypt* ed. Guest, p. 13.

Ali over the Caliphate. More than a decade was to pass before he was sufficiently well established as Caliph in Damascus to consider renewing the action against his Byzantine opponents.[12]

On the side of Constantinople, troubles in her Balkan and Western domains made Constans II willing to abandon, at least temporarily, his struggle with the Arabs. In the Balkans it was the Slavs, advancing toward the Aegean, who were causing the difficulties. They had expanded to a point on the Aegean near Salonika and the mouth of the Vardar River. They had taken to the sea, attacked Salonika itself, and were cutting communication by sea between this city and Constantinople.[13] A naval expedition was found necessary in 658 to contain them.[14] In the West the situation was even more critical. There no firm hand had been felt since the time of Heraclius. Not only had the greater part of Byzantine Spain been lost in the early seventh century, but other areas were in danger as well. The prestige of Byzantium had suffered severely from its loss of Syria and Egypt to the Arabs and from its sea defeats at their hands. In addition, religious differences between Constantinople and the West, as so often in Byzantine history, increased the difficulties. Heraclius's doctrine of Monothelitism, still the official creed of Byzantium, had not been accepted by either the Papacy or the Western Church.

In Africa, for example, its governor, the Patrician Gregory, had revolted against Constantinople and had proclaimed himself Emperor, when an Arab raid of 647 had removed him and his army from the political scene and cut short his career.[15] In 654 another Arab razzia had increased the chaos, though it had done little permanent damage.[16] In Sicily the population, hostile to Monothelitism, was restive. Most dangerous of all was the situation in Italy. The Lombards were on the move again in the face of Byzantine weakness. In 642 the Lombard ruler had attacked and seized Genoa and most of the Byzantine province of Liguria.[17] Like Amr in Egypt, he had razed its walls to prevent this port from falling again into the hands of a Byzantium strong on the

[12] Hitti *op. cit.*, pp. 178-86, 199.

[13] Vernadsky *Ancient Russia*, p. 247.

[14] *Theophanes*, p. 532.

[15] *En Nuwairi* in *Journ. Asiat.* (1841), p. 105-09. *Ibn al Hakim* (trans. by de Slane) in *Hist. des Berbères* Appendix I, 362-63.

[16] *Ibn al Hakim*, trans. *Gateau*, p. 53.

[17] Paul the Deacon *op. cit.*, p. 199. Chron. of *Fredegarius* in *MGH* II, 3.

sea.[18] In the south, the Lombard Duke of Beneventum had been attacking Imperial possessions. Even a Byzantine naval expedition, which in 650 had ravaged his coastal domains and landed troops at Monte Gargano, had done little to curb his aggressiveness.[19]

It was this situation which caused Constans II to take an unprecedented step. He moved his capital, a large portion of his fleet, and 20,000 troops of his Asiatic army to Syracuse in Sicily.[20] Perhaps he instinctively understood the role that Byzantium's North African, Sicilian, and Italian domains were to play in preservation of her naval Empire in the Mediterranean. Certainly Arab land and sea raids into this area already forecast their future hostile intentions and proved there was little time to waste in putting Constantinople's western house in order.

For ten years Constans labored to reconstruct Byzantium's rule in the West. Though he never was able to resolve the religious struggle between Orthodoxy and Monothelitism, he was, on the whole, successful. Africa was brought back to full obedience by the loyal Patrician, Nicephorus, while the pretender, Gennadius, successor to Gregory, fled to the Arabs for refuge.[21] Sicily was thoroughly pacified. So were the other Byzantine island possessions in the West, particularly Sardinia.[22] In Italy, Lombard aggression was halted, but not all the lost ground was recovered, though a full-scale military and naval campaign in South Italy in 663 showed the reality of Byzantine might to the Italians once again.[23] When Constans died in 668, murdered in Sicily by one of his own officers, he left Byzantium's Western provinces in relatively good condition. For thirty years more Byzantium was able to withstand Arab and Lombard pressure alike.

But in his absorption with the West, Constans II did not neglect the East. Apparently by 666 he felt secure enough on land and sea to reopen hostilities with Moawiyah. In that year he sent the Mardaites, a curious group of mountaineers recruited by Byzantium and referred to as the brass wall of Asia Minor, far into the interior of Syria and even Palestine.[24] Very possibly these latter were landed or at least supplied by sea. They proved so effective that Moawiyah was glad to secure peace at the price of tribute

[18] Diehl *Exarchat*, p. 45-46.
[19] Paul the Deacon *op. cit.*, p. 199-200.
[20] *ibid.*, 219-25.
[21] Marçais *Berbérie*, p. 31.
[22] Carta-Raspi *op. cit.*, p. 65-80.
[23] Paul the Deacon *op. cit.*, p. 217-26.
[24] Al Baladuri, p. 159. *Theophanes*, p. 554.

to Constantinople.[25] This Mardaite expedition is perhaps the best
indication of the weakness of the Ommayid naval position along
the Syrian coast just a decade after their victory in the "Battle of
the Masts."

But there are other indications of lack of Arab naval strength
in this period. In 663 the Damascus Caliph transported large numbers of Persians from their homes and settled them in coastal
cities of Syria and Palestine such as Sidon, Beirut, Jubayl, Tripoli,
Acre, and others. He also raised strong fortifications about his
coastal towns.[26] In 669 he added Iraqis to the Persians and settled
them in Antioch and other centers on the maritime coast.[27] Nor
were such defensive precautions confined to Syria. Alexandria's
walls, pulled down by Amr, seem to have been rebuilt at about
this time, for a Western visitor in 670 reports the city completely
surrounded by fortifications.[28]

Constans' death and the confusion that followed when his
successor Constantine IV returned to Constantinople apparently
determined Moawiyah to wipe out his defeat of 666. In 669 he
returned to the offensive on the sea. Perhaps the Mardaites had
convinced the Ommayid ruler of the need to dominate the Mediterranean shores. The distinguishing feature of the Arab naval
efforts that followed lies in their aggressiveness. The first Arab sea
expeditions had been either defensive in character, like those on
Cyprus, or simple razzias. From 669, for the next decade, they
aimed at nothing less than Mediterranean conquest.

One part of the Arab assaults was directed west. In 669 Sicily
was raided.[29] In the following year a large Arab army penetrated
North Africa and set up a permanent fortified base at Kairouan
in South Central Tunisia, whence for years they were to operate
far into the interior.[30]

This Western assault, however, seems to have been largely in
the nature of a feint. The main Arab effort was directed against
Constantinople itself, the heart of Byzantine power. A testing raid
against Chalcedon in 669 probed the defenses of the area about
the capital.[31] Then in 672 the full fury of Arab naval strength was

[25] Al Baladuri, p. 162. [26] ibid., p. 148.
[27] ibid., p. 162. [28] Wiet op. cit., p. 28.
[29] Ibn Idhari Bayan I, 13. Amari Storia I, 215-22.
[30] Amari Storia I, 237-9. Marçais Berbérie, p. 31. Note interior location of
Kairouan far from Byzantine sea power.
[31] Theophanes, p. 532-33. Masudi Prairies d'Or, trans. Meynal, v, 62.

launched upon the Aegean. Crete was attacked, and Rhodes over-run in the same year. A Byzantine counter-raid on the Delta of Egypt in 673 had little effect,[32] for in the same year a vast armada of Egyptian and Syrian naval contingents swept into the Sea of Marmora and began a seven-year blockade and siege of the Byzantine capital. Constantinople's peril was extreme, though land routes and the Black Sea remained open, so that supplies could reach the city. Its salvation came from an interesting development, the use of Greek fire against the blockading enemy fleet. This secret chemical compound, possibly already in use as early as 516, was rediscovered or perfected by a certain Callinicus, a Syrian then in the city, and used in its new form for the first time during the siege. The effect of it was devastating. The Arab vessels were burnt and scattered and driven in confusion out into the Aegean. In 679 they sailed for home only to be further damaged by great storms on their route south. Very few of the great Armada returned safely to Syrian and Egyptian home bases.[33]

The Byzantines followed up their advantage by reappearing in the Eastern Mediterranean on the heels of the retreating Arabs, armed with their terrible Greek fire. The Ommayid ruler hastened to make peace at heavy price. The tribute paid by Moawiyah to Constantinople was renewed, this time at the heavy rate of 3,000 pounds of gold, fifty captives and fifty horses a year.[34] Yezid, who had succeeded his father Moawiyah at this point, was further humiliated by being forced to withdraw from Cyprus the Arab garrison established there thirty years before.[35] The sea was Byzantium's again, and the second round of the naval struggle was in their favor.

Events in Africa as well as in the East were soon to prove how real their naval victory was. During the great attack on Constantinople of 673-679, the Arabs established at Kairouan had been actively raiding into the interior of North Africa and conquering and proselytizing the Berber tribes there. Lacking naval power, they had left the Byzantine-held towns and fortresses along the coast relatively undisturbed. So successful were they that in 681,

[32] *Al Kindi,* p. 38. Wiet *op. cit.,* p. 38.

[33] *Al Kindi,* p. 39. Michael the Syrian *Chron.* ii, 455. For best account see Canard, M. *op. cit.,* p. 77-80. On Greek fire see Zenghlis, C. "Le Feu Grécois" in *Byzantion* (1932) vii, 265-88.

[34] Hill *Hist. of Cyprus* i, 286.   [35] *Al Baladuri,* p. 237.

despite renewed Byzantine naval strength in the Mediterranean, their army commander, Oqba, determined to press further West and led his forces all the way to Tangier and the Atlantic. His disregard of the potentialities of naval power proved disastrous to him. A coalition of Berber tribes under a certain Kosaila threw off the Arab yoke and rose in his rear. The Byzantines along the coast, now certain of naval support and reinforcements, joined him from their coastal stronghold. Oqba's long line of communication was snapped, and he and his army destroyed in battle. The victorious Byzantine and Berber allies pressed on to take Kairouan in 683.[36] Only a few Arabs escaped by retreating all the way back along the coast to their base of Barca on the borders of Egypt. North Africa returned to her older Berber-Byzantine allegiance.

Constantine IV did one more thing to consolidate his Empire. In 681 at an Ecumenical Council at Constantinople he abandoned Monothelitism.[37] In so doing, he healed the religious breach which had separated Constantinople from the Orthodox Papacy and Western Church. But this act did even more. It reconciled the large Melchite population of Syria and Egypt with Constantinople, and thus increased Byzantine influence over that group within the Ommayid domains. It was a strong and vigorous Empire that he left to his successor, Justinian II, upon his death in 685.

Justinian's accession was the signal for renewed hostilities. Abd al-Malik, the new Caliph of Damascus, cut off tribute to Constantinople[38] and sent a large force from Barca under Zohair ibn Quais into North Africa to avenge the defeat of 683. This force was at first successful. Kairouan was reoccupied, and Kosaila slain in battle.[39] But the Arabs almost immediately retreated back to Barca. Their reason for retreat lay in the action of Byzantine sea power. A Byzantine naval expedition sailed to Barca and landed in Zohair's rear. He was thus forced to retreat and was badly defeated by this Byzantine force.[40] At the same time the Mardaites

---

[36] Al Bakri *Description de l'Afrique Septentrionale* trans. de Slane (Algiers 1913), p. 151. Marçais *op. cit.*, p. 29-33. The part played by Byzantine sea power in Oqba's defeat and failure has been consistently ignored by earlier historians. It was the decisive element, far more so than the resistance of the Berbers in the interior. Amari *Storia* I, 240-41. Kosaila commanded a mixed army of Berbers and Rûm in his victorious struggle. *Nuwairi*, p. 130-31.

[37] Runciman *Byzantine Civilization*, pp. 42, 116.

[38] Hill *Cyprus* I, 287. [39] Marçais *Berbérie*, p. 34-35.

[40] Ibn al Athir *Annales du Magreb et de l'Espagne* trans. Fagnan (Algiers 1901), p. 27.

were let loose again on Syria. Abd al-Malik, like his predecessors, was forced to make another humiliating peace. Sea power had proved too much for him. A treaty of 689 between Constantinople and Damascus specified that the Caliph was to pay tribute of 5,000 pounds of gold, 365 captives and 365 horses a year to Byzantium. In return, Justinian II agreed to withdraw 12,000 Mardaites from the Lebanon and settled them in Asia Minor. The revenues of Cyprus were to be divided, and it was to be a neutral territory between the two contending Empires.[41]

This peace, however, was not destined to last for long. In 693 war broke out again. Its occasion was the coinage by Abd al-Malik of the first Arab gold dinars bearing an Arabic superscription and not the image of the Byzantine basileus. This coinage was included in the annual tribute sent from Damascus. When it was received, Justinian II immediately declared war.[42] His action was apparently too precipitate, for he had little success. Unable to use the Mardaites, now in Asia Minor, he could apply little direct pressure on Damascus, and was badly beaten on the borders of Asia Minor. His deportation of the Cypriots from their island raised bitterness among his southern naval forces. So in 698 when the Kibyrrhaeot themal fleet revolted and proclaimed its admiral, Aspimar, Emperor, under the title of Tiberius III and sailed on Constantinople, the city did not oppose these forces.[43] The deposed Justinian went to the Crimea and then to Kazaria, whose ruler's sister he had married. For ten years he lived in exile hunted by his enemies, until 705 when he returned in triumph to Constantinople.[44]

These events in Constantinople disorganized its defensive military and naval organization and allowed the Ommayids to win a great victory in North Africa. In 693, Abd al-Malik had sent a huge expeditionary force of 40,000 there under Hasan ibn No'man. He directed his attention to Byzantine strongholds. Supported by some naval contingents, he reduced them one after another. In 695 Carthage, the Byzantine African capital, fell to the Arabs, who forced its surrender by seizing its aqueduct and

[41] Paul the Deacon *Hist. Misc.* (*Pat. Lat.* ed. *Migne* xcv). *Tabari* in *Journ. of Hell. Studies* xviii, 129. *Al Baladuri*, p. 203. *Theophanes*, p. 555.

[42] *Theophanes*, p. 558. Hitti *op. cit.*, p. 117-19.

[43] Constantine Porphyrogenitus *De Administro Imperio* c. 47, p. 215. Hill *Cyprus* i, p. 89-90.

[44] Vasiliev *Goths in the Crimea*, p. 81-84.

cutting off its water supply.[45] But Byzantines and Berbers fought back. The Berbers rose against the Arabs under a mysterious Queen Kahina of the Jerawa tribe.[46] A Byzantine fleet under John, Patrician of Sicily, retook Carthage.[47] All in vain. The Arabs returned to the attack. Carthage was retaken in 698 and with the death of Queen Kahina, killed in battle in 700, Byzantine Africa was no more.[48]

Immediately Caliph Abd al-Malik showed how much he valued sea power, perhaps because of his early sad experience with it in the hands of his Byzantine enemies. He ordered Musa, the Arab governor of Africa, to set up a naval base there and sent him 1,000 Coptic shipbuilders and their families to assist him in the building of a navy.[49] In addition, he reduced the island of Pantelleria, which lay just off the African Coast, and dominated the straits between the mainland and Sicily.[50] Musa did not build his naval base and arsenal at Carthage. Rather, he chose a location further inland on a lake and dug a canal to connect it with the bay. Carthage was abandoned, and here arose the city of Tunis.[51] This act of Musa shows the deep respect the Arabs had for Byzantine naval power. Tunis, inland and thus protected from naval surprise, was a safe harbor for Arab vessels. Carthage was not. Thus securely established, Musa hastened to construct 100 warships in his new shipyard.[52] In 704 this new fleet joined Ommayid vessels already active in the Mediterranean.[53] A third naval center, North Africa, was added to the older Arab ones of Syria and Egypt.

The new Tunisian naval base soon proved its usefulness. In 703 an Egyptian fleet raided Sicily. A terrific storm arose and threatened it with destruction. The Tunisian base provided its ships with safe anchorage.[54] More important were the actions of Musa's own

---

[45] Al Kairouani *Hist. de L'Afrique* trans. by Pelissier and Remusat in *Explorations Scientifiques de l'Afrique* (Paris 1845) VII, 53.

[46] *Ibn al Hakim*, trans. de Slane. *Hist. des Berbères*, p. 73-74. *Ibn al Athir*, p. 32.

[47] Diehl *L'Afrique Byzantine*, p. 385-86. *Theophanes*, p. 566-67.

[48] *Nuwairi* in de Slane. *Hist. des Berbères* I, 344.

[49] *At Tigani* in *Journ. Asiat.* ser. IV (1852) XX, 65-71. *Al Kairouani*, p. 120.

[50] *Al Bakri* in *Notices et extraits des MSS* XII, 50.

[51] Amari *Storia* I, 248.

[52] *Pseudo Ibn Qutaybah* in Gayangos *The History of the Mohammedan Dynasties in Spain* I, Appendix LXVII. *At Tigani*, p. 69.

[53] Carta-Raspi *op. cit.*, p. 114-15. This expedition sent against Sardinia is considered doubtful by some authorities who question the veracity of the Pseudo Ibn Qutaybah. It seems probable to me.

[54] *Pseudo Ibn Qutaybah* in *op. cit.*, p. lxvi.

newly constructed vessels. In 704 he sent them to raid Sicily and perhaps Sardinia.[55] In 708 he directed them against the Balearics, raiding the island of Majorca and capturing the ruler of the islands, probably the Byzantine governor.[56] In 710 Sardinia was the victim.[57]

These were no haphazard raids. They were part of a careful plan. Musa was engaged in a conquest of North Africa right up to the Atlantic. He used his navy from its Tunisian base to immobilize Byzantine naval threats to his rear from their bases in Sicily, Sardinia, and the Balearics. Oqba's failure to possess such a fleet to guard his rear and flank had cost him his life and army twenty years earlier. Musa avoided this mistake, and his progress from Tunis to Ceuta was swift and victorious.

When he arrived at the straits of Gibraltar with a large Arab-Berber force, he saw Spain across the narrow water barrier that separated it from Africa. In the hands of the weak Visigoths, it was a rich prize to a conqueror. But Musa hesitated. His fleet was apparently not with him, being busy guarding his long line of communications and keeping watch on the Byzantines in Sardinia and Sicily. The only ships available were four belonging to Count Julian, governor of Ceuta, who had gone over to the Arabs. In these four vessels Taric, one of Musa's lieutenants, crossed the narrow strait and landed at the foot of the mountain which still bears his name.[58] His immediate successes caused Musa to send him 5,000 reinforcements. But he had to construct ships on the African side to dispatch them to the Spanish shore. In these vessels he himself crossed with his main army when news of Taric's overwhelming victories reached him.[59] From this point on, the conquest of Spain was completely a land operation in the best tradition of the earlier Islamic campaigns in Egypt and Syria. By 717 the Arabs had not only occupied all of Spain but had spilled across the Pyrenees and added Visigothic Narbonnese Gaul to their domains. Except for the indirect help of the fleet which guarded North African communications in the Middle Sea opposite Sicily, the conquest of Spain involved no use of naval power on the part

[55] *Al Kairouani*, p. 14-15 and 57.   [56] Ibn Idhari *Bayan* ed. Dozy II, 30.
[57] *Ibn al Athir*, p. 51.
[58] Ibn Khaldun *Hist. des Berbères* trans. de Slane I, 136. For a fuller account see Dozy *Recherches sur la Littérature d'Espagne au Moyen Age* 3rd ed. (Leyden 1881) I, 42-57.
[59] *ibid.*

of Musa and Taric. Yet this expedition was extremely significant. From 693 to 717 the Arabs had turned Byzantium's naval right flank by crashing through the North African defenses and spreading up through Spain into Southern France. Islam was now ensconced like a crescent two-thirds of the way around the Mediterranean from the Rhone to Armenia.

If Byzantium failed to react in a naval way to this great series of successes by the Arabs in the Western Mediterranean, the reasons for this failure are easily explained. In the first place, civil disorders plagued the Empire. Justinian II returned from exile in 705 to wreak vengeance on his enemies in the capital, thus further disorganizing the state. The Bulgarians, swarming across the Danube, penetrated to the very suburbs of the city on the Golden Horn. Worst of all, the Ommayids were preparing a vast fleet for a final naval showdown. A Byzantine naval raid on Egypt in 709, which resulted in the capture of Admiral Khalid, may have delayed Arab plans to some extent.[60] But soon after Justinian II's death in 715, which left the Empire without a legitimate ruler, Arab preparations were complete.

This second great attack on Constantinople by the Ommayids was their supreme effort. The naval armada they gathered numbered 1,800 vessels, including naval squadrons from Syria, Egypt, and North Africa. An army, pushing across Asia Minor, seconded the fleet's efforts. First the Aegean islands were overrun and the Dardanelles forced. Then in 717 army and fleet appeared before golden Byzantium. Again as in 626 and 673, the city was in deadly jeopardy. Again, too, a leader was found who saved the Empire. This time it was Leo, Isaurian general, who, made Emperor in this extremity, became Byzantium's savior. He stretched a great chain across the Bosphorus, barring entry to the invading fleet, and manned the walls with seasoned troops who thwarted efforts of the Arab army to storm the walls. The siege dragged on through the winter. The lightly clad Arab troops suffered cruelly from the cold. Meanwhile Leo negotiated with the Bulgarians. In the spring they attacked the Arabs investing the city from the European side and drove them off. This was followed by a sally by the Byzantine fleet, armed as of yore with its terrible Greek fire. This and the defection to the Byzantine side of many of the Christian crews of

[60] Brooks, E. N. "The Relations between the Empire and Egypt from a New Source" in *Byz. Zeit.* (1913) xxii, 381-2.

the Arab vessels turned the tide. Badly beaten, burnt with Greek fire, the Arab vessels retreated precipitately toward the south. Again storms, as in 679, claimed their toll. Hardly one out of ten ships returned to its home base. The army, deserted by the fleet, also fled for the Taurus frontier. But Leo marched after them and massacred the larger portion. Few returned alive to Syria.[61]

The victorious Byzantine naval squadrons again sailed out of the Aegean into the Eastern Mediterranean on the heels of their foes. They carried the naval war to the enemy camp and raided the delta of Egypt in 720[62] and again in 725.[63] The Caliph Omar II, successor of Walid and Abd al-Malik, was forced to reduce the tribute of Cyprus to the older figure set by Moawiyah years earlier.[64] Only in the West did the Arabs have any fight left. There a North African squadron raided Sicily in 720,[65] perhaps emboldened by Byzantine difficulties on the island after the revolt of its governor in 718.[66]

Victorious Constantinople should have finished up the naval war at once. But instead it dragged on for almost three more decades. The reason for Byzantium's failure to capitalize on its great victory lies, as usual, in the sphere of religion. Victorious Leo III, like his predecessors Justinian and Heraclius, chose this moment to embroil his Empire in religious controversy. The dispute was caused by his espousal of the new doctrine of Iconoclasm and his attempt to force it upon a reluctant Empire in 725.[67] The attempt raised a furor in the Imperial capital and in the Greek Aegean areas, where veneration of images was particularly strong. So much so that in 727 the themal fleets of Hellas and the Cyclades, Iconodule in sympathy, chose a certain Cosmas as Emperor and sailed on Constantinople,[68] as the Kibyrrhaeot fleet had done thirty years earlier at about the time of Justinian II. This time, however, the Imperial fleet, which remained loyal to Leo, held firm. Using Greek fire, it scattered and defeated the revolting themal squadrons.

The disorders in the East caused by Iconodule opposition to

---

[61] Vasiliev *Byzantine Empire*, p. 288-89. A fuller account is to be found in Canard, M. *op. cit.*, p. 80-102.

[62] *Al Kindi*, p. 70.

[63] Wiet *op. cit.*, p. 56.

[64] Hill *Cyprus* I, 286.

[65] *Nuwairi* II, 252.

[66] *Theophanes*, p. 611.

[67] Runciman *Byzantine Civilization*, pp. 116-17, 121-23.

[68] Halphen, L. *Les Barbares* (Paris 1930), p. 184-85.

Iconoclasm were matched by a similar opposition in the West in Sicily and Italy. As in the case of Monothelitism a century earlier, the Orthodox Papacy and Western Church refused to go along with the religious decisions of Constantinople's ruler. Revolts flared throughout Italy when Byzantine officials tried to force their religious reforms on a reluctant population.[69] This was just the opportunity awaited by the Lombards. Their ruler, Liutprand, added Luni and perhaps Corsica to his territory, gaining some naval strength found in seaport cities in the process.[70] Leo, his naval forces crippled by the conflict just concluded in 727, could do little but send a small fleet to enforce obedience to his decrees from Pope Gregory and perhaps regain the territory lost to Luitprand. But this force was wrecked by a storm in the Adriatic in 730 and accomplished nothing.[71]

Instead of reconsidering, Leo continued his efforts in the West. He punished the Pope by confiscating the large papal estates in Southern Italy and Sicily and transferring the Episcopal sees in this region from the jurisdiction of Rome to that of the Patriarch of Constantinople. Heavy new taxes were placed on the Italian people as well.[72] This proved even more unwise. The Pope united with the Lombards in 735, and the Byzantine Exarch and his officials were driven from Ravenna and the Pentapolis.[73] Byzantine rule in Italy looked as if it were on the point of disappearing. Two things changed the situation. First, the Pope, though still opposed to Iconoclasm, was loyal to the principle of the Empire and had little desire to exchange a distant Byzantine master for a nearby Lombard one. In addition, the fleet of Venice intervened. Together, Venice and the Papacy in 742 drove the Lombards out of their recent conquests and returned the Exarch to power in Ravenna. Byzantium recovered a portion of her lost Italian domains.[74]

The Ommayids, seeing these domestic difficulties in East and West paralyzing Byzantine naval efforts, returned to the attack. In 726 Cyprus was raided by an Arab fleet and its tribute restored to the higher figure set by Abd al-Malik and Walid.[75] Not for a decade was Byzantium in a position to retaliate. Then in 736 it

[69] Pirenne *op. cit.*, p. 218-21.
[70] "Lunigiana" in *Encyclopedia Italiana* (1934) xxi, 663.
[71] *Theophanes*, p. 631.   [72] Diehl *Exarchat*, p. 410.
[73] Hazlitt, W. C. *The Venetian Republic* (London 1900) i, 23-24. Cessi, R. *Storia della Republica di Venezia* (Milan 1944) i, 13-14.
[74] *ibid.*, p. 17-19.   [75] *Theophanes*, p. 623.

launched another attack on Egypt in which a large number of
vessels was captured.[76] This was followed by another even larger
assault by 360 ships on the land of the Nile then in the throes
of Coptic revolt.[77] Arab retaliation consisted of a raid on Cyprus
in 743 in which they carried off large numbers of its inhabitants
into slavery in Syria.[78]

It is apparent that the Eastern naval warfare was an affair of
raid and counter-raid, with Cyprus and Egypt as the principal
victims, in which both sides seemed relatively evenly matched. Not
so in the West. There the Arab North African flotilla launched
raid after raid upon Sicily and Sardinia without retaliation at the
hands of the Byzantines. In 727, 729, 730, 733, 740, and 752 Sicily
suffered Moslem naval assaults.[79] Sardinia was the victim in 735
and 752.[80] Not all these raids, however, were successful. That of
733 against Sicily and of 735 against Sardinia ended in Arab naval
defeat, with Byzantine defensive forces using Greek fire and in-
flicting heavy losses on their attackers.[81]

In 747 this period of sparring came to an end. A great naval
battle decided the issue contested for a century on the sea by
Byzantine and Ommayid forces. It took place just off Cyprus.
There the Byzantine Kibyrrhaeot fleet cornered a tremendous
Arab armada consisting of 1,000 dromons representing the flower
of the Syrian and Egyptian naval strength. The Byzantine squadron was much smaller, but probably armed with Greek fire. In the
battle that followed, the Arabs were disastrously defeated. Only
three of their ships escaped.[82]

This naval victory by Byzantium was of immense significance.
It settled the long Ommayid-Byzantine naval struggle. The Arabs
of Syria and Egypt were never able to make good their losses.
Egyptian naval forces simply disappeared from the Mediterranean
for more than a century and never really recovered until the
Fatimid period in the late tenth century. We hear no more of
Syrian naval squadrons for a quarter-century and no real revival

[76] Al Kindi, p. 79.
[77] Brooks, E. N. op. cit., p. 381-82.
[78] Theophanes, p. 639. Al Baladuri, pp. 238, 241.
[79] Amari Storia I, 293-301.
[80] Carta-Raspi op. cit., p. 119-23.
[81] Amari op. cit., p. 295-300.
[82] Theophanes, p. 631. Paul the Deacon Hist. Misc. (Pat. Lat. ed. Migne xcv),
col. 1095.

took place until the time of Leo of Tripoli in the late ninth century.[83]

Even the Arab North African naval base soon had its teeth drawn. Byzantine naval victory in the East allowed a shift of forces West. The raid of 752 was the last launched from Arab North Africa for half a century.[84] Byzantium after a century of naval effort had at last reestablished its mastery over the waters of the Mediterranean.

To recapitulate, the Ommayids challenged Byzantium's naval supremacy in the Mediterranean in three waves. The first, primarily defensive in nature, began in 648 and ended indecisively in 655, though this latter year saw a great Arab victory. The second wave of assaults, beginning in 669, represented a more serious effort, including a great seven-year siege of Constantinople. It ended in complete Byzantine victory by 685. The third assault, starting in 693 and the most serious one of all, lasted for almost sixty years until the year 752. It started with Arab successes, particularly in the West, and included a second great siege of Constantinople. After the failure of this supreme Ommayid effort, the contest degenerated into a sparring match of raid and counterraid. Finally, 747 saw Byzantine victory and 752 the disappearance of Ommayid naval power.

Yet perhaps Byzantium's naval victory by 752 was less conclusive than it seemed. She had won the sea. But in the course of their third wave of assaults the Arabs had pierced their opponent's sea and land defenses in the middle Mediterranean. They had turned Constantinople's naval flank and added North Africa and Spain to their domains. It was from these North African naval bases that squadrons were to sail forth in the next century and avenge the great naval disaster of 747.

Another serious consequence of this naval struggle for Byzantium lay in its results in Italy. No doubt the attempt of various Byzantine rulers to force first Monothelitism and then Iconoclasm on a reluctant Papacy and Italian population was in a large measure the cause of Byzantine losses there. But a far greater reason lay in Constantinople's preoccupation with her naval and land struggle with the Ommayids. Except for Constans II, no Byzantine ruler from the time of Heraclius up to Constantine V was able to give any real attention to Italian problems. As a result Byzan-

[83] Brooks, E. N. *op. cit.*, p. 385-91.   [84] Hitti *op. cit.*, p. 602.

tine dominion slipped away. By 747 Byzantine control had been restricted to a few parts in the south and Rome, Ravenna, the Pentapolis, and Venice in the north and center of the peninsula. Rome was really Papal, and Ravenna and the Pentapolis were held only by the influence of the Pope and an all but independent Venice. The year 754 was to see all but Venice and the southern areas slip forever from Constantinople's grasp.

There remains the fundamental question of why Byzantium, despite the losses noted above, finally recaptured control of the sea; of why the Ommayids lost the naval struggle. The answers are few but significant. In the first place, geography played the greatest role in Constantinople's eventual success. The Arab centers of naval power in this period in Egypt, Syria and, after 704, North Africa lay in unprotected areas open to easy naval access. Use of the Nile in Egypt and of a protected canal to Tunis in North Africa was necessary to give even a minimum of security to naval arsenals, shipbuilding, and anchorage of fleets. On the other hand, Constantinople was ideally situated for protection of its flotillas and naval establishments. The Aegean formed a protective belt of islands and bays right up to the Dardanelles, then the Sea of Marmora, another protected body of water, and finally the Black Sea in the rear as a reserve area free of any Arab menace. To reach the nerve center of Byzantine power, the Arabs had to run the gantlet of Crete, Rhodes, and the Aegean Islands, smash through the Dardanelles into the Sea of Marmora, and finally pierce the barrier of the Bosphorus. Twice they tried to accomplish this feat, and twice they failed. In a minor way the Ionian and Adriatic Seas up to Ravenna and Venice represented a similar problem to any invading fleet. So, too, did the Tyrrhenian Sea with its protection of Sicily, Sardinia, and Corsica, though neither of these routes was attempted by the Arabs in this period.

In the second place, Constantinople won the naval struggle because of its invention and use of a secret weapon—Greek fire. Perfected during the first great Arab siege of the capital, it was in large measure responsible for the ultimate success of Byzantium's naval forces. Its formula was the Byzantine Emperor's principal state secret, and it was carefully safeguarded.[85] It seems probable that only the Imperial fleet stationed at Constantinople was equipped with it, except in times of emergency when the

[85] Zenghlis, C. "Le Feu greçois" in *Byzantion* (1932) vii, 265-75.

themal fleets were allowed its use.[86] Arab naval vessels, no matter how well handled, could not cope with Greek fire in this period.

Third, the Byzantine Empire either had available or had access to plentiful supplies of ship timber, naval stores, and iron, all important in the construction of naval vessels. And it was able to deny a large portion of such needs to its Ommayid opponents. Iron was not to be found in either Syria or Egypt, and the region of the Nile was deficient in necessary ship and mast timber. Syria's supply of this latter in the Lebanon and to the north may in this period have been severely limited. North Africa and Spain possessed both, it is true, but all evidence points to the fact that North Africa's iron deposits were not worked in the eighth century,[87] while Spain contributed nothing in the way of naval forces at this time. North Africa's timber and naval stores were all west of Tunis, as well, thus making their use difficult for the Arabs. Byzantine supplies of these essential products, on the other hand, were all but inexhaustible. In the West, Sicily, Calabria, Istria, and Dalmatia, as well as the northwest Ligurian coast, all produced timber and naval stores.[88] From the Tyrol came ample iron. Asia Minor, the Caucasus, and the Crimea were all sources of timber in the East, while iron was available in large amounts in Asia Minor and the Balkans. Just how these supplies were denied the Ommayids will be taken up further on, but it might be well to note that their lack, particularly in Egypt, was a problem that the Arab rulers never were able to solve satisfactorily.[89]

Lastly, the Byzantines triumphed through excellence of organization. Under the impact of Arab and Persian invasion in the seventh and early eighth centuries Byzantine civil and military administration changed drastically. The themal system was developed, putting military *strategoi* in charge of both civil and military organizations within all provinces. This provided an inexpensive

[86] This is largely conjectural, but logical under the circumstances. In 698 and 727, when they sailed on the capital in revolt, the provincial fleets were not equipped with Greek fire. The Imperial fleet was. The same thing is true during the revolt of Thomas the Slav in the early ninth century. Hence ordinarily it can be assumed that only the Imperial fleet possessed this terrible weapon.

[87] Gsell, S. "Vielles exploitations minières dans L'Afrique du Nord" in *Hesperides* (1928).

[88] See Chapter I on negotiations between the Patriarch of Alexandria and Pope Gregory the Great in which the former attempted to secure needed timber supplies from these regions. On timber supplies in Italy in the 5th century, see Sidonius *op. cit.*, p. 99-100.

[89] Wiet *Egypte Arabe*, p. 174-75.

and efficient method of defense and was in no small measure responsible for Byzantium's survival. It was applied to naval as well as military forces probably as early as the time of Constans II and Constantine IV, when the disaster off Lycia in 655 made naval reform all but obligatory.[90]

In its final form in the late seventh and early eighth century Byzantium's naval strength was organized as follows. It consisted of a professional standing navy composed of one Imperial and four provincial or themal fleets. Of these, three were in the East and two in the West. In the East the naval center of power was Constantinople, where the Imperial fleet had its base. It was in the seventh century either directly under the command of a Lord High Admiral, known as the *Strategos* of the Karabisians, or was indirectly controlled by the latter through a subordinate *drungarios* or admiral. The two Eastern provincial fleets were those of the Aegean and Kibyrrhaeots. They were each based on definite territorial naval districts, that of Kibyrrhaeots consisting of the southern coast of Asia Minor, that of the Aegean of the Cyclades and Dodecanese islands. They were each under an admiral or *drungarios* subordinate to the Strategos of the Karabisians. Other themes beside these two maintained smaller squadrons in the East as well, but for naval purposes they were probably under the control of one or the other of these three principal naval commanders. Except in time of crisis the provincial fleets were probably not equipped with Greek fire.[91]

In the West, the two principal provincial fleets were those of Sicily and Ravenna.[92] There may also have been a third, that of Africa, up to the end of the seventh century.[93] The Sicilian naval district included the toe of Italy and its west coast as far as Rome and perhaps farther, that of Ravenna the Adriatic coast and perhaps Rome itself. The African naval command may have included, in addition to Africa itself, Sardinia, the Balearics, Ceuta, and the last Byzantine footholds in Spain.[94] It is tempting to seek the

[90] On the formation of themes prior to the period of the Isaurians see the excellent article by E. Darkko "La militarizzazione dell' Impero Bizantino" in *Studi Bizantini e Neoellenici* (1939) v.

[91] Bury, J. B. *The Imperial Administrative System in the Ninth Century* (London 1909), p. 108-09.

[92] Diehl *Exarchat*, p. 197.   [93] This is, however, largely conjectural.

[94] There was an army of Africa, Sardinia and the Balearics in the late seventh century. This may have included a fleet as well. Carta-Raspi *op. cit.*, p. 88-98.

same unified naval control in the West as in the East. If this be accepted as logical, the Patrician of Sicily, through the *drungarios* of his fleet, exercised the same sort of overall naval command in the West that the Strategos of the Karabisians did in the East. It would then be correct to speak of Sicily after the time of Constans II as a naval theme.[95]

Both Imperial and provincial fleets maintained naval establishments—warships, sailors, arsenals, dockyards, and naval equipment—at the expense of their naval districts, but there can be little doubt that in time of hostilities they supplemented their strength with levies in men and ships upon the maritime ports under their jurisdiction.[96] This was particularly the case as regards transport and supply ships. Perhaps a prearranged levy on each maritime center was the usual method employed, particularly by the provincial or themal fleets.[97]

The eighth century saw little change in this naval system—except perhaps the solidification of the provincial naval districts in the East into definite themes. That may be the significance of the raising of the *drungarios* of the Kibyrrhaeots to the rank of *strategos*.[98] The fact that the office of Strategos of the Karabisians was abolished at the same time suggests, though, a conclusion of a sort quite different from that advanced by Bury. It may simply represent the shifting of command of the Eastern fleets from Constantinople to the more vital Asia Minor frontier by Leo III, when, after the siege of 717-718 had been raised, Byzantium's offensive naval strength moved south into the Mediterranean. The Strategos of the Kibyrrhaeots seems, in the early Isaurian period of Leo III and Constantine V, to have had a fleet far larger than was necessary for defensive purposes. It was this fleet, for instance, which cornered and destroyed the Arab armada off Cyprus in 747.[99] In the West, this same century saw the disappearance of African naval strength, and a serious weakening of Ravenna's naval power,

---

[95] Amari *Storia* I, 175. Vasiliev *Byzantine Empire*, p. 278.

[96] A later example of this system is to be found in the levies of ships demanded from Naples, Amalfi and Gaeta in 813 by Gregory, Byzantine governor of Sicily, for defense against the Moslems. *Codex Carolinus* ed. Cenni letter #3 of Pope Leo III.

[97] See note above. Also note levies on Venice in 806-7 in Bury "Byzantine Naval Policy in Western Waters" in *Centenario della nascita di Michele Amari* (Palermo 1910) II.

[98] Bury *Administrative System*, p. 108.

[99] *Theophanes*, p. 631.

leaving the Exarch only a tiny remnant of ships under his command. Sicily alone remained a Byzantine center of naval power in the West, and its fleet had some real importance.[100]

This Byzantine naval organization was both flexible and workable. It used to the full the naval resources of the Empire and provided for concentration of naval power when and if needed. Like the land themal system which it resembled, it had the further advantage of allowing the main expense of naval defense to fall on local areas and thus cheaply provided protection for the coasts of the Empire from Arab naval assault.

About the naval organization of the Ommayids, unfortunately, less information is available than about Byzantium's fleets. Its main outline, however, is clear. It consisted of three more or less autonomous naval forces, each based, like those of Byzantium, on a separate maritime area. They were the Syrian fleet, the Egyptian fleet and, after 704, the North African flotilla. In addition, a small Red Sea squadron, perhaps operating under Egyptian command, patrolled the Red Sea.[101] In a general way these three fleets matched the Byzantine ones, that of Syria being the counterpart of the Kibyrrhaeot Asia Minor fleet, that of North Africa matching the Sicilian fleet, that of Egypt the Imperial fleet of Constantinople. Each was commanded by an admiral. Of the three, the Egyptian was the most important numerically, and it is possible that on joint expeditions, such as the two sieges of Constantinople and major engagements, such as that off Lydia in 655 or off Cyprus in 747, the Egyptian admiral was in overall command.[102] Syrian and Egyptian fleets often operated together,[103] while the North African fleet in the West was largely autonomous. Only in the second siege of Constantinople were all three fleets together.[104] This is another similarity between Arab and Byzantine naval organization, where Sicilian naval contingents had a similar autonomy in the West.

Egypt was the Ommayids' center of shipbuilding, and Fostat and Kolzoum built the first Arab ships.[105] Moawiyah brought Coptic shipbuilders to construct vessels for the Syrian fleet at Acre, which soon became the most important Syrian naval base.[106] They were similarly sent by Abd al-Malik to North Africa, where they built

[100] Bury "Byzantine Naval Policy" in *op. cit.*
[101] Wiet *op. cit.*, p. 39.   [102] *ibid.*, p. 38.
[103] Against Cyprus in 648 and on many other occasions.
[104] Canard, M. *op. cit.*, p. 80-102.   [105] Wiet *op. cit.*, p. 175.
[106] *ibid.*, p. 176.

the first North African Moslem navy for Musa after 700.[107] Forty years after the conquest, the expenses of the chief of naval construction in Egypt amounted to 7,000 dinars a year.[108] Shortage of timber was the chief problem faced by these Egyptian shipbuilders, and in spite of various expedients it was one they never completely solved.

Just how these fleets were organized, manned and equipped it is difficult to say. In the first years, native Syrians and Egyptians, recruited in coastal ports, probably provided the majority of the naval personnel.[109] A better organization prevailed later on, particularly under Abd al-Malik and Walid. As in the case of Byzantine provincial fleets, contingents from maritime cities were undoubtedly called upon to supplement standing naval forces, but just how this was done is unknown. In general, the Ommayid navies seem more informal and less well organized than their Byzantine opponents.

Byzantine maritime advantages in geography, Greek fire, timber and iron, and organization explain their final victory in 752, but what of the influence of land operation upon this naval struggle on both sides? On the land the Arabs were more at home than on the sea and had real advantages over their opponents. Yet, save for their North Africa campaign from 693-705, Arab land warfare did not affect sea power to any great extent. In the East from 641 to 752, the land frontier between Byzantium and Damascus stayed remarkably stable, running roughly along the line of the Taurus mountains. Occasionally Arab armies penetrated deeply into Asia Minor, as at the time of the second great siege of Constantinople. At other times Byzantine forces, like the Mardaites, pushed far into Syria. But constant border razzias were more normal. The Arabs were far more aggressive in these raids, but the Byzantine themal system managed to provide the interior of the Empire with excellent protection.[110]

In the West, after the Byzantine African defenses had been breached, Arab military power played a far more decisive role, though its operations were, in the case of Spain's conquest, com-

---

[107] *At Tigani*, p. 65-71. *Al Kairouani*, p. 120.

[108] Wiet *op. cit.*, p. 175.

[109] Becker, C. H. in *Cam. Med. Hist.* (Cambridge 1913) II, 352.

[110] Tabari's chronicle of the regular razzias of Arab border troops into Byzantine territory shows how frequent they were. See Hitti *op. cit.*, p. 199-200, on this subject.

pletely divorced from any naval element. When Arab forces passed the Pyrenees and advanced into the Midi, however, they met their first serious opposition—that of the Franks. Until 737 this opposition was not very effective, and the battle of Tours in 732 was merely the checking of an Arab razzia. The main struggle was over Aquitaine, Provence and Languedoc. Here the progress of Arab conquest was steady. Narbonne was taken in 720.[111] In 725 Carcassone fell, and Nîmes and the surrounding area were occupied.[112] Eudes, Duke of Aquitaine, who offered serious resistance was overwhelmed, and Aquitaine overrun.[113] In 735 Arles opened its gates to the Moslems, and they went on to plunder Provence.[114] Charles Martel, Frankish Mayor of the Palace, could answer only with a punitive expedition against Arles, Marseilles, and Lyons. This proved of little value, since in 736 Avignon and the left bank of the Rhone went over to the Arabs.[115]

At last Charles Martel was stung into action. He led a major expedition south, retook Avignon, blockaded Narbonne and burnt Nîmes, Beziers, Agde, and Maguelone in reprisal for their assistance to the Moslems.[116] But this expedition also had little effect, for in 738 Provence under its local ruler revolted against the Carolingians and the Arabs crossed the Rhone again.[117] Only Lombard naval assistance prevented Charles from losing Provence. In 739 another expedition of the Franks to the south was necessary.[118] Its failure to accomplish much can be seen in the fact that it was not until 752 that Pepin finally reconquered Septimania from its Arab invaders, occupying Nîmes, Maguelone, Agde and Beziers.[119] It was not until 759 that the last Moslem stronghold, Narbonne, fell.[120]

The most interesting feature of this struggle lies in the small part played in it by naval power. The Franks had none, and the

[111] Molinier and Zotenburg in Hist. Gén. de Languedoc new ed. ix, 551-52.

[112] ibid., p. 553-56.

[113] Isadore Pacensis Chron. in Recueil Hist. de Franc ii, 721.

[114] Codera Narbona, Gerona y Barcelona bajo la Dominación Musulmana (Institut d'Estudi Catalani Annual), 1909-10, p. 195-96.

[115] ibid.

[116] Lot, F. Pfister, C., and Ganshof, F. Les Destinées de l'Empire en Occident de 395 à 888 (Paris 1928), p. 398-99.

[117] ibid.

[118] Paul the Deacon Hist. of the Langobards, p. 183.

[119] Molinier and Zotenburg op. cit., p. 554.

[120] Codera op. cit., p. 197-8.

only naval forces they used were those provided by the Lombards in 739. The Arabs, here, as in Spain, also appear to have made little use of the sea. That they were better provided for in this respect than the Franks is undoubtedly true, as the unsuccessful Frankish blockade of Narbonne in 739 shows conclusively.[121] Land campaigns, however, were the decisive factor in France, while war on the sea decided the issue elsewhere in the Mediterranean world. The fact that Southern France fell in 752 at the same time that North African Moslem sea-raids on Sicily and Sardinia ceased seems largely a coincidence. The struggle between Franks and Arabs over Southern France was but a sideshow in the great Mediterranean naval conflict, affected by it and affecting it in turn only slightly; it was not part of the main pattern of events.[122]

So far only the naval side of this century-long series of wars between Constantinople and Damascus has been considered, a conflict which brought in the Franks in the last three decades. But what of the economic side? What were its effects upon the trade and commercial life of the Mediterranean. Were they, as has been claimed, extreme? Or were they not particularly significant? Was it this struggle which more than any other factor accounts for the differences between the world of Justinian and that of Charlemagne, Irene, and Harun al-Rashid? Thanks to it did the Mediterranean world of 752 already show signs of an economic pattern very different from that of previous centuries?

It must be admitted that at first Arab conquest made little actual difference in the trade of the Mediterranean world. No catastrophic economic consequences appeared. The Arabs, as desert bedouin conquerors, had neither the ability nor desire to break with Egypt's or Syria's economic past. They were neither merchants nor traders upon the sea, but conquerors, and they left the practice of commerce to those who had controlled it previously—the Christian Graeco-Syrians of Alexandria and the seaport cities of Syria.

More important, they continued up until the end of the seventh

[121] Lot, Pfister, and Ganshof op. cit., p. 413-15.

[122] Pirenne viewed these events somewhat differently, as have most other historians. Pirenne op. cit., p. 156-57. Poitiers was not a decisive battle at all, and the whole struggle between Arabs and Carolingians in Southern France was indecisive. It is the relatively ignored Byzantine naval victory of 747 off Cyprus that deserves attention.

century the administrative practices of Rome and Byzantium in Syria and Egypt; the taxation system (with some changes), the gold currency, the regulations concerning industry. Non-Moslems continued to staff the financial, clerical and administrative bureaucracy; and Greek remained, as in the past, the language of government administration.[123] The old system continued under new management in the Moslem East, just as it had in the Latin West when the German rulers took it over in the fifth century.

There are abundant examples of this continuity, particularly in Egypt. The Arabs took over the Byzantine state mints, dye houses, and papyrus manufacturing.[124] Yet the same special signs of the Trinity are to be found upon this Arab papyrus of the seventh century that the earlier Byzantine product bore.[125] The older Byzantine state monopolies of fine cloth (*tiraz*) at Tinnis, Touna, Damietta and Alexandria were simply continued by the Arab rulers of the land.[126] Even more important, the mints continued to turn out the gold *nomismata* of Byzantium, and until 692 these pieces were the money par excellence of Egypt and Syria.[127] The only money coined with Arabic titles until that time was of silver.[128]

What was true in Egypt was to be found in Syria as well. At Damascus the lack of break between old and new is striking. The Christian ministers and clerks of Moawiyah and Yezid, the use of Greek as the official language, the secular character of early Ommayid rule, the tolerance displayed towards non-Moslems at the Ommayid court—all these are evidences of continuity with the Graeco-Roman past and in sharp contrast with later Ommayid and Abbassid developments.[129] The great Mosque of Damascus, built in the style of a Byzantine church, proclaims the same tendency.[130] Syria and Egypt seem, in the first fifty years after conquest, to be ruled by Arab Byzantine rulers of Damascus.

Nor is there much evidence of any major displacement of population in these lands due to Arab conquest—except, perhaps, in the

[123] Hitti *op. cit.*, p. 217.

[124] Lopez "Mohammed and Charlemagne, A Revision" in *Speculum* (1943), XVIII, 21.

[125] Grohman, A. *Allgemeine Einführung in der Arabischen Papyri* (Vienna 1924), p. 77-92. *The Kurrah Papyri from Aphrodite in the Oriental Institute* (Chicago 1936), p. 70-92.

[126] Grohman "Tiraz" in *The Encyclopedia of the Islam.*

[127] Hitti *op. cit.*, p. 117.   [128] *Al Baladuri*, p. 263.

[129] Hitti *op. cit.*, p. 240-78.   [130] *ibid.*, p. 265-67.

coastal areas of Syria. When Alexandria was retaken by the Arabs in 645, some Greeks left with the withdrawing Byzantine garrison and fleet, but many remained.[131] In the interior of Syria some Greeks also fled the land.[132] But the Arab conquest was so swift and so peaceful that there seem to have been few refugees. In North Africa there is evidence that some of the population left the province after the raid of 647, probably going to Sicily.[133] There was also an exodus from Carthage when the city finally fell to the Ommayids in 698.[134] And there is mention of some of these refugees on Pantelleria in 700 when it fell into Arab hands.[135] But, in spite of these instances, the idea that there were any mass population transfers in the seventh century as a result of Arab conquest is probably exaggerated.

Coastal Syria and Cyprus seem special cases. There more widespread displacement may well have taken place in the seventh century. Coastal Syria appears to have been disrupted by both the Persian and Arab invasions and their aftermaths. The Sassanian monarchs devastated many Syrian cities and persecuted severely the Melchite Greek population. At the time of Arab conquest many fled from the coast to the security of Asia Minor or elsewhere in the Mediterranean world.[136] These displacements continued under the first Ommayids, particularly between 666 and 689 when the Mardaites were actively intervening in the Lebanon. The withdrawal of 12,000 of them by Justinian II in 689 and their settlement in Asia Minor represents a major population shift, as does Moawiyah's placing of Persians and Iraqis along the Syrian coast at about the same time. But it would be unwise to overestimate the importance of these developments. The present Christian character of the Lebanon emphasizes the continuity of Syria with her Graeco-Roman past as far as population is concerned. The same is true of Cyprus. There the first Ommayid Caliph, after conquering the island in 654, destroyed the important city of Constantia and allowed all who wished to leave the island.[137] There

---

[131] *Al Baladuri*, p. 348. *History of the Patriarchs of the Coptic Church at Alexandria* ed. Evarts (Paris 1907), p. 494-97.

[132] *Al Baladuri*, pp. 180, 189, 194, 195, 227, 232.

[133] *At Tigani* in *Jour. Asiat.* 4th ser. (1853), p. 125-26.

[134] Diehl *Afrique Byzantine*, p. 59.   [135] *Al Bakri*, p. 97.

[136] Charanis "The Hellenization of Sicily" in *The Amer. Hist. Rev.* (1946) LII, 80-1.

[137] *Al Baladuri*, pp. 148, 162, 203, 253.

is little evidence that many availed themselves of this opportunity. Thus, despite these exceptions, it seems safe to say that in Syria and Cyprus, as elsewhere in the regions taken by Islam, the major portion of whatever refugees there were, were either members of Byzantine officialdom or Orthodox Melchite churchmen, rather than merchants, traders, or artisans whose loss would be more disastrous from an economic standpoint.[138]

Up until 693 it would also seem wise not to overestimate damage done in land and sea campaigns between Byzantium and Damascus. Only certain areas were affected seriously in land campaigns. They were Syria, the Syrian-Anatolian border region on either side of the Taurus Mountain frontier and North Africa. Syria was a theater of war between 666 and 689 when the Mardaites were particularly active there. North Africa was raided in 647, 654, 670-685, and 688-9. The Taurus region on both sides of the border was the scene of constant conflict. But except for the latter area, not all districts within these scenes of land conflict were equally affected by war. The maritime districts and cities of Byzantine North Africa, for example, seem to have escaped with little molestation from the Arabs of Kairouan between 670 and 685.[139] Not until the great invasion of 693 did they suffer any serious damage. The same is true of Syria, where only certain areas were subject to Mardaite devastations.

On the sea the same picture is apparent. Cyprus was raided in 648 and 654, Sicily in 652 and 669, the Aegean areas in 652, 669, and 672-9. Only the last naval expedition, including as it did a long siege of Constantinople, seems to have caused more than local damage. Egypt suffered one minor raid in 673, and the Syrian coast was probably attacked in conjunction with Mardaite disorders of 666 and 688-9. There were on the sea, as on the land, long intervals between raids. Any damage done could easily have been repaired. Neither war damage nor population shifts brought any essential breakdown of the Mediterranean economic structure established by Rome and reconstituted by Justinian.

In fact, the theoretical and financial unity of the Mediterranean area remained. The Caliphs of Damascus by periodic payments

---

[138] Both Charanis and Lynn White, it seems to me, overestimate the scope of Greek migrations from these areas in the seventh century. See Charanis *op. cit.*, and White, Lynn "The Byzantinization of Sicily" in *Amer. Hist. Rev.* (1936) xxxxii.

[139] Marçais *Berbérie*, p. 29-31.

tribute to Byzantium recognized, at least theoretically, that Constantinople's rulers still were the overlords of Syria and Egypt. They acknowledged it even more by their continued use and coinage of Byzantine *nomismata*. The whole Mediterranean remained an area in which the golden coinage of Constantinople was still the great international medium of exchange.

It must be admitted, however, that Arab conquest did bring some changes. The most important one was to stop Egypt's tribute grain from being sent to Constantinople. This grain was collected as of old in Egypt by the Arab rulers, and Alexandria continued to be supplied with free wheat, but the supplies that had gone north to Byzantium now travelled south to provision the holy cities of Mecca and Medina. To assist in the delivery of this grain, Amr, Egypt's conqueror, had in 643 put the Nile-Red Sea canal back into operation, thus establishing a water transport route to the south.[140] This change in grain destination had repercussions upon Constantinople. Heraclius abandoned free distribution of grain in the capital, and while the job of provisioning this metropolis remained one of the important responsibilities of the Imperial government, new sources of grain had to be found.[141] It seems probable that the nearby agricultural areas of the Balkans, Asia Minor, and perhaps South Russia made up the deficit caused by the loss of Egypt's old contributions. If so, this may have directly benefited the peasant population of the Empire, who gained a valuable new market for their grain, a fact that may explain the independent, prosperous, free peasants revealed in an analysis of the Farmers' Law.[142]

Another change was the abandoning of much of Justinian's regulation of exports and imports in the seventh century. The Arabs, controlling both the old Sassanian domains and Syria and Egypt, had no interest in maintaining the old customs stations between the two areas. On the other hand, Constantinople did not—judging from all available evidence—discriminate in this period against trade with Syria and Egypt, except perhaps in the matter of ship timber. To do so would have been an admission that these provinces had been irrevocably lost, not merely occupied temporarily

[140] Weil *Geschichte der Chalifen* (Manheim 1846) I, 119-29. Lane-Poole *Egypt*, p. 20.

[141] *Chron. Paschale* ed. Dindorf (Bonn 1832) I, 711.

[142] Vernadsky, G. "Sur l'origine de la loi agraire" in *Byzantion* (1925) IV, 169-80. Ostrogrovsky, G. "Agrarian Conditions in the Byzantine Empire in the Middle Ages" in *Cam. Econ. Hist.*, I.

by the Arabs. Since the Byzantine rulers up to 693 were unwilling to admit that Egypt and Syria were foreign, they did not apply Justinian's entry system to them, though customs duties on their wares were no doubt collected. In addition, though the Imperial monopoly of purple silk was maintained at Constantinople as state control over *tiraz* was in Arab Egypt, other controls were not strictly enforced. For example, the *navicularii* or state-controlled merchant marine, so prominent in earlier periods, seem to have disappeared at about this time.[143] With the end of Egypt's tribute grain they had no function. Free merchant commerce in the Mediterranean area apparently became the rule. The Rhodian Sea Law, probably dating from this period, makes this abundantly clear. Under its provisions, shipmasters were free agents, able to go where they wished to pick up cargo.[144] No trace of a government-regimented merchant marine appears in the seventh century after the Moslem conquest, in startling contrast to late Roman and earlier Byzantine developments. It is possible to overemphasize this point, but in general the seventh century in the Mediterranean seems to have been a period of free unfettered commerce.

It was this freedom of trade, despite war and naval raids, which explains Egypt's great prosperity up to 705. Arculf, a European traveller who visited it in 670, reported Alexandria was a rendez-vous for the commerce of the entire world and that innumerable people came there to buy goods.[145] So prosperous was the land of the Nile about 700, as a matter of fact, that its Arab governor reported to Damascus that his treasuries could hold no more revenues and asked for advice. The Caliph ordered him to use the surplus in the construction of mosques.[146] Not only was Egypt's Mediterranean commerce important at this time, but her traffic with the South and East appears to have increased. The Sassanians had, in the late sixth century, thwarted any expansion of Egypt's trade through the Red Sea and Indian Ocean. Now, with the Sassanians gone, this trade route again became an active one. The Red Sea canal assisted in this development. In fact, so important did the Red Sea commerce become that the Ommayids maintained a naval squadron in its waters to protect the trade routes to Mecca

---

[143] Charanis, P. "The Social Structure of the Later Roman Empire" in *Byzantion* (1944-5) xvii, 50-51.

[144] Ashburner, A. *The Rhodian Sea Law* (Oxford 1909).

[145] Wiet *op. cit.*, p. 28.   [146] Lane-Poole *Egypt*, p. 24-26.

Medina and perhaps all the way to Aden. In 684 this squadron supported Egypt's governor in a revolt against the Caliph of Damascus,[147] and in 692 transported troops to the Hijaz.[148]

In the interior of Syria a similar prosperity prevailed. There the city of Damascus was the beneficiary of the vast sums in booty and tribute that rolled into the coffers of the Caliphs from both the East and the West.[149] The elimination of the old Roman customs barriers between this region and Iraq may also have assisted trade to the East and hence prosperity. Only coastal Syria, disturbed by movement of its population and raids from the sea, failed to share Syria's high level of commercial and industrial wealth. And here more examination of seventh-century evidence is necessary before any definitive conclusions can be reached. This maritime area was still able under the first Ommayids to supply the Arab fleet with large naval contingents. And nearby Cyprus, similarly disturbed by raids, was able to send a yearly tribute of 7,200 dinars to Damascus as well as a similar sum to Byzantium— surely an indication of some real commercial prosperity.[150]

Concerning Constantinople and the Balkan and Anatolian provinces of the Empire, we have little evidence upon which to base an opinion. Border raids were no doubt destructive in Eastern Anatolia, as were the years of the first great assault upon Constantinople and the Aegean area. But there is no evidence that any serious economic crises, such as that which Heraclius faced, disturbed the state. The themal system proved a cheap and efficient system of defense, and Constantinople's trade remained important. No drop in quality or weight of the gold coinage appears in this period.[151]

In addition, there is evidence of a growing Black Sea trade which enriched the Byzantine metropolitan capital. This commerce was with Cherson and the Kazar kingdom in the South Russian-Caspian area. In 626 the Kazars had been loyal allies of Heraclius in his struggle with Persians.[152] Relations had remained close since then. Justinian II, for example, late in the century married a Kazar princess and fled to that kingdom after his expul-

---

[147] Wiet *op. cit.*, p. 39.
[148] *ibid.*, p. 44.
[149] Hitti *op. cit.*, p. 229-31.
[150] Hill *Cyprus* I, 286-87.
[151] Lombard "L'or Musulman du VIIe au XIe siècle" in *Annales* (1947) II, 144-46.
[152] Vernadsky *Ancient Russia*, p. 220-22.

sion from his capital in 695.[153] This Kazar alliance allowed Byzantium to tap trade routes to China which by-passed Arab-controlled ones through Persia. The hostility between the Kazars, whose state was particularly based upon trade, and their Ommayid Arab neighbors testifies to the importance of the commerce which travelled over these routes.

The first half-century of Arab rule and Syria and Egypt, then, seems to have brought no catastrophic results to the economic life of the Eastern Mediterranean. Nor is there evidence either that this period saw much falling off of economic prosperity in the West. No doubt there were repercussions from the population shifts that took place, particularly in Syria, and international commerce was hampered by the naval warfare that was waged between Damascus and Constantinople. But the effect of these factors was in the seventh century apparently rather slight.[154]

A good case in point is North Africa. Though it suffered Arab razzias from 647 on, there is little evidence that its basic productive capacities were destroyed or its prosperity seriously impaired. The Moslem raiders of 647 were surprised at the riches they found there.[155] In the period from 695 to 705 when Arab conquest was completed, its riches in gold, olive oil, grain, horses, and camels still amazed its conquerors. The booty sent to Damascus by the victorious Musa was immense, including even some industrial products, such as fine rugs.[156] Such wealth is an index of the seventh-century prosperity of the African shores.

Italy presents a very similar picture, with the exception of Genoa and the Ligurian coast, which will be considered separately. There is little evidence of any breakdown in Italian prosperity in the seventh century. Commerce with the East continued active, particularly from Ravenna, which had close trade connections with Constantinople[157] and probably Alexandria. Greeks settled in this center had made it practically an Hellenic city. There was a large Greek colony at Rome as well, and Greek merchants of fine textiles were not unknown there.[158] The Church as well was filled with

[153] Pernice, A. *L'Imperatore Eraclio*, p. 152-55.
[154] Lopez provides the best arguments for a continuation of relatively undisturbed commerce in the Mediterranean throughout the seventh century. Lopez "Mohammed and Charlemagne—A Revision" in *Speculum* (1943) xviii.
[155] Diehl *L'Afrique Byzantine*, p. 558-60. Ibn Idhari *Bayan* i, 5.
[156] Marçais *Berbérie*, p. 23-25.   [157] Diehl *Exarchat*, p. 279-80.
[158] *Ibid.*, p. 278-79.

these Easterners, and in 678 there were four Greek monasteries in Rome alone. Nor were Syrians unknown. Four of the Popes of the late seventh and early eighth centuries were Syrians, and a Syrian monastery was functioning at Rome at this time. This may show closer connections with Syria than is often imagined. Diehl has noted that the increase of Greek and Oriental relics and customs in Italy was constant during this period—another indication of continuity with sixth-century developments.[159]

France and Spain also continued to have important commercial links with the Eastern Mediterranean, although perhaps upon a somewhat reduced scale. France was the special economic preserve of Syrian merchants, and it seems possible that the dislocation that their homeland suffered at this time may have affected their ability to supply the markets of France with Eastern wares. Yet as late as 716 Southern France was importing Eastern spices, papyrus, and other products. Evidence of this fact is contained in a diploma of a Merovingian monarch dated in this year which gave the monastery of Corbie special privileges in importing Oriental goods without payment to the royal fisc at the port of Fos. This grant confirms earlier such privileges from the previous century, thus showing that it was no special dispensation and that the monastery had been importing such Eastern wares during the seventh century, if not earlier.[160] Marseilles continued to be an important port at this same time, and olive oil, probably from North Africa, as well as Eastern wares, were numbered among its imports.[161] Spanish ports also in this late Visigothic period seem to be very active in their trade with the Eastern Mediterranean.[162]

Yet there is evidence of some economic strain in France and Spain in the late seventh and early eighth centuries. Perhaps this was due to their great degree of economic passivity which made them—far more than Italy and North Africa—depend upon Easterners from Syria and Egypt. Both Italy and North Africa appear to have traded more with Greek areas of Asia Minor than was the case with the countries further West. Also, both had some merchant shipping of their own, largely lacking in the Frankish and Visigothic domains. This made them less dependent upon the arrival of Eastern merchant fleets. Thus dislocation of Syrian ship-

[159] *ibid.*, p. 255-56.
[160] Pirenne *op. cit.*, p. 89. Heyd *op. cit.*, p. 89-92.
[161] Pirenne *op. cit.*, p. 93-94.   [162] *ibid.*, pp. 87, 94-95.

ping, due to difficulties in the home ports, was immediately noticeable in Spain and France and less so in Italy and North Africa.
One further factor affected France, the lessening importance of
her slave trade. The large number of captives who were brought
back as booty from Arab raids on North Africa, Anatolia, and
Central Asia flooded the markets of the Eastern Mediterranean.
Those dispatched from Southern France could have few takers.
This loss of a valuable export market may have seriously unbal-
anced the export-import trade of the Midi's port cities with the
East.

Whatever the causes of this economic strain, it is reflected in
the currencies of both the Visigoths and Merovingian Franks in
the seventh century. More and more silver, a currency having
mainly a local value, was coined and less and less gold. Such gold
as was coined in France was in the form of *triens*, each having the
value of one-third a solidus. Very frequently such coinage was
poor in weight and quality, often being silver with a wash of
gold.[163] In addition, Spain in the seventh century shows another
evidence of economic difficulties—persecution of Jews. This persecution, which began early in the seventh century, steadily increased in intensity.[164] Though its basis was largely religious, it
may very well have had some economic causes. Certainly the
decree of Egica, king between 687-702, which forbade Jews to
engage in any foreign commerce suggests such a possibility.[165] As
prosperity decreased, popular opinion was eager to blame the
Jews, active in foreign trade, as the responsible agents. Yet such
developments in the West were certainly not important before 716.
Up to that time the tide of trade and commerce, though restricted
at times, continued to flow through the Mediterranean from East
to West and bring prosperity to almost all the lands on its shore.
Syrians and other Eastern merchants continued to land with their
wares in Spain and France as well as in Italy and North Africa.
They are found as well far in the interior all through the seventh
century.[166]

If there is little break in the economic system that prevailed
about the Middle Sea in the first years after Moslem conquest,
however, there is much dislocation apparent in the second half-
century. The contrast between the years 700 and 752 is strik-

[163] Lombard *op. cit.*, p. 143-44.   [164] Pirenne *op. cit.*, p. 84-85.
[165] *ibid.*, p. 85.   [166] Heyd *op. cit.*, p. 21-22.

ing. In 700 there still existed a unified, prosperous Mediterranean. In 752 what was the picture? An Egypt in disorder, Syria in the doldrums, North Africa and Spain in chaos, France stagnate, Eastern Syrians and Egyptians no longer in Western markets, and France and Spain on a silver coinage—a world in which only Byzantium, Italy, and Kazaria have escaped economic ruin. On the political side one sees both Merovingians and Ommayids replaced by Carolingians and Abbassids with capitals in Aix-la-Chapelle and Bagdad, respectively, far from the shores of the Mediterranean. Obviously something important had happened, something that needs explanation. What were the causes of this profound economic and political revolution?

In the first place, there is no evidence of any large shifts of population in any section of the Mediterranean in this second period. Nor was war devastation so severe as to affect the prosperity of any large area. As in the first fifty years of Ommayid-Byzantine hostilities, important land campaigns were confined to three regions: the Syrian-Anatolian frontier, North Africa and Southern France. The North Africa area was the scene of fighting from 693 to 705 when it was finally captured by the Arabs. But the campaigns there were swift. Except for Carthage, which passed back and forth between the two antagonists, like Alexandria before its final capture by the Moslems, all the Byzantine-held towns seem to have surrendered almost without a struggle. After the death of Queen Kahina, the Berbers submitted with almost equal rapidity.[167] Fighting in Spain was purely nominal, one battle, as in the case of Syria and Egypt, sufficing to give the land to its Islamic conquerors. Only in Southern France was there any long and protracted campaigning. In this region between 717 and 752 there was heavy damage done by war. This devastation was largely the work, though, of the Carolingians and not of their Moslem opponents. It was the result, apparently, of deliberate effort on their part to break down opposition to their rule by the native population of Aquitaine and Languedoc.[168] Asia Minor's Byzantine-Arab frontier was also, as earlier, the scene of constant war and devastation.

On the sea again the pattern is identical with that of the earlier period. Damage in naval raids was neither heavy nor constant for

[167] *Nuwairi* in de Slane *Hist. des Berbères* I, 344.
[168] *Cont. de Fred.* in *MGH Script. Rer. Merov.* II, 168-93.

any particular area. Arab fleets attacked the Aegean and Constantinople in 717-18. They descended on Cyprus in 726 and 743. They raided Sicily and Sardinia at regular intervals from 704 to 753. In return, Byzantine raids were confined to Egypt in 709, 720, 725, 736, and 739. Naval assaults, like land warfare and population transfers, then, do not seem to explain adequately what happened to the Mediterranean world by the year 752. Where, then, lies the answer?

The explanation of the political and economic changes which took place lies in the changed nature of the contest between Ommayids and Constantinople between 693 and 752. The first two waves of the Arab assault found war waged by purely military means. In the third wave a new economic factor enters the picture. To military and naval hostility was added economic war.

The Arabs fired the opening guns in this economic conflict in the reign of the Caliph Abd al-Malik. In 692, he struck the first Arab gold dinars and sent them as tribute to Justinian II in Constantinople.[169] He halted, as well, export of Egypt's papyrus to Byzantium and the West.[170] In addition, he removed from this product the old Byzantine Christian markings of the Trinity and had Arab inscriptions substituted.[171] What he was doing seems clear. He was setting up his domains as a separate economic unit and applying economic pressure to his opponents. It was a declaration of economic independence from Byzantium that none of his predecessors had dared to make.

Justinian II answered with war in 693 when he received the new tribute money, hostilities that went very badly for him.[172] But he may have done more. He may have cut off trade with his opponents. That is the only reasonable explanation of his brutal depopulation of Cyprus, which depended on trade with Syria for its livelihood. If this explanation is correct, it explains why the Kibyrrhaeot fleet, based as it was on a region which had an important trade with Egypt, mainly in timber, rose against the government and sailed on Constantinople to depose Justinian's successor. It also explains why merchants of Ravenna, from earlier days equally important suppliers of ship timber to Egypt, should

[169] Hitti *op. cit.*, p. 117.   [170] Lopez *op. cit.*, p. 21-28.
[171] *Theophanes*, p. 558.
[172] *Zonaras* (ed. Bonn) xiv, 229-31. *Cedrenus* (ed. Bonn) i, 772.

have played a part in his downfall.[173] It is further interesting to note that one of Tiberius III's early acts upon replacing Justinian II's successor on the throne of Constantinople was to repopulate Cyprus again in 698. He not only brought the Cypriots back to their island from those regions of his own Empire to which they had been deported, but attempted to draw back those who had fled to Moslem Syria.[174] He also probably made some sort of economic peace with the Ommayids, for there seems little evidence of any more economic pressure exerted during his reign from Damascus.

With the return of Justinian II to power again in 705, though, economic warfare appears to have recommenced. It apparently was set off by the Byzantine raid on Egypt in 709[175] or some other act of economic aggression by Constantinople. Whatever the cause, in 709 the Caliph Walid, successor to Abd al-Malik, continued along the economic path begun by his father. This is referred to by Hitti as "Arab nationalism," an apt phrase. It involved the use of Arabic instead of Greek in all government administrative documents.[176] Such a change in the language of administration was not possible all at once. Egyptian papyri reveal that the first entirely Arabic one dates from 709, the last bilingual Arab-Greek one from 719, and the last Greek one from 780.[177] It was Walid, however, who started this important development.

Also, it was he who in this same year first introduced, or at least enforced, controls over Egypt's population and perhaps that of other sections of his Empire. A strict passport system was put into force, and no Egyptian was permitted to leave his own district, let alone the country.[178] That this was directed against Byzantium can be seen by the provision in this control system for the search of all Nile shipping and the hanging of any Greeks found thereon.[179] Egypt from this time on became a police state where foreigners and Egyptians alike could move only with the permission of the government. And finally the *barid*, or secret service, set up originally by Moawiyah, was so much expanded that its activities soon

---

[173] Diehl *Exarchat*, p. 279-80.

[174] Const. Porph. *De Admin. Imp.*, c. 47, p. 215.

[175] Maqrizi *Kitat*, ed. Bouriant in *Mem. de la Mss. Franc. au Caire* (1900), p. 633-35.

[176] Hitti *op. cit.*, p. 217.   [177] Wiet *op. cit.*, p. 47-49.

[178] *ibid.*, p. 43-46.   [179] *ibid.*

earned its members the name of "The Demons of the State."[180] When Omar II, Walid's successor, applied regulations to the Christian and Jewish communities, requiring them to wear a distinctive dress to separate them from the Moslems of his Empire, the web of controls was complete.[181] From this time on, the Ommayids had an Arab-Moslem state self-consciously organized and directed against its neighbors. Gone were the free-trade days of the seventh century. A new era was at hand.

Byzantium's rulers reacted by imposing controls and economic pressures of their own. They, too, apparently tightened up on their subjects leaving their Empire for Arab lands, as the experience of a Western pilgrim in Cyprus in 722 proves clearly enough. While on his way to the Holy Land he was seized and kept in prison for some months by the Byzantine governor of the island, who insisted he was an Arab spy. It was with difficulty that he convinced the authorities of his innocence and proceeded on his journey.[182]

But it was the economic methods of warfare used by Justinian II and his successors that are most interesting and most important. The full story of their system is difficult to piece together. The main outlines of it, though, stand out clearly enough. It was a return to the controlled trade system which Justinian and his successors had used against Sassanian Persia, by which the routes and character of foreign trade were both carefully directed for the benefit and defense of the Empire. In addition, it was a system in which naval power was used to assist in such channeling.

Perhaps this earlier system had never been totally abandoned in the seventh century. There are indications that it continued to be used in Italy and in commercial contacts with the Kazars. The difficulties and differences between Kazar rulers and Constantinople in 686 and 687 over Cherson and the Crimea, a struggle which appears to have ended in a sort of condominium over that important seaport, suggest a Byzantine policy of channeling all trade through this one controlled city. This was not too popular with Byzantium's northern ally, but it appears, however, to have been the solution finally agreed upon.[183]

---

[180] *ibid.*, p. 163-64. Hitti *op. cit.*, pp. 195, 322-25.
[181] Hitti *op. cit.*, p. 234.
[182] *Pilgrimage of St. Willibald* in Tabler et Molinier I, 256.
[183] Vasiliev *Goths in the Crimea*, p. 81-84.

It is the case of Genoa and Luni, however, which best reveals this trade control system in operation in the seventh century. Prior to 642 Genoa had been an important commercial center on the Ligurian coast. Situated in the center of this province, one Roman road led from it directly through a pass in the Apennines to the rich plain of Lombardy. Another Roman coastal highway linked the city with Rome to the south and Nice and Provence to the west. Until 642 it was also the administrative center of Byzantium's Ligurian province.[184] In that year it and most of the maritime region about it fell into the hands of the Lombard monarch.[185] What happened? Genoa and its surrounding territory lost their commercial importance. It became purely agricultural, the roads to it decayed and the valleys leading inland from it were fortified against any enemy attack from the sea.[186]

But to the east, further along the coast, lay Luni, a smaller, less important port without a good road into the interior. Luni, however, either remained in Byzantine hands or was soon recovered by them, possibly at the time of Constans II.[187] What was its fate? It prospered and grew. A new route into the interior was developed. This was the road between Rome and Lombardy, the Via Francigena, which avoided the seacoast carefully at all other spots but took a turn to the sea and went to Luni. After its conquest by the Lombard kind Luitprand about 725, and under Charlemagne, it remained of some commercial importance.[188]

The meaning of this is clear. The Byzantines, controlling the sea, used their sea power to channel all trade along this coast into the city they controlled and denied it to Genoa and other centers they did not. Thus Constantinople rendered Lombard land aggression valueless, and gave an incentive to towns which she controlled remaining loyal. Having the power of economic life or death in their hands, they dealt it out in controlled trade according to their political interest.

There is good reason to think that in 715 or 716, or close to these dates, Byzantium applied this economic warfare, backed by its

---

[184] Lopez, R. S. "Aux Origines du Capitalism Génois" in *Ann. d'Hist. Econ. et Soc.* VI, 430-31.

[185] Paul the Deacon *Hist. of the Langobards*, p. 199. Luni was not included in the conquests of 642 according to Paul.

[186] Lopez *op. cit.*, p. 431-2.

[187] "Lunigiana" in *Encycl. Ital.* (1934) XXI, 663.

[188] *ibid.*

fleet, to the Ommayid domains and some other neighbors as well. One reason for picking this date is that in 715 the Byzantine-held port of Comacchio, predecessor to Venice at the entrance of the Po, entered into an agreement with the Lombard ruler for the regulation of Eastern commerce between Comacchio and the Lombard domains.[189] It is tempting to think that in this year Comacchio became Byzantium's controlled-trade gateway to the Po River valley as Venice was to become later in the century. Even more important, in 716 a treaty was negotiated with the Bulgarian ruler, though not put into effect until 718, which carefully regulated commerce between the two peoples. It established a passport system and provided that Bulgarian merchants should bring their wares to either Constantinople or Salonika where carefully supervised trading was to take place.[190]

The supposition that this same control system was also applied to Arab domains is strengthened by the fact that in 716 the last large shipment of Eastern goods is recorded at Fos,[191] and that in that same year the Lombard kingdom gave up its use of papyrus.[192] The Byzantines had apparently closed the Mediterranean to trade and shipping from Arab-held lands unless it followed their prearranged routes and regulations. That a great Moslem armada sailed on Constantinople the next year is not surprising, for the Byzantine blockade was a death sentence to Egypt's and Syria's shipping and economic life. Its defeat led to an implementation of the Byzantine system.

Byzantium, however, could not do without all products from the Arab world. The spices and Eastern wares that the latter handled as middlemen were essential to the economic health of the Byzantine Empire. Thus no complete blockade of the Arabs was ever attempted. One or perhaps two controlled entry and exit ports were set up for this commerce. We know from Arab geographers that in the next century Trebizond was the entry used for all Arab trade with Byzantium.[193] Though it is mere supposition, this system may date back to 716 or earlier. For Trebizond as the center of

---

[189] Pirenne op. cit., p. 176. [190] Theophanes, p. 775.

[191] Heyd op. cit., p. 89-92.

[192] So did Germany at about this same time. Lopez "Mohammed and Charlemagne," p. 26-28.

[193] Lopez "Silk Industry in the Byzantine Empire" in Speculum (1945) xx, 26-7. Al Istakhri trans. Defremery in Jour. Asiatique (1849) xiv, 462. Masudi Prairies d'Or trans. Meynal (Paris 1861) ii, 3.

Byzantine Arab trade accomplished a number of objectives for the rulers of Constantinople. First it gave them a port on the Black Sea which was safe from naval attack and thus secure. Second, by setting it up as their Arab trade terminus, they drew the spice and silk trade that they so badly needed away from Egypt and Syria, the naval centers of their Ommayid rivals, to Mesopotamia which held no naval danger for them.

In addition to Trebizond, however, Constantinople itself may have served as a second trade port of entry and exit. In the late ninth century, when the *Book of the Prefect* gives us the regulations governing the capital's commerce, it is clearly indicated that Western Arab traders were encouraged to come to the city on the Golden Horn, where they were given special trade advantages and privileges.[194] Perhaps this was also the case in 718. The mosque Leo III is said to have built at Constantinople for Moslems certainly suggests such a possibility.

But it was one thing to set up this system of trade control and another to enforce it both on Arab enemies and one's own subjects. Two things, however, made this control easier than would otherwise have been the case. The first was Byzantine naval strength which, victorious in 718, sailed into the Mediterranean. The other was Byzantium's possession of the islands of this sea. The Balearics, Sardinia, and Corsica formed a series of island barriers along the North African and Spanish coasts. In addition, Byzantine control of the straits of Messina and both sides of the entrance into the Adriatic made extremely difficult the passage of any ships they wished to exclude from travel to or from the West.

Another factor assisted them. The route along the southern Mediterranean coast from Egypt to North Africa was a very dangerous one to shipping, though not impossible. It lay along the Syrtis Gulfs where the north wind blew without any land masses intervening to give shelter and mitigate its blasts.[195] Few indeed were the harbors where safe anchorage could be found from Barca to Tripoli. The usual East-West route was therefore by way of Crete and Cyprus and along the southern coast of Asia Minor, though the direct Alexandria-Crete route was also used. Byzantine naval power along these coasts could thus effectively cut trade not only with the West, but even between Egypt and Syria and Moslem North

---

[194] *Book of the Prefect* v, 1-2, 4-5; ix, 6; x, 2. Al Istakhri *op. cit.*, p. 462.
[195] Procopius mentions the dangers of this coast. *Procopius* vii, 371-3.

Africa. If a ship escaped interception at one spot it stood a good chance of meeting its nemesis at another. Byzantium was thus in a position to blockade the Mediterranean both in the center and along the Western North African coast and the East-West circle route as well.

Byzantium's own subjects proved perhaps even more intractable than the enemy. Trade with Moslem areas was their economic life-blood. The Byzantine economic blockade must have raised pro-tests. Perhaps it explains the revolt of Sicily's governor in 718, and an additional reason besides Iconoclasm for the naval revolt of the Cyclades and Hellenic themal fleets in 727. It may have been a subsidiary cause of the defection of Luni and Corsica to the Lombards in 725 and of the Pentapolis and Ravenna in 735. Prob-ably it was capable of only partial enforcement up to the great naval battle of 747. After that time it could become really effective.

If the foregoing explanation of this economic blockade seems conjectural, a glance at the shores of the Mediterranean in this period shows that the blockade not only existed but was amazingly effective. Consider the East first, against whose Syrian and Egyp-tian coasts both naval and economic measures were primarily directed. Syria by 752 had lost its important trade position. Not only had its coastal cities so little life that they were not even able to muster a fleet for twenty more years,[196] but the Ommayid Ca-liphs had fallen after their naval and economic defeat at the hands of Byzantium. The Abbassid Caliphs, basing their power on a Mesopotamia through which a rich stream of trade passed on its way to Trebizond, were in control. Damascus fell to the level of a second-rate provincial center.[197]

Egypt's plight was even more serious. Ommayid regimentation and Byzantine naval and economic war had done their work all too well. In 705 Egypt was a prosperous land, its treasury filled to overflowing. In 725 the first of the great Coptic revolts, which were to last more than a century, broke out. It was suppressed with difficulty.[198] Arab tribes were then brought in and given lands in the Berbers region, perhaps as a garrison against further Coptic disorders.[199] In addition, the Melchite clergy were given back their churches and persecution of them was ended.[200] Perhaps this was

---

[196] Hill *Cyprus* I, 291.
[197] Kremer *Culturgeschichte des Orients* I, 183.
[198] Wiet *op. cit.*, p. 56-58.   [199] *ibid.*, p. 61-63.
[200] *ibid.*, p. 56-59.

done not only as punishment for the Copts but also because Leo III's Iconoclastic doctrines made them hostile to Constantinople and thus no longer a menace to their Ommayid masters. In 739 an even more serious Coptic rising took place. It was apparently synchronized with an invasion of Coptic Nubians from the south and a large Byzantine sea raid on the Delta. It, too, was put down with difficulty.[201] In 745 another revolt occurred, this time by Arab tribes in the Delta who objected to the heavy taxation to which they were being subjected.[202]

It has generally been assumed that these Coptic revolts were primarily religious in character. But perhaps they show something else.[203] The Copts, who were the agricultural and, even more important, the business class of Egypt, were adversely affected by the heavy taxation and the lack of prosperity of the land. Is it not logical to see in these revolts a reflection of the results of a Byzantine economic and naval blockade of Egypt? Why else should the Copts, loyal to their Arab overlords from conquest times, have suddenly turned upon them?

When North Africa is considered, again the same pattern of events repeats itself. By 740 economic conditions had so deteriorated that Moslem taxation seemed like exaction. In addition, the Berbers, undoubtedly resenting the social and political superiority which their Arab rulers were insisting on in their dealings with them, were eager to achieve an equality their masters were unwilling to grant. As a result, there came the great revolt of Kharijism which shook African Arab control to its very foundations for more than sixty years.[204] And it is interesting to note that the original rising was not just by the Berbers but by the lower classes in the North African cities, a rather good indication of the economic basis of these disorders.[205] Even in Spain, where Berber revolts and disorders followed each other one after another during these years, one may see a reflection of the same bad economic conditions.[206]

[201] *ibid.*   [202] *ibid.*

[203] Neither Hitti, Wiet nor Lane-Poole gives much attention to the economic side of these revolts, preferring to view them as the results of the religious persecution of Omar II. For example see Hitti *op. cit.*, p. 234.

[204] Ibn Khaldun *Hist. des Berbères* I, 216-17, 237. *Nuwairi* in de Slane *Hist. des Berbères* I, 319.

[205] Gautier stresses the economic side of these disorders and the part played by the cities. Gautier, E. F. *Les Siècles Obscurs du Magreb* (Paris 1927), p. 103.

[206] Lévi-Provençal *Histoire de l'Espagne Mussulmane* (Cairo 1944), p. 24-38.

If these conditions were current in Moslem lands, East and West, is it surprising that France, commercially passive and dependent on traders from Syria and Egypt for her economic life, should have suffered economic stagnation after 716? From that time on, no Syrians came to her southern French ports and few traders from anywhere else. Those cities destroyed by the Carolingians in 739 were not rebuilt.[207] In the middle of the century gold was coined for the last time for fifty years.[208] The Mediterranean Sea, which once served as a pathway for commerce to the mouth of the Rhone, was largely deserted. The old era had passed for the West, and a new one was at hand. Only Italy, still controlled in certain areas by Byzantium, failed to suffer. Her sea lanes were open—at least to Constantinople. Italy, however, was an exception. Elsewhere the middle of the eighth century saw a triumphant Byzantium dominating a shattered Mediterranean world.

Pirenne obviously saw an important fact, but picked the wrong villain. It was not the Arabs but Byzantium who destroyed the ancient unity of the Mediterranean.[209] In her war to the death with the Ommayids, Byzantium used naval and economic means to reach victory in the period from 715 to 752. In so doing, she destroyed the older economic pattern of Mediterranean life and set the stage for a new one which was to emerge.

[207] Buckler, F. W. *Harunu 'l Raschid and Charles the Great* (Cambridge, Mass. 1927), p. 7.

[208] Prou, M. *Catalogue des Monnaies Carolingiennes de la Bibliothèque Nationale* (Paris 1896).

[209] Pirenne in his *Mohammed and Charlemagne*, while he claims to describe a Moslem blockade of Europe actually shows clearly that relations with Byzantium were Charlemagne's chief problem and concern. He also admits that Byzantium had the only effective Mediterranean fleet in this period. Pirenne *op. cit.*, p. 162-63. Why he did not draw the obvious conclusions from this I cannot say. Only Runciman seems to have realized how Byzantium's sea power channeled trade in this period, though he does not give it sufficient weight. Runciman *Byzantine Civilization*, p. 166-167.

4. The Byzantine Dominion

It was an exhausted Mediterranean world which, in 752, witnessed a Byzantium finally victorious over its Arab Ommayid opponents. Constantinople had proved in the heat of naval and economic conflict its right to rule the waters of the Middle Sea. It had humbled its old rivals for this leadership, Egypt and Syria. But in so doing, it and its Arab opponents had destroyed the unity of Romania. Leadership in the Islamic world backed away from Mediterranean Syria and Egypt, which had been the basis of Ommayid strength, to the interior of Western Asia. Bagdad, Persian in thought and culture and looking East toward Central Asia and the Indian Ocean rather than West toward the Mediterranean, became the new capital of the Abbassid Caliphs. Well might Einhard refer to Harun-al-Rashid as King of Persia and Theophanes speak of the Abbassids in the same vein.

In the West, the Franks too, though to a lesser degree perhaps, felt the same breakup of the old Mediterranean synthesis. Though they had, like the Emperors of Constantinople, humbled their Moslem opponents, the rulers of Spain, and had won for the Frankish state a clear title to the coastline of the Mediterranean from the Pyrenees to Italy, it was a hollow victory. This coast, with its blackened, burnt cities, faced a sea which brought little economic life-blood to its towns. Those Syrian traders who had linked it to the great cities of Alexandria and Antioch came no more to its shores. And the center of power of the Frankish state retreated from the Mediterranean, as did that of Islam. The Salian Merovingians, depending upon France as the basis of their power, lost out to the Ripuarian Carolingians, more Germanic in their background. The new Frankish Carolingian state was centered not at Paris but at Aix-la-Chapelle, and looked to the Rhine, Moselle, and North Sea rather than to Rhone, Seine, and Loire.[1] Europe began to come into being on the ruins of Romania in the West.

For almost half a century after 752, Byzantium possessed the only effective naval power in the entire Mediterranean-Black Sea

---

[1] Pirenne's basic thesis on this point seems very reasonable. Pirenne *Mohammed and Charlemagne*, p. 184-8.

area. She preserved that maritime supremacy she had won in 747. The Imperial fleet at Constantinople and the themal fleets of the Aegean, Kibyrrhaeots, and Sicily had no real rivals. Possessing such islands as Sicily, Crete, Cyprus, Sardinia, and perhaps the Balearics, as well as all the most important strategic straits on the East-West trade routes. Constantinople's naval control could be strict and total, as its ships patrolled hostile coasts and prevented Byzantium's enemies from using the waters of the Mediterranean.

There is ample evidence that this was so. Egypt and North Africa remained navally impotent throughout these five decades. The former abandoned naval power altogether.[2] The latter lost the island of Pantelleria and forsook any naval activity from its Tunisian naval bases.[3] Rather, the African Moslems retreated to the Sousse area in the south, further from the range of Sicily's raiding squadrons.[4] Well might the Arab historian Ibn-al-Athir recall this period in the history of the Magreb in the following words: "Their vessels cruised the shores . . . and more than once they captured the ships of Moslem merchants they found in their way."[5] The fortification of Tripoli in 796 and the construction of *ribats* or strong points at Monastir and other places along the North African coast are a proof of how effective this type of naval power really was.[6] The same situation as regards Egypt and the East is revealed in a statement attributed by Masudi to Harun-al-Rashid. When the latter thought of constructing a canal across the isthmus of Suez he abandoned the plan on the grounds that Byzantine ships would sail through and raid the holy cities of Mecca and Medina.[7]

Bulgarians and Carolingian Franks found themselves equally impotent before Constantinople's maritime strength in these same years. In the year 763 Constantine V could ship an army by sea to the mouth of the Danube and thus take his Bulgarian enemies in

[2] Brooks, E. N. "The relations between the Empire and Egypt from a New Source" in *Byz. Zeit.* (1913) xxii, 383-4.

[3] Though in Moslem hands in 700, in 835 Pantelleria was definitely Byzantine. It probably passed into their control about 752. *Ibn al Athir* trans. in Vasiliev *Byzance et les Arabes* i, 360.

[4] This shift of the center of power in Tunisia from the region about Carthage is not the least interesting feature of this period. It was an important shift, due, I think, to Arab fears of Sicily's raiding squadrons.

[5] *Ibn al Athir* trans. Fagnan (Algiers 1901), p. 90.

[6] *Ibn Idhari* i, 107. *Nuwairi* in Ibn Khaldun *Hist. des Berbères* i, 394. *Ibn al Athir*, p. 149.

[7] Masudi *Prairies d'Or*, iv, 98.

the rear and force their defeat.[8] In 773 he could again gain victory by using an armada of 200 ships to assist his armies in the same manner.[9] Charlemagne in 787, victorious in northern and central Italy, was to find his efforts south of the Duchy of Spoleto equally thwarted by Byzantium's naval strength.[10]

There were only two small regions, as a matter of fact, where any non-Byzantine naval power was found at this time. They were Spain and Syria. In both places, however, this naval strength was organized on a purely local basis. Spain's maritime power, for example, seems to have come from a small area between Tarragona and Tortosa and to have been used as part of the Wali of Saragossa's frontier forces defending Spain against Carolingian attacks. Up to 798, it appears, such naval forces were used only three times, raiding Marseilles in 768,[11] threatening Italy in 778,[12] and attacking Narbonne in 793.[13] Furthermore, it is well to note that in this period, as well as later, the Ommayids of Spain directed their naval attacks against the Empire of the Franks and not that of Byzantium. Since during these years a serious struggle was going on between these two latter powers in Italy, this fact is of real interest.[14] It seems to indicate that Spanish naval power operated in this period either in alliance with or with the tacit consent of Constantinople's rulers, who were delighted to see their Frankish rivals diverted by another enemy.

Syria's fleet, which gradually recovered to some extent from the great defeat of 747, was similar to Spain's in that it, too, was essentially a frontier force of local nature. But it differed from the latter in that it was definitely directed by the Abbassid Caliphs against Byzantine territory. Yet so weak was it that its first offensive operation did not take place until 773. Then Cyprus was raided, and its Byzantine governor captured.[15] This raid took place, however, only when Constantinople's naval squadrons were busy

[8] *Theophanes*, p. 671. Lombard, M. *Constantin* v (Paris 1902), p. 48.

[9] *Theophanes*, p. 687.   [10] Gay *L'Italie Meridionale*, p. 46-48.

[11] *Chron. of pseudo Fredegarius* in *MGH Script. Rer. Merov.* II, 197.

[12] Jaffé-Wattenbach *Regesta*, no. 2424.

[13] Böhmer-Muelbacher *Regestrum*, p. 138.

[14] The close relations between the Ommayids of Spain and Byzantium lasted long after the Carolingians, in fact up to the 11th century. These relations were based on similarity of interests and common opposition to Carolingians, Ottos, and the Moslem rulers of Sicily and North Africa. Lévi-Provençal *Hist. de l'Espagne Mussulmane* (Cairo 1944), pp. 175-78, 376-82.

[15] Brooks, E. N. *op. cit.*, p. 384.

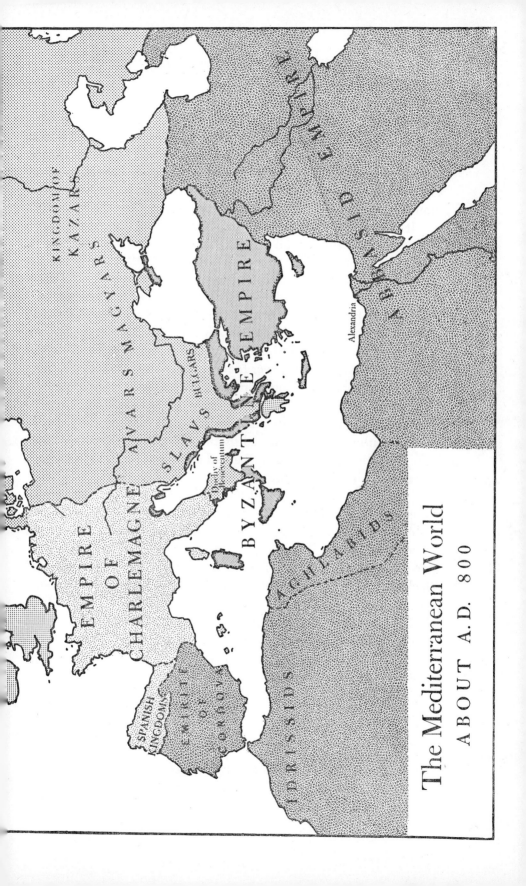

The Mediterranean World
ABOUT A.D. 800

KINGDOM OF KAZA

AVARS MAGYARS

SLAVS

BULGARS

EMPIRE
OF
CHARLEMAGNE

Duchy of
Beneventum

BYZANTINE EMPIRE

SPANISH
KINGDOMS

EMIRATE
OF
CORDOVA

IDRISSIDS

AGHLABIDS

ABBASID EMPIRE

Alexandria

in the war against the Bulgarians. Not until 790 were Syrian flotillas again used, this time raiding both Crete and Cyprus.[16] These raids apparently called forth a large measure of Byzantine naval strength, and a large-scale sea battle was fought off Cyprus in the bay of Attalia between the two antagonists. In it a Byzantine admiral was captured,[17] but Moslem losses must have been heavy indeed, for another sixteen years were to elapse before we hear of any more offensive operations by the Syrian-Tarsus border fleet.

It is the situation in Spain and North Africa, however, which best shows in this period the naval impotence of Byzantium's Islamic antagonists. The Abbassids attempted, after replacing the Ommayids as Caliphs, to establish their power fully over Egypt, North Africa and Spain. They sent strong armies, largely composed of Persian troops, to overrun these territories and force them to accept them as overlords. In vain. Spain slipped away in 756 into the hands of Ommayid Abd-ar-Rahman I,[18] and only one Abbassid expedition had the sea power to reach its coast.[19] It landed at Beja in the south after a short trip from Africa, was badly defeated, and received no reinforcements from the sea. In 788, Morocco revolted and became an independent state under Alid Idrissid rulers, without being molested by the Abbassids.[20] Finally, in 800, the Aghlabids received from Bagdad a grant of de facto independence over the Tunisian coast.[21]

Only Egypt could be held under direct rule, and here control was compromised by revolts by both Arabs and Copts. The revolts became so endemic, in fact, that they rendered possession of Egypt a doubtful asset.[22] Why did these territories slip away from Abbassid control? It could not have been that the Caliphs of Bagdad lacked troops. They did not, as their successful campaigns against the Isaurians proved again and again. It was largely because they lacked any effective naval power. Without it they could neither reach Spain nor supply adequately loyal troops in distant North

[16] Brooks, E. N. "The Byzantines and Arabs at the time of the Early Abbassids" in *Eng. Hist. Rev.* (1900) xv, 745-46.

[17] *Baladuri*, p. 154. Weil *Geschichte der Chalifen* ii, 157.

[18] *Ibnu'l-Tiqtaqa-al Fakri* trans. Amari (Paris 1910) in *Archives Marocaines* xvi, 240-43.

[19] *ibid.*, p. 268-75.

[20] Mas Latrie *Traités de Paix et Commerce, etc.* (Paris 1865), p. 5.

[21] Amari *Storia* i, 268-77.

[22] Wiet *Egypte Arabe*, p. 61-63. Lane-Poole *Egypt*, p. 31-38.

Africa. And so they had to sit by and watch these Western portions of their domains become detached by local rulers and set up as independent or quasi-independent states.[23]

It was the same naval power of Byzantium which dictated the location of the capitals of these new Moslem principalities. Like those of earlier Arab times, they were all inland in this period. Egypt's capital remained Fustat, Aghlabid Tunisia's was Kairouan, the Idrissids built theirs at Fez, and the Ommayids of Spain had their governmental center at Cordova. They shared the common characteristic of being far enough from the sea to be safe from naval surprise. Thus once again the non-maritime character of the Islamic Mediterranean world of the late eighth century and the thoroughness of Constantinople's control of the seas is emphasized.

In the years after 800, however, the situation began to change. Byzantium appears to have begun to neglect her sea power. This decline probably began at the time of Irene, but its full consequences were not apparent until the end of her reign. Her successor, Nicephorus, found a naval situation which can only be described as critical. Four non-Byzantine areas began to increase their fleets and naval power—Spain, Syria, North Africa, and the Carolingian Empire.

Spain, though potentially dangerous, was the least serious problem, since her fleet was directed against the Carolingians in alliance with Byzantium. But its naval operations did broaden in scope to include most of the Western Mediterranean. The Balearics, which were apparently deserting their old allegiance to Byzantium to seek Carolingian protection, were raided in 798.[24] And between 806 and 815 attacks by sea were made with regularity on Corsica and the Frankish-held coast from the Tiber to the Rhone. In 806, for example, a Frankish squadron was defeated off the former island when it was raided by Spanish Moslems.[25] These latter were defeated in their turn in 807 in the same waters and lost thirteen ships.[26] This apparently did not deter the Spanish Islamic flo-

---

[23] It is also true, however, that a similar breakup of Abbassid power took place in its Eastern provinces where sea power could not be a decisive factor. Abbassid disintegration was thus also due to the faulty administrative system used by these rulers. See Appendix III and Hitti *op. cit.*, p. 331.

[24] *Ann. Reg. Franc.* in *MGH Script.* I, 104.

[25] *Eginhard* in *MGH Script.* II, 45. *Ann. Reg. Franc.* in *MGH Script.* I, 193.

[26] Ganshof "Note sur les Ports de Provence du VIIIe au Xe siècles" in *Rev. Hist.* (1938) CLXXXIII, 31.

tillas, for they made new incursions in 808, 809, and 810.[27] In 813
another expedition from Spanish ports raided Nice, Città Vecchia,
and Corsica, but on its way home was surprised and badly mauled
off Majorca by a pursuing Frankish fleet under the Count of Ampurias. Five hundred Corsican captives taken by the raiders were
rescued.[28] Finally, in 815 another descent was made on the Balearics, now apparently under Frankish protection.[29]

The most interesting of these Spanish naval enterprises, however, took place in the Eastern Mediterranean. Thither in 814 a
group of 10,000 Islamic Spanish refugees, exiled after a revolt in
Cordova by the Ommayid ruler al-Hakim, sailed to find new
homes. They arrived in Egypt apparently unopposed by either
Byzantines or Abbassids. By 816 they were powerful enough to
take over the city of Alexandria and rule it for almost a dozen years.
The confused state of Egypt, then in complete disorder, made
their seizure of power possible.[30] When they were finally expelled,
it was a land expedition by the Abbassid governor which accomplished their discomfiture.[31] Apparently the rulers of Bagdad had
no naval power at their disposal for this task in that section of
the Mediterranean.

If the activities of these Spanish Moslems against the Franks
in the Western Mediterranean and against Abbassid Alexandria in
the East were not too displeasing to Byzantium, other activities
by Moslem fleets were. In 806 Syrian flotillas, quiescent for almost
two decades, again took offensive action. In conjunction with
Harun-al-Rashid's land campaign across Anatolia to Heraclea they
raided Cyprus.[32] In the next year they followed this up with an
assault on Rhodes.[33] Only Constantinople's payment of tribute to
Bagdad secured peace.

[27] *Ann. Reg. Franc.* in *MGH Script.* i, 194. Buckler *op. cit.*, p. 23-24.

[28] *Eginhard* Ed. Duchesne, p. 258. Amari *Storia* i, 354-55.

[29] Campaner y Fuertes *Bosquejo Histórico de la Dominación Islamica en las islas Baleares* (Palma 1881), p. 10-17. It is interesting that a careful distinction in our sources is almost always made between the Moslems of Spain and those of Africa. Those from Spain are called *Mauri*; those from Africa, *Saraceni*. No doubt the differences in the policies of these two groups towards the Carolingian domains in Europe were well understood by Carolingian chroniclers.

[30] Wiet *op. cit.*, p. 68-72.

[31] *Al Kindi*, p. 180-84. Lane-Poole *op. cit.*, p. 35-38.

[32] *Theophanes*, p. 749. Abu-al Fida *Annales Moslemica* trans. Reiske and Adler, ii, 91. Cyprus seems to have been completely Byzantine in this period, for here Constantine V sent exiled iconodules in 770. *Theophanes*, p. 688.

[33] Masudi *Prairies d'Or* ii, 337.

In addition to the Syrian fleet, naval danger came from another quarter. Aghlabid North African flotillas, perhaps encouraged by Byzantine weakness, again took to the water after half a century of impotence. In 805 they raided the Peloponnesus and assisted the Slavs in their siege of the city of Patras,[34] perhaps as part of an overall Abbassid plan to put pressure on Constantinople by land and sea. This attack was followed by a ten-year truce negotiated between the Patrician of Sicily and the Aghlabid ruler.[35] Though this truce was renewed for another ten years in 813, it seems to have been rather ineffective. It did not prevent African Arabs from making unsuccessful assaults on Sardinia in 812 and 813.[36] In this latter raid they lost 100 ships which foundered off the island in a storm.[37] Yet in 820 Sicily itself was attacked and much booty taken.[38] In 821 it was Sardinia's turn to be the victim.[39]

While Syrian, North African, and Spanish Moslems were thus again taking to the sea with greater vigor to dispute Byzantine primacy of this element, Charlemagne was not idle either. Perhaps the deterioration in relations which followed Irene's deposition in 802 and Nicephorus's accession as Emperor in Constantinople spurred him on to naval efforts. Perhaps his sons, Louis in Aquitaine and Pepin in Italy, confronted by Ommayid Spanish and Byzantine maritime strength in their duties as viceroys, convinced him of the necessity of some naval action. At any rate, at about this time Charlemagne decided on a navy and ordered 1,000 ships built in his Empire.[40] Just where they were to be constructed is problematical, but it is interesting to note that the first years of the ninth century did see a sudden flurry of Carolingian strength on the sea.

In the Western Mediterranean two centers of naval power appear to have been set up by Charlemagne. One was along the coast of the Spanish March where both Tortosa and Barcelona fell into his hands by 812. The other was along the northwest coast of Italy. By 806 and 807 there was sufficient maritime strength developed along the Ligurian and Tuscan coasts for Charlemagne's lieutenants to dispute control of the waters off Italy with Spanish

---

[34] Const. Porphyr. *De Admin. Imp.* c. 49, p. 217.

[35] Vasiliev, A. *Byzance et les Arabes* I, 64, gives the best account of this truce. See also Amari *Storia* I, 332, 356-7.

[36] *Codex Carolinus* ed. Cenni, IX, X.   [37] *Ibn al Athir*, p. 182.

[38] Amari *Storia* I, 358-59.   [39] *Ibn Idhari* I, 120.

[40] Pirenne *op. cit.*, p. 248.

Moslem pirates. His Spanish flotilla, on the other hand, was able to win a major victory under the command of the Count of Ampurias off Majorca in 813. That this victory was no minor one can be seen in the fact that there were no Ommayid Spanish raids on Frankish territory again until 838.[41] And sufficient naval strength remained along the Carolingian coast of Italy for vessels from Luni and Pisa to launch an assault on Bone in North Africa in 828,[42] probably in alliance with Byzantium.

But it was in the Adriatic that Charlemagne was even more active, if less successful in the long run. Here Venice, possessing great naval and commercial strength and owing allegiance to Byzantium, was his prime objective, though he also sought to add maritime Istria and Dalmatia to his domains. Charlemagne realized, apparently, that possession of Venice would assure him not only the major naval strength in the Adriatic but also access to the markets of the East. After 802 he and his son Pepin made every effort to secure domination of it. At first he was rather successful and by 805 had secured practical adherence of the city to the Empire and victory for the Carolingian party led by Fortunatus, Patriarch of Grado.[43]

But then Byzantium interfered actively. Alarmed at this turn of events, her ruler sent a fleet under Nicetas, which in 807 recalled Venice and Dalmatia to their older allegiance.[44] Fortunatus fled to Aix-la-Chapelle, and the Byzantine party gained the ascendency again. Pepin, without sufficient Adriatic naval power, had to be content with a truce with the Venetian authorities.[45] Constantinople still was not satisfied, however, and in 808 sent another fleet to Venice under Paulus, Strategos of Cephallonia. Venetian contingents joined this squadron in an attack on Comacchio, the trade gateway to the Po, still held apparently by the Carolingians.[46] The attack failed, but did spur Charlemagne to a final effort. His son Pepin gathered an army and a fleet and prepared

---

[41] Meanwhile an expedition was sent to Corsica by the Carolingians in 825. "Capitula de expeditione Corsicana" in *Capit. Regum. Franc.* ed. Boretus I, 325. On raid on Marseilles in 838 see Campaner y Fuertes *op. cit.*, p. 16-17.

[42] *Vita Hlud. Imp.* in *MGH Script.* II, 632.

[43] Dandolo *Chron.*, p. 23. John Diac. *Chron. Ven.* ed. Monticolo, p. 100.

[44] Eginhard *Annales* in *MGH Script.* II, 184. For fullest account see Brown, H. *Studies in Venetian History* (London 1907) I, 10-47.

[45] Bury, J. B. *Eastern Roman Empire*, p. 322-26.

[46] *ibid.*

an all-out attack on Venice in 809.[47] The assault overran Venice's mainland possessions like Malamacco, but failed to penetrate to the Rialto in the lagoons whither the government had been moved.[48] Venice remained Byzantine and outside the Carolingian Empire.

By 812 Charlemagne gave up his attempt. He made a peace with Byzantium in which, in return for an alliance, trade privileges and recognition as Emperor, Venice with her mainland possessions, Istria and Dalmatia were recognized as Byzantine.[49] When he died in 814 the situation remained the same. Louis the Pious and Lothair remained allied to Constantinople, which gave a very grudging recognition of their title of Basileus and did not really carry out the provisions of the *pactum* of 812.[50] But naval power in the Adriatic remained in Byzantine hands, or rather those of the all but autonomous Venetian state.

On the whole, then, up to 821, despite the increase of naval power in the hands of Syrians, North Africans, Carolingians and Spanish Moslems, Byzantium managed to hang on to her naval superiority. Not even land pressure by Abbassids and Bulgarians shook her position seriously in respect to naval power. But in 821 came disaster, which, added to outside naval pressure, finally cracked her position of naval dominance in the Middle Sea. This disaster came not from outside forces, but as a result of civil war—the rising of Thomas the Slav between 821 and 823, which crippled Constantinople on the sea.

This revolt was a curious one. In it were mingled many elements of discontent. It was supplied and assisted by the Caliph al-Mamun of Bagdad, who furnished troops and sent his Syrian fleet to raid the islands and the coast of Asia Minor in support of Thomas's efforts. It was Iconodule in sympathy, for Thomas apparently claimed his major objective was the deposition of the Iconoclast Emperor and the return of images, outlawed again since Irene's time. It had the backing of the provincial fleets of the Aegean that sailed on Constantinople as they had done in 698

[47] Const. Porphyr. *De Admin. Imp.*, p. 124.
[48] John Diac. *Chron. Ven.*, p. 106.
[49] Gasquet *Byz. Empire*, p. 287-318. Hazlitt *History of the Venetian Republic* I, 46-52. Cessi, R. *op. cit.*, p. 31-33.
[50] Lopez's account of the meaning of this treaty and its results is to be found in Lopez, R. S. "The Silk Industry in the Byzantine Empire" in *Speculum* (1945) XX, 31-5.

against Justinian II's successor and in 727 against Leo III. It even appears to have been a proletarian rising in Asia Minor with peasant backing. Perhaps the very diversity of these elements caused its lack of success. But the chief stumbling block was the Imperial fleet at Constantinople. As in 727, it remained loyal and scattered the provincial squadrons with Greek fire and drove them from the Sea of Marmora. Thomas was as unsuccessful on the land as on the sea. Bulgarians attacking his troops on the European side put them to rout and spoiled any chance of a successful land assault on the capital. By 823 he had been defeated and killed, and his revolt had collapsed.[51] But from the naval standpoint Byzantium was crippled. The provincial fleets, scattered and burnt in civil war, were badly needed to buttress Constantinople's slipping naval fortunes, as Syrian, North African and other maritime enemies gathered their strength.

In 827 these enemies struck. The Spanish Moslems of Alexandria were the first to exploit Byzantine weakness. Expelled by the Abbassids from this city, they crossed to Crete and landed there all but unopposed. Soon the island was in their hands, and they had built a strong fortified pirate nest at Candia.[52] From this center they were for almost a century and a half to be the terror of the Aegean and a thorn in Byzantium's side. The lack of resistance which they encountered seems to have been directly the result either of the destruction of provincial fleets in the revolt of Thomas a few years earlier, or of the dissatisfaction of the island population of the Aegean, Iconodule in sympathy, which made them disloyal to Constantinople and almost welcome the Spanish pirate exiles. Perhaps it was both.

At the same time, further to the West an even more important event was taking place. The Aghlabids of North Africa opened an attack on Sicily, the key to the central Mediterranean. This was no small-scale affair, no raid. It was an expeditionary force which aimed at conquest of the entire island. It was made possible in part because of the defection of Byzantium's Sicilian fleet, which, under its admiral Euphemios, went over to the Moslems after an unsuccessful revolt had failed.[53] It is interesting to note that there was

---

[51] There have been many full treatments of the revolt of Thomas the Slav. The best is to be found in Vasiliev *Byz. et les Arabes* I, 22-49. See also Vernadsky *Ancient Russia*, p. 302.

[52] *Tabari* trans. in Vasiliev *Byz. et les Arabes* I, 287. *Al Kindi*, p. 180-84.

[53] Vasiliev *Byz. et Arabes* I, 67-71.

some hesitation in North African ranks about engaging in this expedition. Only after weighing all factors was the decision made to go ahead.[54] The final expedition which sailed from Sousse numbered, in addition to Euphemios's vessels, seventy to one hundred ships and several thousand men.[55] With its landing on Sicily, as with the occupation of Crete, a new era began. The age of Byzantine domination came to an end and a new period of Islamic control of the seas came into being. The battle off Cyprus in 747 was avenged. The new rulers of the Mediterranean, the Moslems of North Africa and Crete, came into the heritage that Constantinople had held so long and the Ommayids had sought in vain to seize.

Thus to catalogue the gradual changes in naval power in the Mediterranean during these seventy-five years of Byzantine maritime supremacy, though, is to explain only a portion of the Mediterranean picture. For if 752 saw the rulers of the city on the Golden Horn undisputed masters of the blue waters for three-quarters of a century, it saw them less successful on the land. Shift of power from Damascus to Bagdad in the Islamic world, though important, did not end hostilities between the Arab Caliphs and the Emperors of Byzantium. If Moslem naval power was crippled at that time, their land forces certainly were not. And as soon as the Abbassids were firmly established on their throne in Mesopotamia they attacked Byzantium's eastern frontiers even more fiercely than their Ommayid predecessors had done.

Byzantium, on the land, weakened by the internal Iconoclast struggles and foreign enemies, had real difficulty in the late eighth and early ninth centuries in holding its own. Practically every ruler of Constantinople at some time during this period was forced to pay large sums of gold in tribute to Bagdad's rulers. In 772, for example, Constantine V, perhaps the ablest of the Isaurian line, was forced to pay a large sum to secure peace on his Eastern frontiers.[56] His preoccupation with savage Iconoclast persecutions and difficulties with Bulgarians in the Balkans and Franks in Italy made it impossible for him to concentrate strength in the East. Similarly such tribute payments were renewed by Irene in 781, when Moslem armies marched all the way across Anatolia to the Bosphorus.[57] The

---

[54] *Riad an-Nufus*, p. 78. [55] *Ibn Idhari*, p. 146. *Nuwairi*, p. 174.

[56] Brooks "The Byzantines and the Arabs" in *Eng. Hist. Rev.* (1900) xv, 728-47; (1901) xvi, 84-92.

[57] Brooks, *op. cit.*, 737-9. *Theophanes* ed. De Boor, p. 456.

year 798 saw new golden streams flow to Bagdad after a Moslem army reached Ephesus.[58] And Irene's successor, Nicephorus, was similarly forced to pay tribute after 806, when Harun-al-Rashid's troops in even greater force reached Heraclia itself across from Constantinople.[59]

These preoccupations with campaigns against Arabs and Bulgarians in Asia Minor and the Balkans explain why Byzantine intervention in the third spot where it was under pressure from the land in this period, the Italian peninsula, was so weak and ineffective. In addition there is another reason—the Iconoclasm which Constantinople's rulers, except Irene, professed. Neither the Papacy nor the Western Church would accept this doctrine, and attempts by Leo III and Constantine V to force them to do so weakened still further the frail ties which bound Rome and Italy to Constantinople. By the middle of the century, Byzantine control over the Pentapolis, Ravenna, and Rome was merely nominal. When the Lombard monarch took Ravenna and advanced on Rome in the 750's, it was not to Iconoclast Constantinople that the Papacy turned for assistance. Rome looked across the Alps to Pepin, Mayor of the Palace and ruler of the Franks. With him a bargain was struck. The Pope acquiesced in the deposition of the last shadowy Merovingian Monarch and crowned Pepin King of the Franks. In return, the latter led his army across the Alps into Italy and deprived the Lombards of their recent conquests.[60] But these domains were not returned to Constantinople's officials, despite the embassy from Constantine V which visited the victorious Frankish king.[61] Instead, Pepin gave Rome, Ravenna, the Pentapolis, and Corsica to the Papacy, this territory being called the donation of Pepin.[62]

In this guise began Frankish intervention in Italian affairs to the detriment of Byzantine interests and the final turn of Rome west toward the Carolingians instead of east toward Constantinople. This also marked the beginning of a long struggle between the Franks and the Papacy on the one hand and Byzantium on the other for influence over Italy. This contest lasted with varying degrees of intensity throughout the period we are considering.

[58] Weil op. cit., ii, 157.   [59] Masudi Prairies d'Or, ii, 337.

[60] Pirenne op. cit., p. 210-35.

[61] Jaffé Regestrum, pp. 126, 149. Ann. Laur. Min. in MGH Script. i, 112-13. Epist. Mer. et Carol. xvi, pp. 545, 650.

[62] Pirenne op. cit., p. 224-6.

Byzantium used naval and economic power and diplomacy to make up for her lack of armed strength. Her diplomacy was particularly tortuous. First she supported her old enemy, the Lombard king, until Charlemagne in 774 crossed the Alps and ended Lombard power in north and central Italy by annexing all Italy from Rome north to his Empire. Then Constantinople threw her support to the still independent Lombard Prince of Beneventum and gave asylum to the exiled ruler of Pavia.[63]

When Irene came to the throne in 781 this diplomacy took two new forms. Irene was Iconodule, so she attempted to detach the Pope from his Carolingian protector on religious grounds, and at the same time she offered marriage to Charlemagne and thus sowed suspicion in the mind of the Supreme Pontiff in Italy. Though her one attempt at armed intervention in Southern Italy in 787 was not a success,[64] up to 800 at least she managed to hold her own. Then Charlemagne in that year assumed the title of Emperor with the Pope's blessing, and the breach widened. Irene's successor, Nicephorus, who came into power in 802, refused to recognize this title, and more open warfare broke out between the two Empires.[65] Not until 812 did peace come, when Constantinople, hard pressed by Bulgarians and Abbassids, agreed to accept the ruler of Aix-la-Chapelle as Basileus. With varied stresses and strains, the situation of 812 continued until Louis the Pious lost control of his Empire to his warring sons, and the Carolingian Empire began to dissolve in the middle of the ninth century.[66]

Yet it should be emphasized that though Byzantium was unable to recover the Exarchate of Ravenna and Rome in these seventy-five years, she did maintain some control over Italian territory, particularly in the south. Naples, Amalfi, and Gaeta in Campania,

---

[63] *Codex Carolinus* ed. Cenni, letters Nos. XVIII, XXXVIII, LX, LXV, LXXI, LXXII.

[64] See letter of Pope Hadrian to Charlemagne in *Codex Carol.*, p. 617. Gay *Italie Meridionale*, p. 46-48. Buckler *op. cit.*, pp. 16, 26-27.

[65] Bury *Eastern Roman Empire*, p. 317-18. Gasquet *op. cit.*, p. 287-318.

[66] Just how sincere this peace was on the part of Byzantium remains a question. See Cessi, R. "Pacta Venetia" in *Archiv. Veneto* new series (1928-29) V-VI; and Cessi, R. *Venezia Ducale* (Padua 1928-29) 2 vols. The expedition of Carolingian controlled ships against Moslem Bone suggests that as late as 828 Louis the Pious regarded it as a binding alliance. The various embassies sent by Constantinople to Aix-la-Chapelle up to 840 also suggest a fairly strong tie. On these, see Vasiliev *Byz. et Arabes* I, 185-87 and Gasquet *op. cit.* On Bulgarian pressure on Byzantium and its effects on Frankish-Byzantine relations, see Runciman *History of the First Bulgarian Empire* (London 1930), p. 67-73.

Calabria and a good part of Apulia remained Byzantine. Beneventum also stayed in the orbit of Byzantine influence.[67] So, too,
did Venice, Istria, and Dalmatia nearby. All this was in spite of
few, if any, land forces used or available. How this came about can
be understood only if the full system of Byzantine Mediterranean
control is examined.

These continuing land pressures from Franks, Bulgarians and
Abbassids, despite Byzantium's domination of the seas, explain
why the rulers of Constantinople could not relax their economic
vigilance in the Mediterranean and Black Sea areas during this
period. Rather, they tended to continue and perfect the economic
warfare that characterized the earlier part of the century from
716 to 752. The system that assisted in humbling the Ommayid's
sea power seems to have been perfected as an economic defense
of an empire under pressure from all sides. Byzantine territory
continued to be organized economically as well as navally and
militarily as an armed camp directed against her enemies North,
South, East and West.

The result was a continuance of the conditions that characterized the earlier part of the century. Syrian and Egyptian merchants
and shipping were barred from reaching the Western Mediterranean, and there is little evidence that many of them did so. Perhaps the Abbassids, who appear to have continued the economic
and passport controls of the Ommayid police state, may have
assisted in the process.[68] But it seems to have been mainly a result
of Constantinople's policies. All wares from the East which Byzantium needed for herself and her Western trade which had to be
imported from Arab middlemen in Persia and Iraq continued to
be channeled through Trebizond on the Black Sea.[69] Perhaps some
trade was allowed under strict control with Syria and Egypt, but
if so, it appears to have been required to go direct to Constantinople itself. In addition, some Eastern silks and spices and other
products that reached the Byzantine Empire came through Kazar

[67] Bury *East. Rom. Empire*, p. 308-11. Gay *Ital. Mer.*, p. 18-19.

[68] Al Mansur, interested in shifting the commerce of the Indian Ocean from the
Red Sea to the Mesopotamian route, apparently filled up the Nile-Red Sea Canal
with sand in 762. Weil *op. cit.* I, 119.

[69] *Al Istakhri* trans. Defremery in *Journ. Asiat.* (1849) XIV, 462. Masudi *Prairies
d'Or* II, 3. In this regard it is interesting to note the path of the plague mentioned
by Theophanes in the 8th century. It went from Egypt, to North Africa, to Sicily
and *then* to Constantinople. This shows how little trade there was between Egypt
and Byzantium in this period. *Theophanes*, p. 442-43.

hands to the controlled entry port city of Cherson, similar in its operation to Trebizond.

For northern trade, Cherson again seems to have been the great outlet for Russian furs, slaves, and other northern products which were then controlled by the Kazars as middlemen as well.[70] Trade with the Bulgarians was apparently directed to Salonika and Constantinople by the treaty of 816 between the two countries, if not earlier.[71]

In the West, similar trading portals for commerce with the Franks seem to have been established in Byzantine-held Italy as they had been in the case of the Lombards earlier. They were Naples, Gaeta, Amalfi, and perhaps Salerno on the west coast (Salerno apparently having replaced Luni, now in Carolingian hands), and Venice on the east coast. To these cities and these alone were spices and fine silks allowed to be shipped for sale in Italy, and once a year merchants from these centers went to Pavia where they exposed for sale these Eastern wares in the Po River valley to merchants from Northern Italy and perhaps the entire West.[72] Trade was, however, apparently more freely allowed with the Lombard duchy of Beneventum in south Italy and with Rome itself.

On trade allowed with Moslem North Africa, information is much scantier, but certain facts suggest that in the first decades of the ninth century, if not earlier, this commerce was channeled through Sicily. Perhaps that is the meaning of the commercial clauses in the truces arranged in 805 and 813 between the Aghlabid rulers of Tunisia and the Byzantine governors of Sicily. If so, it explains the presence of Sicilian merchants in North Africa and Moslem merchants in Sicily expressly protected by the provisions of these treaties.[73] Here most probably olive oil, as of old, represented the most important export which the Magreb had to offer in return for Eastern wares supplied by Byzantium.

Concerning Spain's trade less is known. But it seems possible

---

[70] On Kazar-Byzantine friction over the trade role of Cherson and the Crimea in the late 8th century see Vasiliev *Goths in the Crimea*, p. 89-97. On the role of Cherson in the early ninth century see Const. Porphyr. *De Admin. Imp.*, p. 71.

[71] *Theophanes* ed. Bonn, p. 775. Runciman *Bulgarian Empire*, p. 144-48.

[72] Solmi *L'Amministrazione finanziaria del regno italico nell'alto medio eva* (Pavia 1932), pp. 86, 94-96, 105. See Lopez, "Silk Trade," p. 35-41, for an excellent summary of Solmi's main points.

[73] For a summary of these treaties see Amari *Storia* I, 357.

that it was much less subject than other regions to control by Byzantium. Spain, as an important ally, may have been allowed to trade directly with the East without interference. Two facts seem to bear this out. First, the Rhademite Jews are reported in the early ninth century to have traded directly with Egypt and the East from Marseilles by way of Spain.[74] And second, the sailing of Cordovas' exiled Moslems directly to Alexandria without molestation from Byzantium seems to point to some close trade connections between the two areas. If so, Spain seems to have been the only country in the Western Mediterranean not subject to Constantinople's trade control in this sea.

It would be impossible to expect such a trade system to be completely maintained, any more than were England's Navigation Acts in the Atlantic in the eighteenth century. Important leaks developed, and it seems possible that there was special laxity in enforcement at the time of Irene, when naval power was neglected. There continued, in the first place, to be some sea trade between Syria and Egypt, a trade which could be protected by Syria's fleet which the Abbassids did continue to maintain, though in no great strength. Also, there undoubtedly continued to be traffic, probably hugging the African coast, between North African Sousse and Gabes and Egypt and Syria.[75] It was difficult, if not impossible, for Byzantium from its island bases of Crete, Sicily, and Cyprus and even Malta and Pantelleria to shut off such sea commerce completely. But it would be unwise to overestimate the amount of traffic on either of these routes in the eighth and early ninth centuries. Ibn Khordadhbeh, writing on those routes used in early Abbassid times, carefully shows that the main road between Rakka

[74] Ibn Khordadhbeh *Book of Routes* ed. De Goeje in *Bibl. Geog. Arab* (1899) vi, 114-16. These Rhademite Jews represented a group of international neutrals between the contending Carolingians, Spanish Ommayids, African and Near Eastern Arabs and Byzantium. They were apparently tolerated by the dominant Byzantine fleet, perhaps because their Western headquarters was in Spain. They were similar in function to the Jewish Kazars who fulfilled a like role on the other side of Byzantium. Their presence suggests some continuance of the older trade order of things, but very little. Jews monopolized the eunuch trade a few years later from Verdun to Spain. *Mir. St. Bertiniani* in *Acta Sanctorum Sept.* ii, p. 597. Neither the Rhademites nor any other Jews were allowed to trade in slaves or much else *inside* the Byzantine Empire, however. See Starr, Joshua *The Jews in the Byzantine Empire* (Athens 1939).

[75] The embassy taking the elephant from Alexandria to Carolingian Europe in 802 returned by way of Tunis and Alexandria, thus showing some traffic by sea along the African coast in this period. Buckler *op. cit.*, p. 25.

in Syria and Egypt ran not along the coast but inland by way of Damascus, coming close to the sea in only southern Palestine.[76] Similarly the major route between Egypt and North Africa did not follow the Roman coastal road in this period, but went far inland by way of a series of desert oases. The use of these interior routes, just like that of the Via Francigena between Rome and North Italy which similarly avoided coastal regions, suggests that Byzantine naval power made coastal land traffic dangerous, though not impossible, to Egypt from either Syria or Tunisia.[77]

This impression is heightened when the embassies which travelled between the Carolingians and the Abbassids are considered. The first of these was sent by Pepin to Bagdad in 765,[78] the last by the Caliph al-Mamun to Louis the Pious in 831.[79] They were particularly numerous in Charlemagne's later years, when both Islamic and Carolingian rulers shared a common hostility to Constantinople and to the Ommayid Emirs of Spain. But communication proved very difficult indeed with Byzantium holding command of the East-West sea lanes. Most of these embassies thus found it necessary to travel the long way around by way of North Africa and Alexandria to Carolingian-held Italian ports, and round trips generally took at least three years. In 801, for example, to emphasize the difficulties of sea transportation, the famous elephant Abu'l-Abbas, a gift to Charlemagne from Harun-al-Rashid, was taken by land from Egypt to North Africa and entrusted to a ship only from North Africa to the port of Luni where it was disembarked for its final journey to Charlemagne's court.[80] In 806 another embassy, which had been dispatched from Aix-la-Chapelle to Bagdad in 802, in returning to Italy just barely escaped capture by a Byzantine squadron (possibly that of Nicetas) to arrive post haste at the Italian town of Treviso.[81] On the whole, considering

[76] Mez *The Renaissance of Islam* (London 1937), p. 497. This route was as follows: Aleppo, Hamat, Hims, Baalbek, Damascus, Tiberius, Ramle, Gifar, Cairo and Alexandria.

[77] On the abandonment of the coastal road in Liguria see *Honorantie Civitatis Papiae* ed. Solmi in *L'Ammin. financ. regno italico* (Pavia 1931), p. 21. On the development of an interior route, the Via Francigena, see Lopez "Orig. du Capit. Genois," p. 434. On land routes from Egypt to Tunis see Mez *op. cit.*, p. 501.

[78] Buckler *op. cit.*, p. 9.   [79] *Ann. Reg. Franc.* a 831. Buckler *op. cit.*, p. 40.

[80] Mas Latrie *op. cit.*, p. 11.

[81] *Ann. Reg. Franc.* a 806. Buckler *op. cit.*, p. 30. In 801 an embassy from the new Aghlabid ruler of Tunis reached Pisa and went on from there to Charlemagne's court. *Eginhard* in *MGH Script.* I, 190. Note that they did *not* go by sea to Marseilles, but preferred the long overland journey to Aix-la-Chapelle from Pisa.

elapsed time and difficulties of transit, those embassies which passed between Charlemagne and nearby Aghlabid Tunisia probably maintained more satisfactory contacts.

But it was not only in commerce and travel between North Africa and the Moslem Near East that leaks appeared in Byzantium's system of sea control. More serious were those from nominally Byzantine-controlled Italian ports, particularly Venice. Since 742 this city had been autonomous, though under Constantinople, and at that time already possessed a fleet of sixty to eighty ships which traded with the East.[82] Though on the whole loyal to its Byzantine ties, its commercial interests extended beyond the Empire. Venetian merchants, despite Byzantine regulations, were active in both the slave and timber traffic to Moslem shores. In 748 they even bought slaves in Rome for this lucrative trade, which brought them to North African ports in a commercial capacity.[83] So flagrant did this trade become that Leo V, the Byzantine Emperor, in the early ninth century forbade his subjects, and the Venetians in particular, to trade with Syria and Egypt.[84] Yet there can be little doubt that this order was not obeyed, since in 827 or 828 Venetian ships brought back from troubled Alexandria the valued relics of St. Mark.[85]

It may have been a similar effort to halt forbidden trade between Aegean and Asia Minor coasts and Egypt and Syria which provoked Moslem retaliation and caused a great exodus of Christians from Syria and Palestine to Cyprus and Anatolia in 813.[86] Such efforts may also lie behind the fact that Thomas the Slav received the support of both the Byzantine provincial flotillas and Caliph al-Mamun in his great revolt of 821-823.[87] Possibly a strict enforcement of trading regulations with Syria and Egypt was ruining the prosperity of the very maritime districts upon which the themal fleets were based. Such illegal trade may also explain why the Spaniards, expelled from Alexandria, sailed directly to Crete. Perhaps they had long had commercial connections with the island during their years in control of that great Egyptian seaport.

[82] Hodgkin *Italy and Her Invaders* vi, 490.
[83] *Liber Pont.* ed. Duchesne (Paris 1886) i, 433.
[84] Dandolo *Chron.*, p. 167. This was probably a general rule for the *entire* Empire, not Venice alone.
[85] Dandolo *Chron.*, p. 170.   [86] *Theophanes*, p. 778-80.
[87] Michel the Syrian *Chron.*, ed. Chabot iii, 37.

In the West also, trade was carried on between Byzantine-held territory and the Arab world, the chief offenders being the Tyrrhenian cities of Amalfi, Naples and Gaeta. Naples, at the time of Irene, for example, changed from direct Byzantine rule to autonomy under a certain Duke Stephen of a local Neapolitan family.[88] Then, under Leo V, when Byzantine economic regulations were being tightened up elsewhere, it is interesting to note that Naples lost its autonomy and came under the rule of a foreign Greek *protospatharios* named by the governor of Sicily.[89] This change was of short duration, however. In 821 this latter was driven out, and Naples returned to what might be called dominion status under a descendant of Stephen.[90] It is indeed tempting to see in these changes a desire on the part of the Neapolitans to escape from a strict enforcement of Byzantium's rules. It was probably by way of these maritime centers, particularly Naples, that North African and Spanish wares reached Rome in Carolingian times.

Nor were the cities along the southern French and Italian coasts from Narbonne to the Tiber completely inactive at this time. Some trading was done by Spanish Moslems, who brought their wares to Arles in the late eighth century,[91] not to mention the Rhademite Jews. Some traffic also continued between Luni and Pisa and North Africa.[92] Perhaps Naples, Gaeta, and Amalfi, as well, traded along the northern Tyrrhenian coasts. There is even mention of an English merchant at Marseilles in this period, and some evidence of trade between Moslem Spain and England.[93]

But such exceptions do not affect the general trade pattern of the period. By and large, major international Mediterranean-Black Sea trade routes continued to be channeled even more effectively in this period to those areas to which Byzantium wished to direct them. If Tunisian merchants traded with the East and with western Italian ports, if Venetians, Neapolitans, and Amalfitans continued to send their products to Arab lands in North Africa and the East, if the maritime regions of Asia Minor, Crete, and Greece maintained some commerce with Syria and Egypt despite Con-

[88] Capasso ed. *Monumenta ad Neapolitani ducatus Historiam pertinentia* (Naples 1881) II, 251-53.
[89] Capasso *op. cit.*, I, 205.
[90] *ibid.*, p. 207. Gay *Ital. Mer.*, p. 18-19.
[91] Theophilus *Carmina contra iudices* in MGH *Poeta Latini Medii Aevi* I, 499.
[92] Ganshof "Notes sur les Ports de Provence" in *Rev. Hist.* CLXXIII, p. 29-36.
[93] *Annales Petavini* in MGH *Script.* I, 17.

stantinople's plans to the contrary, such trade was relatively minor. It could not possibly match the great free trade between these same regions in the period prior to 716. Those areas which kept an important and vital international commerce were *those chosen by Byzantium to do so*. They were Cherson, Trebizond, Constantinople, Salonika, Sicily, Gaeta, Amalfi, Naples, Bari, and Venice and perhaps some Spanish ports. Other neighboring centers and regions either lost importance from 716 on or handled local, rather than international, trade and commerce.

Perhaps it is this system of trade control which best explains Charlemagne's long struggle with Byzantium up to 812. At first Charlemagne appears to have been reluctant to follow his father's policy of intervention in Italy. Not until 774 did he cross the Alps. But gradually, particularly in his later years, he began to understand the economic importance of trade to his Empire. It was not alone the need of Papal support which is the key to Charlemagne's Italian policy and hostility to Constantinople. He also saw the need of controlling the sources of the wealth that the Mediterranean could bring to his shores. He saw, as well, the grip that Byzantium had on this trade and he attempted to break it. He complained once to a Greek ambassador, according to Einhard, that he wished his Empire were close enough to trade with the East.[94]

His building of a fleet in the Mediterranean and his encroachment upon the Balearics, Sardinia, and South Italy, his attempts on Venice, Istria, and Dalmatia, all form part of a concerted drive toward the trade sources of wealth denied his state. So, too, do his many conferences with envoys from the Patrician of Sicily, the Viceroy of Byzantium in the West,[95] his offers of marriage to Irene[96] and his negotiations with Abbassid rulers and governors.[97] Even his assumption of the title of Emperor in 800 may represent a step in this same direction.

But he showed his concern and understanding of the system best by his own economic efforts. He himself attempted to apply economic coercion against Byzantium's monopolistic trade outposts in Italy, particularly against Venice. Though Venice in 774 had assisted him with naval power in his conquest of Pavia, he wanted

[94] Eginhard *Vita Carol.* in *MGH Script.* II, 455-57. *Mon. St. Gall* in *op. cit.*, p. 761.
[95] Bury *East. Rom. Emp.*, p. 317-8. Buckler *op. cit.*, p. 17. Amari *Storia* I, 315-17.
[96] *Ann. Reg. Franc.* a 802. Buckler *op. cit.*, p. 320-21.
[97] Buckler *op. cit.*, has the fullest account of negotiations between Charles and the Caliph of Bagdad, though he may push his theories a little too far.

more from it. In 787, when a Byzantine expedition landed in Southern Italy, he applied economic pressure to the Venetians by confiscating their factories in the Pentapolis and ending their extensive trading privileges within his domains.[98] So effective were these measures that for a few years from 802 to 805 he actually had Venice largely under his control. When Byzantine intervention with sea power turned the balance against him in 806, he employed commercial blockade as well as military force against the city.[99] By 812 he had won what he wanted. Byzantium, menaced on all sides, decided to come to terms with her most distant opponent, the Carolingians. By terms of this treaty it appears Charlemagne won at least the right of all the merchants of his Empire to trade freely within the Byzantine Empire. In return Venice's privileges were returned her, and her mainland possessions were given back, while Istria and Dalmatia were recognized as belonging to Constantinople.[100]

It proved a hollow victory. Charlemagne died before the treaty was put into effect. So, too, did Byzantium's ruler who had granted the concession. Louis the Pious never received cooperation from the Byzantines,[101] though up to at least 828 relations between the two Empires remained very close. Carolingian subjects never received that freedom of trade which Charlemagne so wished. Intermediaries under control of the Eastern Emperors continued to be the sole distributors of the valuable Eastern wares to the Frankish West. Perhaps Constantinople could not afford to change her system. Even had she been really willing to allow Carolingian traders free access to her commerce, she was unwilling to allow them to trade directly with Egypt and Syria. To do so would have destroyed her Empire. And so, as the Carolingian state weakened, Byzantium continued her directed monopolies to those Italian cities which acknowledged her overlordship. Not until the eleventh century was the system shattered. Charlemagne failed, then, in his

[98] *Codex Carolinus* (Rome 1761) No. LXXXIIII. Brown *Studies in Venetian History* I, 15-20.

[99] *ibid.*, p. 25-47. Fortunatus, pro-Carolingian Patriarch of Grado, was rewarded for his service in bringing Venice to Charles' side in 803 by an imperial diploma giving him the right to trade untaxed in any part of the Empire. Charlemagne thus understood economic pressure quite clearly.

[100] Cessi, R. "Pacta Veneta" in *op. cit.* and *Venezia Ducale.*

[101] On Byzantium's uncooperative attitude towards the Carolingians see Lopez "Silk Industry" in *op. cit.*, p. 35-41. Pirenne implies the same thing in his *Mohammed and Charlemagne*, p. 174-85.

major objective, and his Empire, enfeebled in the hands of unworthy successors, was unable to realize his hopes. Not he but the
North African Moslems finally broke the Byzantine-directed and
controlled Mediterranean system, and they did it not by diplomacy
or negotiation but by destroying Constantinople's naval Empire
and setting up one of their own.

But Byzantine trade controls did more than channel international commerce during the period from 716 to 827 to certain
spots and deny it to others. They had another important and perhaps utterly unforeseen effect on the character of trade in the Mediterranean and Black Sea. The controls resulted in a change in the
intermediaries who handled the bulk of commerce between East
and West. Up to 716, despite some activity by native Italian and
North African merchants, the bulk of the East-West trade had
been handled by Syrians, Egyptians, Greeks, and Jews; Easterners
who exported wares to the West settled in colonies there and
shipped back Western wares to the East.

From 716 on, Byzantine economic measures blocked the Syrians
and Egyptians from Western markets.[102] But they did even more
than that. By the close of the century the trade system that they
established eliminated a major portion of the Greek merchants of
the Constantinople, Aegean, Asia Minor region from this carrying
trade as well.[103] They shut themselves and their opponents, the
Arabs, in an economic strait jacket from which there could be no
escape, and condemned themselves to an economic passivity
hardly less outstanding than that displayed by Syria and Egypt.
It happened in the following way. In setting up certain trade portals through which commerce had to pass, Byzantium destroyed
all freedom of action by her own merchants outside the Empire.
She did even more. In effect, she gave a monopoly of distribution
of her valued products, particularly silks and spices, to the merchants of those entry ports themselves or to those who came there
to trade. From Cherson, for instance, the Kazars distributed Byzantine wares to Russia and their own domains; from Trebizond,

[102] This seems the true explanation of the disappearance of most Syrian traders
from Western markets—a problem noted but not explained by Pirenne or any other
historians save Runciman in his *Byzantine Civilization*, p. 166-67.

[103] The disappearance of Greek merchants from even Byzantine controlled sections of Italy is equally significant and has been less carefully examined than the
disappearance of the Syrians. See Heyd *op. cit.*, p. 55-56.

Armenian and Arab merchants performed like functions; from Sicily, North African Moslem merchants appear to have distributed the products of Constantinople to the Western Magreb peoples. But most important of all were the distribution activities of the favored maritime cities of Venice, Amalfi, Naples, and Gaeta.

Once these cities began to amass profits in the distribution of these wares, they went one step further. They went to the source of supply in their own ships, to Constantinople particularly. They soon had control of not only the distribution trade but of the carrying trade as well. Constantinople remained the heart and center where all trade routes met from North, South, East, and West, but it did not do much of the importing and exporting on its own. The economic strength of the Byzantine state became more and more concentrated on its periphery, as her privileged border cities used their own ships more and more to trade with the center of the Empire as well as outside it. In Italy, where our information is fuller, the system can be best studied. Up to 716 Greek merchants were thickly settled in Italian centers and handled a major part of the maritime commerce between this land and the Eastern Mediterranean. By 800 most of them, as well as the Syrians and Egyptians, appear to have disappeared.[104] It is the merchants of Venice, Amalfi, and Bari, for instance, who handle this important carrying trade.

Perhaps a modern parallel will make what happened even clearer. In the late sixteenth century the Dutch had a monopoly, thanks to Portuguese refusal to sell spices beyond Lisbon, of the distribution trade of this valuable commodity. Their ships met Portuguese fleets at Lisbon, bought the spices in bulk and made the middleman's profit in peddling them throughout Western Europe. Soon they did more. In the 1600's they began to go to the source of supply, the Portuguese East. Soon the carrying trade from the East as well as the distribution trade was in their hands. That was exactly the result of Byzantium's very similar practices.

This had two very important consequences for Byzantium. In the first place, it built up maritime power in border areas such as Italy, which were all but impossible to control with the limited land forces at Constantinople's disposal in this period. Cities like Venice and Naples had to be given what amounted to dominion

[104] Pirenne *op. cit.*, p. 255-60.

status for all practical purposes.[105] Thus, except when actual naval power was dispatched to them, as in the case of Venice in 806 and 808, they could not be controlled adequately. Their naval and commercial strength was therefore frequently used in ways quite contrary to Byzantine policy, particularly in trade with forbidden Moslem ports of North Africa, Egypt, and Syria. Venice's activities, which called for Leo's prohibition against trade with the Moslem East in the early ninth century, are a case in point.[106] Like the reaction of the American New Englanders to Britain's navigation acts in the eighteenth century, so that of Italian cities to Byzantium's very similar restrictions left much to be desired from the standpoint of the mother country.

Second and perhaps even more important, the growing strength of the maritime possessions on the outskirts of the Empire, as in Italy, had a very important effect upon naval strength toward its center. As important carrying trade fell more and more into distant hands, a progressive decline in the strength of the themal fleets of the Aegean and Kibyrrhaeots, depending upon maritime-impressed contingents, is noticeable. This, rather than any positive neglect, accounts for the weakness of Byzantium's naval power in the early ninth century. Neither the provincial fleets of Sicily nor the Aegean could stand up against naval forces which one hundred years earlier they could have defeated easily.[107]

Byzantium's own system then led to economic passivity at her center of power and also naval weaknesses, which she was incapable of remedying without changing her entire structure of economic, military and naval defense. She joined her victims, Egypt and Syria, on the economic sidelines, still rich, still powerful but unable adequately to maintain the system of Mediterranean control which she had built against her opponents.

The net effect, then, of Byzantine policies was to begin the transformation of Italian merchants from privileged ports into the great middlemen between the West and the Eastern wares which Byzantium controlled. But the Italians were not alone in this new

[105] Nothing better explains Venice's independent course in the Carolingian period than this fact. See Brown *op. cit.*, p. 115-47 and Cessi *Venezia*, p. 33-34. On Naples, see Gay *op. cit.*, p. 43-48.

[106] Dandolo *Chron.*, p. 167.

[107] Naval weakness then is the *result* of the economic passivity of Byzantium in the eighth century rather than *positive* neglect of her naval forces as Bury and others have stated.

role. Toward the end of this period, they had competitors in this traffic to a lesser degree—the Moslem merchants of North Africa. As Byzantine naval strength declined, the Arabs from the Magreb ports began to fulfill the same functions for Moslem North Africa and perhaps Spain that their Italian merchant brothers were doing for Europe. They went to passive Syrian and Egyptian ports and distributed their wares to the Moslem West. Trading with Sicily, they performed a similar function with Byzantine products. It was they who, after 827, even more than the Italians, were to gain the heritage of wealth that the Middle Sea brought to those who controlled it.

The major trade routes of this period followed the interests of Byzantium in the Mediterranean-Black Sea area. Constantinople was their focal point. The routes whereby most Eastern spices, silks, and other products reached Constantinople and the Mediterranean world in general appear to have been the old Sassanian ones. These were either by land across Persia or by sea up the Persian Gulf to Basrah and Bagdad.[108] Maritime trade with the Far East was particularly important from Iraq ports, and in this period Moslem merchants were active in large numbers as far away as China.[109] Bagdad became a great metropolis, thanks to this commerce in large measure, second only in wealth and population to Constantinople itself.[110]

From Mesopotamia some of these Eastern wares went on to the Black Sea, which was Byzantium's entry port for Arab trade. In passing through to Trebizond they made Armenia, at this time an extremely rich and prosperous area, a sort of buffer state between the two Empires, though more generally under Abbassid influence.[111] From Trebizond they went on to Constantinople, the major distributing point for the Mediterranean. Some Eastern products also reached the Byzantine capital by way of Cherson with the Kazars serving as the intermediaries along the central Asian route.

From Byzantium the major Mediterranean trade routes were those to Sicily and the Italian cities of Amalfi, Naples, Bari, and Venice. The Adriatic route seems to have been the one most used. The Venetians and others exposed their Eastern and Byzantine

[108] Wiet *op. cit.*, p. 166-68. See Al Mansur's statement that Mesopotamia in 758 was the center of commerce. Yaqubi *Geog.*, p. 237.

[109] Hitti *op. cit.*, p. 305-06.   [110] *ibid.*, p. 301-04.

[111] Der Nersessian *Armenia and the Byzantine Empire* (Cambridge, Mass. 1947), p. 7-10.

spices and silks for sale at Pavia.[112] Here they were bought and carried across the Alps by Western merchants,[113] largely Germans, to reach Northern Europe by way of Mayence and the Rhine, though other passes leading to the upper Rhone may also have been used.[114] The Amalfitans, Neapolitans, and Gaetans apparently supplied Rome and the West with these products,[115] the North African Moslems the Magreb and even Spain.

In addition, another route became of importance in this period to Northern Europe, that of the Russian rivers to the Baltic and North Seas. This might be called an alternate to the route which led to Italy, and over it Eastern wares soon found their way in ever-increasing amounts to build up new settlements such as Kiev and Novgorod on Russia's river arteries. Down these rivers flowed slaves and furs to pay Byzantium for the products she sent them.[116]

While these routes were followed by most international trade, the importance of the older paths of commerce declined markedly. Particularly is that true of the route to the Far East by way of Egypt. It is possible that the Abbassids, eager like the Sassanians to increase the prosperity of Mesopotamia, discouraged use of the Red Sea route for Eastern wares.[117] But more plausible is the explanation that Byzantium discouraged commerce from the Mediterranean side. Whether both were responsible or not, it is interesting to note the small importance of the Red Sea commerce of this period in comparison with its flourishing condition in Byzantine and early Ommayid times. By 800 it had all but disappeared, with only the Rhademite Jews, those last vestiges of the older order of things, travelling the route across the isthmus down the Red Sea to Aden and on to China.[118] The Nile-Red Sea Canal had been

---

[112] Solmi *op. cit.*, pp. 86, 94-6, 105. Ganshof "Note sur un passage de la vie de St. Guerard" in *Mélanges Iorga* (Paris 1929), p. 295.

[113] Tyler, J. E. *The Alpine Passes* (Oxford 1930), p. 148-49.

[114] *ibid.*

[115] Sabbe, E. "L'importation des tissus Orientaux en Europe Occidentale au Moyen Age. IXe-Xe siècles" in *Revue Belge de Philol. et d'Histoire* (1935) xiv, 813-23.

[116] On pre-Varangian trade in Russia, see Cross, S. F. "The Scandinavian Infiltration into Russia" in *Speculum* (1946) xxi, 514. Also Meyendorf, A. F. "Trade and Communication in Eastern Europe A.D. 800-1200" in *Travels and Travelers of the Middle Ages* ed. A. P. Newton (London 1926).

[117] Arab tradition says Al Mansur closed the Red Sea canal in 762 to starve Medina, but more probably to draw trade to Iraq, the Abbassid center of power and influence. Wiet *op. cit.*, p. 166-67.

[118] *Ibn Khordadhbeh*, p. 513.

allowed to fill up with sand.[119] The Red Sea fleet of Ommayid times had disappeared, and pirates frequented the entrance to this route off the island of Socotra.[120] Only a few small vessels, known as ships of Koulzoum, operated in its waters, transshipping some Eastern wares from the Persian Gulf by sea to Egypt.[121]

On the Mediterranean side a similar lack of activity in comparison with earlier periods is apparent. Alexandria was still a great port, but much less so than earlier, and economically passive, traded with by Syrian and Magreb merchants from Sousse or Venetian and Greek sailing masters who were ignoring Byzantine prohibitions. It fell an easy prey to Spanish exiles in 815.[122] If it traded much with Constantinople direct there is little evidence of it.

Almost equally inactive were the Syrian ports at this time. Beirut still had some importance, but there is no evidence that this coast had recovered from the passive character that it had had since 716. Syrian ships themselves were inactive in international trade except for some which may have gone to Constantinople.[123] The exodus of many Christians from these shores in 813 under Abbassid pressure may have further heightened the depression in trade that afflicted this coast.[124]

What was true of these Syrian and Egyptian termini of the Mediterranean trade routes was equally true of their old Western termini. Though both Luni and Marseilles may have had some temporary importance in local trade with North Africa and Spain respectively,[125] the important international East-West trade no longer went to Southern France and up the Rhone Valley route. Rather Italy and particularly the Po Valley took its place. After 828 even local trade to the Carolingian-held coast from Città Vecchia to Barcelona seems to have dried up. Only the Rhademite Jewish traders still followed the old route from Marseilles and

[119] It began to fill up at the beginning of the eighth century according to Lane *Egypt*, p. 20, and Heyd *op. cit.*, p. 40-41. This coincides with the opening of Byzantium's commercial blockade of Egypt about 716. See Chapter III.

[120] Wiet *op. cit.*, p. 167-68.

[121] *ibid.*

[122] Maqrizi *Kitat* ed. Wiet (Cairo 1927) III, 181-91. *Al Kindi*, pp. 158-70, 180-84.

[123] Lopez "Silk Industry," p. 28-31.

[124] *Theophanes*, p. 778.

[125] Lopez "Orig. du Capit Génois," p. 434. Sabbe "L'importation des Tissus," p. 840-3.

Spanish ports to Egypt.[126] About Spain less is known, but its importance in international commerce does not appear to have been great at this time,[127] though its Byzantine alliance may have kept it free from interference as far as Alexandria.

The results of these changed trade routes and changed intermediaries in the Mediterranean were disastrous to the economy of many of the regions about its shores. In fact, so serious were the resulting dislocations both East and West that only Italy and Byzantium really escaped their full effects. And even here the level of prosperity, though high, did not approach that of the earlier Justinian period.[128]

In the Western portions of the Middle Sea this is shown by a number of facts. First is the continuing decay of the cities along the coast of Southern France and Northwest Italy despite the temporary Carolingian naval revival under Charlemagne and Louis the Pious. Genoa, for example, remained a dead city, and the main traffic to the North from Rome continued to follow the interior Via Francigena route.[129] The same is true of the Midi coast. Maguelone, for instance, destroyed by the early Carolingians, was not rebuilt, but remained a deserted city.[130] What development there was in this area was agrarian, not commercial or urban. Charlemagne and his successor granted vast domains to monasteries like Aniane and Gellone and they filled the land with *cellae* dependent upon the mother houses.[131] Also some Spanish refugees were granted lands in this region by Louis the Pious.[132] How agrarian and little affected by commerce this portion of the

[126] The land route from Spain to France was the one followed in this period, not the sea route. See *Mir. St. Bertiniani* in *op. cit.*, and for later date *Vita Johannis Abbatis Goriensis* in *MGH Script.* IV, 369-75. On Liguria see Lopez *op. cit.*, p. 434.

[127] The fact that Moslem Spain was on a silver standard throughout the eighth and ninth centuries seems to point to rather unfavorable economic conditions there. *Ibn Khaldun* I, 464. A. Vives y Escudo *Monedas de las dinestias arábigo-españolas* (Madrid 1893), p. ix. So too do the political and social troubles which afflicted the Spanish Ommayid rulers in this period, particularly the risings in the cities. See Lévi-Provençal *Hist. de l'Espagne Mussulmane*, pp. 113-21, 158-67.

[128] For an excellent panorama of economic conditions in the Byzantine Empire in the eighth and early ninth centuries, see Diehl *Byzantine Portraits* (New York 1927), p. 73-147.

[129] Lopez *op. cit.*, p. 435-41.

[130] It was not rebuilt until the eleventh century. Arnaud de Verdale *Catal. Episcop. Magal.* ed. Germain in *Mém. Soc. Arch. Mont.* 1st ser. (1881) VII, 508, 510.

[131] Imbart de la Tour "Les colonies agricoles et l'occupation des terres desertes à l'époque Carolingienne" in *Mélanges Paul Fabre*, p. 147.

[132] *ibid.*, p. 148.

Carolingian Empire was can be seen in the fact that silver was the money in use, coined on the basis of the Carolingian penny and of little value in international trade.[133]

Spain presents a somewhat similar situation. Here, too, silver in the form of dirhems was the coinage struck by the ruling Ommayids.[134] There is other evidence of economic difficulties. Revolts were constant against the Emirs of Cordova, and they appear to have been concentrated in cities like Cordova and Toledo, where they were put down with difficulty. Perhaps these risings were religious and social in character, but they suggest poor economic conditions as well.[135] By the middle of the century so widespread had they become among both Mozarab and native Christian population that they threatened the very existence of the Ommayid government.[136]

North Africa was slightly better off than Spain and France, though such a foundation as Fez emphasizes the agrarian character of the Western portion of the Magreb at this time.[137] There was also a continuance up to 800 of the terrible disorders and revolts of the Berber tribes with their Kharedjite ideas and of the Arab ruling military *jound* as well.[138] Perhaps these disorders were

---

[133] There has been much controversy concerning Europe's silver coinage in this period, particularly as to the cause of it. Pirenne regarded it as evidence of economic retrogression. Dopsch held contrary views. Lopez appears to believe it simply showed Carolingian political weakness and the aping of the Spanish Moslem silver standard. One thing, however, is certain. It did make the international trade of Europe more *difficult*, since silver was *not* acceptable in the Byzantine and Arab markets of the Mediterranean (except Spain), which were on a gold standard. It was much like the modern situation where Britain and other countries of the so-called "sterling bloc" have a "dollar shortage" with attendant trade difficulties. It is significant that Europe's trade with that portion of the Moslem world in the East which was on a silver standard (Iraq, Persia and Turkestan) boomed in this period and helped create the Varangian route. The hordes of Arab coins found along this Varangian route are *silver*, not gold. Can a common silver standard help explain this trade as well as the lack of it with North Africa, Egypt, Syria and Byzantium?

[134] *Ibn Khaldun* I, 464.

[135] Lévi-Provençal *op. cit.*, p. 113-21. He also claims that Moslem conquest of Spain did not at first change the agrarian character of the land as it had existed under the Visigoths. Lévi-Provençal *L'Espagne Mussulmane au Xe Siècle* (Paris 1930), p. 159-62.

[136] Lévi-Provençal *Hist. de l'Espagne Mussulmane*, p. 158-67.

[137] Fez was an administrative and agricultural settlement in the eighth century, not a commercial one. It was also far inland, as were *all* Moslem capitals throughout this period. Lévi-Provençal "La fondation de Fes" in *Ann. de l'Institut Oriental d'Alger* (1938) IV, 22-35.

[138] Gautier *op. cit.*, p. 266-73. Marçais *Berbérie*, p. 43-53.

a cause of the low economic state of the area. Perhaps they were the result. But certain facts seem clear. During the fifty years up to Aghlabid independent rule over Tunisia, the prosperity of this region was so limited that the only way the expenses of government could be met was by a yearly subsidy of 100,000 gold dinars forwarded from Egypt[139]—a far cry from the wealthy North Africa of Byzantine times.

Furthermore, the period saw the almost total decay of older Roman and Byzantine urban centers along the coast. Not just Carthage but also the other cities nearby became lifeless and deserted.[140] It was in the southeastern portion of Tunisia that new centers arose—Sousse, Sfax, Gafsa, Kairouan and other cities nearby, almost all of them having little connection with North Africa's older past and far away from menacing Byzantine Sicily. After 800 this region began to develop some real prosperity, but it was a slow process. In spite of these dislocations, however, the current money in North Africa[141] continued to be the gold dinar and not the silver coinage which Ommayid Spain and Carolingian France followed. Perhaps Africa's valuable olive oil, much needed in international trade, assured it some economic health.

Egypt's condition has already been briefly touched upon, but more careful examination of its economic situation in the late eighth and early ninth centuries is revealing. Though the gold Islamic dinar continued as the medium of currency, economic conditions were anything but satisfactory.[142] The situation deteriorated even beyond that which prevailed from 716 to 752. Under the first Abbassids, revolts by Copts and Arab tribes who had settled in the land were constant and appear to have been caused in no small measure by over-taxation. Finally, in 815, the country entered a sixteen-year period of all but complete chaos. Right up to 831 little order could be maintained. Internal strife was added to by outside aggressions like those of the Spanish refugees in Alexandria. Trade, manufacturing, and commerce were at a standstill, linen weavers of Tinnis starving,[143] Coptic fellaheen deserting the land despite prohibitions against it,[144] and Arab nomads devastating large areas despite frantic efforts of Abbassid governors and

139 *Ibn al Athir*, p. 157.
140 Marçais, *op. cit.*, p. 76-87.
141 *ibid.*, p. 58-60.
142 Lane-Poole *Egypt*, p. 31-38.
143 Michael the Syrian *Chron.* I, 516.
144 Wiet *op. cit.*, p. 63.

rulers to restore order.[145] It was a great change from the Egypt of Byzantine and early Ommayid times.

About Syria's economic status less is known, except that here too the gold dinar remained the current medium of exchange. This is curious in view of the fact that the silver dirhem was the money par excellence in nearby Mesopotamia. It suggests that some trade with Egypt and Constantinople survived. But evidence from Cyprus, that no-man's land between Syria's maritime coast and the Byzantine Empire, suggests that the trade between these regions was not very vital. As in the case of the old Roman cities of North Africa this period saw urban decay in Cyprus. There was a complete desertion of every important city on the island. When prosperity returned in the tenth century, the new cities were located some distance away from their Roman and Byzantine predecessors.[146]

Only the Byzantine Empire proper and Italy escaped the economic doldrums that afflicted the Mediterranean world. Constantinople remained the great commercial and industrial center of the Middle Sea. Its gold currency remained pure and abundant and its prosperity assured. If the Isaurian Emperors were not the builders that Justinian had been, if evidences of their iconography are scanty, this may be more because of their Iconoclasm than anything else. True, there is little evidence of the cultural ferment that characterized the sixth century in literature either, but again preoccupation with religious controversy more than any lack of intellectual vigor may be the cause of this. The Iconodule successors of Leo III, Constantine V and others of the Orthodox party apparently destroyed most of the Iconoclastic productions. The balance of trade of Constantinople and the Empire in general appears to have been favorable and its economic vigor great. How else can one explain the vast sums sent Bagdad in tribute gold in the eighth century?[147]

The same thing appears to be true of Italy, except for its northwestern coast. Here commerce fertilized most of the peninsula with golden trade streams. This is true not only of Byzantine-held

---

[145] *ibid.*, p. 61-64.

[146] Even the capital of the island was moved inland to Nicosia in this period. Hill *Cyprus* I, 261-70. Probably the Graeco-Roman site of Antioch was also abandoned during this period.

[147] Lombard, M. "L'or Musulman du VIIe au XIe siècles" in *Annales* (1947) II, 146-49.

areas but of other sections as well. Carolingian territory shared
with other regions in this prosperity. Such a commercial career as
that of Fortunatus shows the trade possibilities which existed.[148]
So, too, does the wealth at the court of the Lombard Prince of
Beneventum.[149] Both Arab gold dinars or *mancusi* and Constantinople's *nomismata* circulated freely, and the Carolingians coined
gold in the North, though apparently in the form of the two foreign gold mediums of exchange.[150]

Equally prosperous was a new area whose commercial possibilities had up to this time been relatively limited. This was Russia.
As the trade routes shifted and Constantinople became their hub,
the old Baltic-Black Sea route became again important. Along the
rivers of Russia arose new settlements dedicated to trade, and the
wares of Byzantium and of the Eastern Islamic world as well found
their way up these rivers to the Baltic and North Sea. Down these
trade routes from the North, adventurers from Scandinavia began
to venture toward the great city of Micklegrad on the Bosphorus.
The Varangian route came into being. Russia was about to be
born, to be weaned on the gold of Byzantium and the silver of
Moslem Turkestan.[151]

The period of Byzantine domination of the Mediterranean and
the last years of its struggle with the Ommayids saw, then, a great
transformation take place in the Mediterranean. Byzantium used
her naval power to channel trade as suited her interests. The result
was a series of economic dislocations; severe economic depression
in Spain and Egypt, virtual abandonment of cities in Southern
France, Northwestern Italy, Cyprus and the northern coast of
Africa, unimportance of the old Syrian, Red Sea and Rhone Valley
trade routes and a new enhancement of the Adriatic-Po-Rhine
and the Varangian routes to the northern sections of Europe and
of the Black Sea-Caspian and Trebizond-Armenian-Mesopotamian
routes to the East.

It also saw a restriction of the use of gold in international trade
to a much smaller area than had been true at the time of Justinian

[148] On the trading career of Fortunatus, see the excellent account in Brown
Studies in Venetian History I, 25-47.

[149] On the wealth of Arichis, Prince of Beneventum, see Gay *op. cit.*, p. 46-48.

[150] Lopez "Mohammed and Charlemagne," p. 33-34. For a full survey see St.
Monneret de Villard "La Moneta en Italie durante l'alto medio evo" in *Revista
Ital. di Numismatica* (1919-20) XXXII-XXXIII.

[151] Cross *op. cit.*, p. 505-14.

or Moawiyah. Now gold was restricted to the Central and Eastern Mediterranean, where North Africa, Syria, and Egypt used the Moslem dinar, the Byzantine Empire the *nomismata* and Italy both. The gold *solidi* that Charlemagne and Louis the Pious coined in the North Sea area of their domains probably had little connection with these developments, or may represent the end of the Varangian route.[152]

But the silver areas had increased both east and west of this gold center. In the West, Spain followed the Moslem dirhem, and most of Western Europe except Italy and a few northern areas the new Carolingian silver penny. In the East, Mesopotamia, Persia, and Turkestan continued on the old silver dirhem modeled after the Sassanian standard currency. And this coinage was the master of the Indian Ocean as well.

Finally, Byzantine domination resulted in a change of intermediaries between East and West in the Mediterranean, the deliberate end of Syrian and Egyptian carrying trade and international merchants and the inadvertent end of her own. To Italian traders and to a lesser degree those of Moslem North Africa went the job of serving as the great Mediterranean middlemen, linking the spices, silks and manufactured products of the East with the slaves, iron, timber, and olive oil of the West. And in this change more than anything else lay Byzantium's failure. Her system had created maritime strength in areas she could not control adequately. In 827 the North Africans attacked upon the sea, destroyed her naval and commercial monopolies and brought into being a new Mediterranean system in which Islam ruled the major portion of the waters of the Middle Sea.

[152] The suggestion that this gold arrived in northern Carolingian ports from along the Varangian route has not been advanced with sufficient force. For other explanations see Pirenne *op. cit.*, p. 245. Less satisfactory still seem the explanations of Dopsch in his *Wirtshaftsentwicklung der Carolingerzeit* 2nd ed. (Vienna 1922) II, 306-20.

5. The Islamic Imperium

The assault on Sicily and the conquest of Crete in 827 mark the beginning of a new era in the maritime history of the Mediterranean. With these two events unchallenged Byzantine dominion came to an end, and naval control began to pass to the Islamic peoples who inhabited the southern shores of the Middle Sea from Tarsus to the Pyrenees. This change, however, did not take place all at once. The rulers of Constantinople continued throughout the period to control some important naval forces. They went on struggling valiantly on the sea in both the East and the West against their Islamic enemies. They were able to delay completion of Aghlabid conquest of Sicily until 902. They rallied sufficient naval strength to maintain control over important sections of Southern Italy and the Adriatic Sea. They remained masters of the Black Sea, though not without difficulty. They attempted to recapture Crete by sending expedition after expedition to dislodge the Moslem pirates from the island. But they were, except for limited periods, on the defensive during most of these years, and their successes were far outweighed by their failures. By the tenth century effective control of the Mediterranean was in the hands of their Moslem enemies.

The most telling assaults upon Byzantium's naval supremacy were made by North African flotillas in Sicilian and Italian waters and by Moslem Cretan fleets in the Aegean and Ionian seas. Of the two the westernmost attack was in many ways the more significant. It began with the landing of a large North African expedition in 827 at Mazara on the southern Sicilian shore. Upon disembarking this force marched across the island to besiege its capital, Syracuse. A Moslem fleet sailed to make the blockade complete on the seaside as well. Constantinople immediately took alarm and rallied her naval strength to relieve the besieged city.[1] A call to Venice brought Venetian naval contingents to the scene.[2] A Carolingian naval force from Tuscany under Boniface, probably

[1] Vasiliev, A. *Byzance et les Arabes* I, 73-74.
[2] Dandolo *Chron.* in *Mur. Rer. Ital. Script.* XII, 170. John *Chron. Ven.* in *MGH Script.* VII, 16.

in alliance with Byzantium, staged a diversionary assault on the seaport of Bone on the North African shore.[3] But, more important, Constantinople sent a large portion of her Eastern fleet to the scene. This squadron defeated the African flotilla and drove the remnants into Syracuse's harbor. Unable to extricate their remaining vessels, the Moslems burnt them and retreated from the city.[4] By 829 they had only Mazara, their original landing point, and nearby Mineo still in their possession.

Undiscouraged by this initial failure, they returned to the attack the following year. Another large African fleet brought further reinforcements to the Moslem army still on the island.[5] And in addition there arrived a Spanish force from Tortosa to add to Islamic strength. This latter body, however, helped but little. Defeated in the interior by Byzantine troops, the Spanish withdrew.[6] But the Africans did not follow suit. Instead they proceeded to besiege the important city of Palermo on the western side of the island. No Byzantine fleet arrived in time to aid the city, and in 831 it fell into Aghlabid hands.[7] From that time on it was to be a most important base and the center of Islamic power on Sicily. All but autonomous, though nominally subject to North African rule, it was the port par excellence from which Moslem fleets put out to harry the coasts and commerce of Italy and the Byzantine parts of the island.

This advance naval base of Palermo was soon strengthened by new developments. In the first place, the island of Pantelleria was seized by an Aghlabid fleet in 835.[8] This removed the threat to communications between Sicily and Africa which this island in Byzantine hands represented and made reinforcements from Africa much easier to send. Secondly, Palermo entered into an alliance by 836 with the cities of the Campanian coast of Italy, principally Naples.[9] This alliance may have resulted from assistance that a Palermo flotilla rendered the Neapolitans in their struggle against their inland enemy, the Lombard Prince of Beneventum.[10] It probably also was based on long years of commercial contact,

[3] Manfroni *Storia della Marina Italiana* (Livourni 1899) I, 36-40.

[4] *Nuwairi* in Vasiliev *op. cit.*, p. 382.   [5] *ibid.*, p. 383.

[6] *Ibn Idhari* ed. Dozy, p. 92. *Ibn al Athir* ed. Thornberg VI, 238.

[7] *Cronica di Cambridge* ed. Cozza-Luzi, p. 24. John Deac. *Gesta Episcop. Neapol.* in *MGH Script. Rer. Lang.*, p. 430.

[8] *Ibn al Athir* VI, 239.   [9] Vasiliev *op. cit.*, I, 177-8.

[10] John Deac. in *op. cit.*, p. 431.

despite Byzantine objections, between these cities and Moslem North Africa. Whatever its cause, the friendship of Naples was invaluable to the Sicilian Arabs. It weakened Constantinople's naval power in Tyrrhenian waters at a very crucial time. Neapolitan desertion of Byzantium probably explains why Byzantine naval forces were unable to intercept successfully another African flotilla which carried a new governor to Palermo in 835.[11] It may also explain the successful raid of a Moslem squadron on the Aeolian islands in the same year.[12] In the former engagement it is also interesting to note that the African fleet had a number of *harraqas*, naphtha flame-throwing vessels with which the Africans could counter the Greek fire of their Byzantine enemies—the first mention of the use of such ships by the Moslems and perhaps their new secret weapon.[13]

By 838 the Emir of Palermo felt strong enough to attack the naval fortress of Cefalu located on the north Sicilian coast. The land and sea assault was unsuccessful, thanks to the arrival of a relieving fleet which was sent by Constantinople and forced Moslem withdrawal.[14] But this check did not halt the advance. In 843, supported by Neapolitan ships, the Islamic forces seized the city of Messina dominating the straits between Calabria and Sicily.[15] Apparently there was not sufficient local Byzantine naval power in Sicilian waters to protect this important center.

A further cause of these successes in Tyrrhenian waters was that Constantinople had her hands full elsewhere in the West. Similar Moslem attacks were proceeding apace in the Ionian and Adriatic Seas. They began with the seizure of Brindisium in 838 by a fleet made up of either Cretan or African Moslem pirates or perhaps a combination of both. A Venetian flotilla of sixty war vessels summoned to the defense of the region suffered disaster off Crotone in the Gulf of Tarentum and was largely destroyed by the Moslems.[16] Then the local Southern Italian situation made intervention

---

[11] *Ibn al Athir* vi, 239. [12] Vasiliev *op. cit.*, p. 132.

[13] The *harraqas* mentioned by Ibn al Athir were flame-throwing vessels and the possession of vessels so armed may explain the successes of North African fleets and Byzantium's failures. Could Euphemios' treachery have delivered the secret of Greek fire to the Aghlabids eight years earlier? On *harraqas*, see Lane *An Arabic-English Lexicon* i, 552.

[14] *Ibn al Athir* vi, 240.

[15] *Ibn al Athir* vii, 3. Abu'l Faraq *Historia Dynastorium* ed. Pocock (Oxford 1663), p. 167.

[16] *Chron. Salern.* in *MGH Script.* iii, 503 on seizure of Brindisium, later given up.

even easier. A struggle for control of the Lombard Duchy of Beneventum between two rival claimants was going on. In 841, one
claimant, Radelchis, called in African and Sicilian Moslem mercenaries. His rival, Sikenolf, countered by hiring Spanish Islamic
adventurers. Such freebooters were little interested in anything
except booty, and in 841 some of Radelchis's mercenaries seized
Bari and the surrounding territory, cooperating fully with pirate
fleets already operating off the coast.[17] Soon another strong Moslem
advance pirate state, like Palermo, was in existence to last more
than thirty years. Its ruler, known as the Soudan or Sultan appears
to have been autonomous of any Cretan or African control and to
have applied directly to Bagdad for recognition of his power and
position.[18]

The defeat of Venice, the establishment of this new Moslem
state at Bari, and the capture of Tarentum by Cretan pirates at
about the same time opened the Adriatic to Arab raiding fleets.
In 841 their ships started their marauding by capturing and burn-
ing Ancona and Osero on the island of Cherso and seizing on their
way home some merchantmen of Venice returning from Sicily.[19]
In the next year they returned to the northern Adriatic and defeated a Venetian squadron in the Gulf of Quarnero.[20]

These successes on the eastern side of the Italian peninsula were,
however, not matched on the Tyrrhenian side. Naples, after helping
the Sicilian Arabs take Messina, apparently deserted this alliance,
perhaps because pirate fleets were establishing themselves too
close to her shores for comfort and interfering with her commerce.
Thus Sergius, Duke of Naples, formed an alliance with the nearby
maritime cities of Amalfi, Gaeta, and Sorrento. Their combined
fleets defeated the Moslem freebooters on the sea and forced them
to abandon pirate nests on the island of Ponza, just off Naples,
and at Licosia, a promontory in the Gulf of Salerno.[21] Thwarted
in this direction, the Moslems turned their attention to Papal

---

Tarentum was taken in the next year. *Chron. Salern.* in *op. cit.*, III, 508. On Venice's
defeat see Dandolo *Chron.*, p. 175 and John *Chron. Ven.*, p. 114.

[17] Vasiliev *op. cit.*, I, 209-12. Erchemperti *Hist. Lang.* in *MGH Script.* III, 247.
Chron. Salern. in *op. cit.* III, 508-10.

[18] *Baladuri* I, 371-72. Some authorities believe Soudan is a personal name and not
a title, a belief which others dispute.

[19] Dandolo *Chron.*, p. 175. John *Chron. Ven.*, p. 17.

[20] John *Chron. Ven.*, p. 18.

[21] John Deac. *Gesta Episcop. Neapol.* in *op. cit.*, p. 432.

domains and in 846 landed troops who defeated garrisons at Città Vecchia and Nova Ostia and raided the outskirts of Rome itself.[22]

The Pope hastened to appeal for naval assistance to the Campanian allied cities. They apparently were willing to oblige and sent a fleet to protect the Papal coast, but a storm which wrecked the Moslem flotilla off Ostia made this assistance unnecessary.[23] Perhaps it was this resistance of the Neapolitan coast which emboldened the Byzantine authorities of Sicily and caused them to send a small squadron of ten warships in 848 on a raid that took them into the Bay of Mondello just eight miles from Palermo itself.[24] But once the direct threat of Moslem penetration of Italy's coast had been checked, Naples and the neighboring cities again entered into close relations with their erstwhile Islamic foes. For the next twenty years or more, relations between them and Palermo were friendly and peaceful.

A full decade passed after this time with little naval action on the part of the Moslems against their Christian neighbors in either Tyrrhenian or Adriatic Seas. This was probably due in part to struggles between Cretan Moslems and the Aghlabids on the sea.[25] In 858, however, this peaceful period came to an end when Cefalu, attacked by land and sea, finally fell to Palermo,[26] and a Byzantine fleet of forty vessels was defeated off the coast of Apulia.[27] These losses stirred Constantinople to a new effort on the sea. A great Byzantine armada of 300 sail was dispatched from the East to Syracuse. It sailed through the straits of Messina to retake Cefalu. Off the north coast it met an opposing Arab fleet. The result was a tremendous Moslem victory with 100 ships lost by Byzantium, its greatest naval defeat since 840.[28] After this serious check Byzantine power in Sicily suffered still another disaster, loss of the in-

[22] "Vita Sergius II" in *Liber Pont.* ed. Duchesne II, 99-101. *Chron. Casinensis* in *MGH Script.* III, 225-26.

[23] "Vita Leonis IV" in *Liber Pont.* II, 127.

[24] *Ibn al Athir* VII, 4.

[25] *Ibn Idhari*, I, 104. The struggle between the brother of Emir al Abbas of Tunisia and Cretan Moslems may reflect the fact that Bari and Cretan Moslem pirate fleets were interfering with Aghlabid commerce with the East along the circle route that passed by Crete and Southern Italy as well as Christian shipping.

[26] *Ibn al Athir* VII, 40. *Ibn Idhari*, I, 104-05.

[27] *Ibn al Athir* VII, 41-42. *Nuwairi* in *op. cit.*, p. 384. Ibn Idhari says this was a Cretan Arab expedition, not Byzantine. This seems possible, but the Cretan Arabs may have been allied to Byzantium at the time. *Ibn Idhari*, I, 106.

[28] *Ibn al Athir* VII, 42. Amari *Storia* II, 182.

terior fortress of Castrogiovanni in 859.[29] Constantinople's holdings on the island were reduced to the eastern coast about Syracuse and some of the interior. Two-thirds of Sicily was now in Arab hands.

Eight years later the Moslems determined to complete their conquest, and the ruler of Palermo sent a land army and his *harraqas* against Syracuse. A relieving Eastern Byzantine fleet drove off the attackers in 868.[30] But this check was avenged in 870 when Malta was taken by the Aghlabids, thus assuring them complete control of the African-Sicilian straits.[31] In 878 a final large land and sea assault was launched on Syracuse.[32] This time no naval assistance arrived, and it fell to the Moslem forces. On the whole island of Sicily, only Taormina and a small region just across the straits from Reggio remained Byzantine.

One reason the Moslems were able to conquer Sicily was because their threat to the Italian mainland claimed the attention of their opponents. Allied to Naples on the west coast and having firm bases along the Adriatic at Bari and elsewhere, their raids into the interior of southern and central Italy were by the 850's extremely devastating. In fact, it looked as if they might take over the entire region. The alarmed Carolingian ruler of Italy, Louis II, with Papal blessing decided to take action against them. But he had little success. Without a fleet he could not dislodge the Moslems from the coastal strongholds from which they were able to raid far into the interior. His long siege of Bari, for instance, was rendered all but useless with the sea lanes in Moslem hands.[33]

Finally in 867 the tide began to turn. Both Venice and Constantinople intervened in Italian waters. Venice, perhaps allied to Louis II, won a naval victory off Tarentum, thus avenging its defeat in that sea twenty-seven years previously.[34] And the Byzantine Emperor Basil I sent a squadron of 100 ships under the Patrician Nicetas to the rescue of Ragusa, besieged by a joint Tarentum-Cretan force.[35] Victorious at Ragusa the Byzantines turned to Italy. In 870 a larger fleet, including Ragusan and Dal-

[29] *Ibn al Athir* vii, 97. Bury *East. Roman Empire*, p. 397-98.

[30] Ibn Khaldun *Hist. de l'Afrique et de Sicile*, p. 125. *Ibn al Athir* trans. Fagnan I, 148.

[31] *Ibn al Athir* i, 240. *Nuwairi* trans. Gaspar ii, 86.

[32] *Theophanes Continuator*, p. 309-15. *Ibn al Athir* i, 253-54. *Ibn Idhari*, i, 52.

[33] Bury *East. Roman Empire*, p. 315.   [34] Dandolo *Chron.*, p. 184.

[35] *Theoph. Cont.*, p. 280-91. Const. Porphyr. *De Thematibus* (ed. Bonn) ii, xi. Amari *Storia* i, 519-20.

matian naval contingents, appeared off Bari, already blockaded
on the land by Louis II's troops. Their intervention proved decisive, and the city finally fell to the Carolingian monarch. But at
this point quarrels broke out between Louis and the Byzantines.
Byzantium proved hostile to his South Italian ambitions. Thanks
to this enmity, Louis turned north to die a disappointed man. Basil
I reaped the fruits of his efforts.[36] In 873 his forces retook Otranto,
and in 876 Bari fell into Byzantine hands.[37] Only Tarentum appears
still to have remained Saracen. From it or perhaps from Crete
sailed the Moslem squadron which in 875 raided Venice and burnt
the port of Comacchio at the mouth of the Po River—the last
Islamic raid on the upper Adriatic.[38]

While Byzantine naval power was being thus reasserted with
Venetian assistance on the east coast of Italy, less progress was
made on the west coast. True, a small force of ten warships under
George, Governor of Calabria, appeared in the Tyrrhenian Sea.
But it accomplished little. Moslem pressure increased along this
Italian coast. In 868 and 872, Islamic raids were unsuccessfully
made on Gaeta and Salerno, respectively.[39] And Papal territory
suffered severely from such depredations. Pleas for protection
were sent by Pope John VIII to Charles the Bald, to Byzantium,
and to the cities of Amalfi, Gaeta, and Naples.[40] He had little
success. Constantinople, distrustful of Papal wooing of the Carolingians and with her hands full in Sicily and the East, did little.
Charles the Bald had no naval power to send. The Campanian
cities did not wish to offend their Moslem friends. As a result only
the payment of 25,000 silver *mancusi* to the raiders brought some
peace to the estates of the Church in central Italy.[41]

The pressure did not relax until 880, when a sizable Byzantine
flotilla appeared off Sicily and won some successes. This fleet interrupted the commercial traffic between the Moslems and the
cities of Southern Italy and captured so much olive oil in so doing
that it is said that the price of this commodity fell markedly in the
markets of Constantinople.[42] Apparently the Byzantines stationed

[36] Amari *Storia* i, 520-23.
[37] Gasquet *Byz. Emp.*, p. 459-60. Vasiliev *Byz. Emp.* i, 396-97.
[38] John *Chron. Ven.*, p. 20.
[39] *Ibn al Athir* i, 239. John Deac. *Chron. Episcop. Neapol.* in *op. cit.* ii, 317.
[40] See letters of John VIII in Labbe *Sacrosancta Concilia* ix.
[41] Labbe *op. cit.*, p. 74. On the role of John VIII in these struggles, see Engreen
"Pope John VIII and the Arabs" in *Speculum* (1945) xx.
[42] *Theoph. Cont.*, p. 302-05.

this squadron permanently at Termini in Western waters. Its effectiveness probably was responsible for the return of Naples, long disloyal to its Byzantine allegiance in 884.[43] It did not, however, prevent the establishment of a Moslem pirate nest at Monte Garigliano in 882 or 883.[44]

Byzantine naval strength apparently was strong enough for Palermo to take alarm, and in 885 a truce was arranged between the antagonists.[45] In the same year Byzantium made a full-scale Western effort, landing a large army in Southern Italy under Nicephorus Phocas. For two years he labored, using force and diplomacy. By 886 he had firmly reestablished Byzantine power in Southern Italy. Calabria and Apulia were organized into definite themes, and Beneventum recognized Byzantine authority, as did the Campanian cities.[46] With Sicilian Moslems quiet and naval power of Byzantium operating again in the Tyrrhenian Sea, it looked as if an era of peace had come. But this was not to be. After the death of Basil I, in 886, the Moslems returned to the offensive and in 888 attacked Calabria.[47] Contingents of the Imperial fleet sailed westward to Reggio and through the straits of Messina. Near Milazzo off the north coast of Sicily they met a large Moslem armada. It was almost a repetition of 859. The Byzantines were badly worsted, and their ships destroyed.[48] By the time peace had been made in 895, Constantinople had lost its brief control of the waters off Sicily and western Italy.[49]

Seven years later the Aghlabids struck their final blow against Byzantium. Ibrahim, the abdicated African ruler, in 902 led a huge land and sea expedition from Palermo against the remnant of Sicily still in Byzantine hands, Taormina and the surrounding countryside. It fell to the Moslems, leaving only one stronghold, New Taormina, still unconquered. From Sicily, Ibrahim then continued his victorious march across the straits into Calabria. Only his sudden death at Cosenza relieved a frightened Italy of the specter of sharing the fate of Taormina, as the Islamic army withdrew to Sicily.[50] Then the troubles that attended the fall of the Aghlabid dynasty

[43] Gasquet *op. cit.*, p. 422-23.
[44] *Leo of Ostia* in *Mur. Rer. Ital. Script.* IV, 316-17.
[45] *Ibn al Athir* I, 261. [46] *Ibn Idhari* I, 157. *Ibn al Athir* I, 262.
[47] Amari *Storia* I, 568. [48] *Ibn Idhari* I, 157-58.
[49] *Cronica di Cambridge*, p. 66.
[50] *Ibn al Athir*, I, 248-50. John Deac. in Gaetani *Vita Sanct. Sic.* II, 61.

and the establishment of the Fatimids in Kairouan gave the Italians a breaking spell despite Byzantine naval and military weakness.

To sum up, by 902 Sicily had fallen to the African Moslems, despite a long and bitter Byzantine struggle to hold it. But Byzantium had mustered at the time of Basil I enough naval strength of her own and from Western allies like Venice to win back Bari and Tarentum from the Moslems, establish firm control over the themes of Calabria and Apulia, and reestablish some sort of sovereignty over the disloyal Campanian cities of Naples, Gaeta, and Amalfi. Only the pirate nest of Monte Garigliano remained a thorn in the side of the southern Italian countryside.

Disorders in Africa and Sicily soon gave an opportunity to wipe out this Moslem advance base. In 909 the Fatimids took over Tunisia and became the rulers of Kairouan. Their attempts to establish authority over Sicily, however, were at first less successful.[51] In 913 Palermo revolted and sent its fleet against Fatimid Africa in the next year. Much of African sea power was at that moment engaged in trying to add Egypt to Fatimid domains, and so at first the Sicilians had little opposition. They destroyed an African squadron off Lanlay near Medhia and, landing forces, sacked Sfax and attacked Tripoli.[52] Not until 917 were the Fatimids able to reestablish their authority over the island, using the fleet they had sent against Egypt.[53]

During this interval the Byzantine governor of Calabria bought peace from Sicily for his provinces with a payment of 22,000 gold pieces a year.[54] And more important still, though an attack by Naples, Capua, and Amalfi upon Monte Garigliano had failed in 908, in 915 success came at last to the enemies of the Moslem freebooters. Freed of danger of Sicilian interference, a joint Byzantine-Italian land and sea force under Nicolas Pincingli and including Papal, Italian, Neapolitan, and Gaetan levies launched an assault on the Moslem stronghold. Its inhabitants were wiped out, and

---

[51] *Ibn al Athir* I, 309. *Ibn Idhari* I, 235.

[52] *Ibn Idhari* I, 236-40. Ibn Khaldun *Hist. des Berbers* trans. de Slane, Appendix II, 524.

[53] *Ibn al Athir* I, 245-46. *Nuwairi* II, 261.

[54] Amari *Storia* II, 180-81. *Cedrenus* ed. Bonn (1838-9) II, 355. Byzantium with her hands full with Bulgarian hostilities was glad to purchase peace from the Sicilian Moslems.

Italy south of Tuscany was freed of its Moslem tormentors for the first time since 842.[55]

One reason for Byzantium's weakness upon the sea about Italy and Sicily in this period lies in the difficulties the Byzantines were experiencing in the East, particularly in the Aegean off Crete. Constantinople found it difficult to deal with enemies in both the Aegean and the West at the same time. Byzantine attempts to end the Cretan menace began almost immediately after its conquest by Spanish Moslems from Alexandria in 827. A first expedition by Photinos was a complete failure.[56] So, too, was a second attempt to recapture the island by Crateras, Strategos of the Kibyrrhaeots, with seventy warships drawn from his own theme and those of Hellas and the Aegean.[57] The Cretan Moslems countered these attempts with raids of their own on the Thracian coast and the Cyclades.[58] In 839 they won another important victory over Byzantium in destroying a Greek fleet off the island of Thasos.[59] Constantinople then prepared in 843 a large fleet at the capital under Theokistos to subdue these troublesome pirates. Intrigues by the Cretans were apparently so successful that it failed even to sail.[60]

Not until 853 did Byzantium take any new naval action in these waters. Then an attack was launched not upon Crete but upon the Delta of Egypt, which apparently was in close alliance with the corsairs of Candia. This expedition plundered Damietta and found arms which were being sent to the Moslems of Crete.[61] Again in 859 another descent was made on the Egyptian Delta.[62] Perhaps these raids had some effect on Crete, as did Aghlabid attacks, for not until 862 did the islanders disturb Byzantine territory again. In that year they attacked Mitylene and plundered Mt. Athos.[63]

---

[55] Luidprand *Antapodesis* in *MGH Script*. III, 297-98. Amari *Storia* II, 190-97. Gay *op. cit.*, p. 161.

[56] *Theoph. Cont.*, p. 76-77. See Brooks "The Arab Conquest of Crete" in *Eng. Hist. Rev.* (1913) XXVIII.

[57] *Theoph. Cont.*, p. 79-81.   [58] *ibid.*, p. 137.

[59] Vasiliev *Byz. et les Arabes* I, 90.

[60] *Theoph. Cont.*, pp. 200, 203.

[61] *Tabari* trans. in Vasiliev *Byz. et les Arabes* I, 315-17. Al Kindi, p. 203. Vasiliev may overrate the importance of this raiding expedition. It did not result in any real rebuilding of the Egyptian fleet, for when a new Moslem naval expedition was planned against Byzantium in 877 new ships had to be built in both Syria and Egypt. *Theoph. Cont.* v, 68.

[62] *Al Kindi*, p. 203.

[63] Petit, L. "Vie et Office de Sainte Euthyme le Jeune" in *Revue de l'Orient Chrétien* (1903) VIII, 189-90.

Four years later, in 866, they established a semi-permanent base on the island of Neon off the Chalcidic peninsula.[64]

Under Basil I, however, Byzantium's naval renaissance was reflected in the Aegean as well as Western waters. In 879 a large fleet under Admiral Nicetas Orifa destroyed a Cretan squadron in the gulf of Corinth and secured peace in the Aegean for more than two decades.[65] Not until 901 did new Cretan raids take place. They were against the Cyclades, and some ships penetrated even into the Sea of Marmora.[66] In 904 came the greatest blow of all. Leo of Tripoli, joined by some Cretan ships, launched a full-scale attack on Salonika, the second city of the Empire. The assault, led by ships using flaming projectiles, was completely successful, and 22,000 of the city's inhabitants were carried into slavery in Moslem lands.[67] Apparently these raids stung Constantinople into taking more aggressive naval action, for in 910 another large-scale expedition sailed against Crete. Like its predecessors it, too, ended in failure, and Candia remained a thorn in the side of Byzantine power in the Aegean.[68] As a matter of fact, not until 923, when Leo of Tripoli's corsair fleet was badly beaten off Lemnos by the revived navy of Romanus Lecapenus, was Crete's threat to Byzantium's sea security even curbed.[69]

The Moslems of Candia were not, however, Constantinople's only naval enemies in the East during this period, though they were the most dangerous and persistent. Syria and Tarsus also had some naval strength at this time. This strength seems, however, to have been relatively neglected until a Byzantine expedition sometime between 828 and 841 plundered the port of Antioch.[70] This apparently convinced the Abbassids that some naval protection along these coasts was necessary beyond that provided indirectly by Cretan and African flotillas further west. The Caliph al-Mutasim, therefore, ordered ships built in Syria and perhaps

---

[64] *ibid.* They may even have established an advanced pirate base at Athens in this period.

[65] *Theoph. Cont.*, p. 298-300.   [66] *ibid.*, p. 298.

[67] *ibid.*, p. 366-8. John Cameniati "De Excidio Thessaloniciensi" in *Corp. Script. Hist.* (ed. Bonn), p. 491, 598.

[68] Const. Porphyr. *De Ceremoniis*, p. 651-58. Another unsuccessful attack was made in 902, or perhaps this expedition and that of 910 were actually the same one.

[69] *Theoph. Cont.*, p. 405. Runciman *The Emperor Romanus Lecapenus and his Reign* (London 1919), p. 89-90.

[70] Michael the Syrian *Chron.* III, 101.

Tarsus. In 842, this fleet, numbering 400 sail, was sent toward the Aegean. It met with disaster, being shattered by storms off the coast of Asia Minor with the loss of all but seven vessels.[71] A few years later the Byzantine raid on Egypt in 853 convinced the governmental authorities there of the need of organized Egyptian naval power, though how much was actually accomplished in providing it is debatable.[72]

By the second half of the ninth century more permanent naval strength had been established in these areas, principally in the border of Tarsus, where it appears to have operated under the command of the Emir who also was in charge of the Abbassids' frontier land forces used against Byzantium. It was strong enough, perhaps backed by some Syrian and even Egyptian contingents, to stage an assault on the Byzantine Anatolian naval base of Attalia in 860 in conjunction with land assaults on Asia Minor by Abbassid forces.[73] In 873 a Tarsus-Syrian fleet, perhaps stiffened by Cretan contingents, raided Euboea in the Aegean.[74]

Byzantine naval revival in the late years of Basil I, marked as it was by victories over Cretans in the Aegean in 879 and Aghlabids and Sicilians in the West between 880 and 886, helped check this Tarsus-Syria-Egypt naval effort. Probably more important was the fact that domestic difficulties caused the Eastern Moslems to neglect their naval adversaries of Constantinople. These difficulties were caused by the expansion of Ibn Tulun's power—from Egypt over the coasts of Syria and Tarsus. Tarsus, which had the most formidable fleet, managed to hold out until 888 before it succumbed to Tulunid power. It was in this interval that Cyprus was recovered by Basil and was ruled for seven years as an organized theme by Alexius of Armenia.[75]

With the breakup of Tulunid authority, which culminated in an Abbassid reconquest of Egypt in 904, the maritime strength of both the Tarsus and Syrian coast again became formidable. From Tripoli and other Syrian coastal cities Leo of Tripoli sailed with pirate fleets which not only sacked Salonika in 904 but remained the terror of the Aegean for a generation. From Tarsus came the

[71] Vasiliev *Byz. et les Arabes* I, 192-93.

[72] Bury *East. Rom. Empire*, p. 291-93. Maqrizi says that this expedition resulted in naval reforms in Egypt. This seems very questionable. Egypt had no important naval power until Fatimid times in the next century.

[73] *Tabari* III, 1449.   [74] *Theoph. Cont.*, p. 59.

[75] Wiet *op. cit.*, p. 94-95. Const. Porphyr. *De Themat.*, p. 40.

flotilla which in the same year defeated the weak Tulunid fleet in the Nile and assured easy Abbassid reconquest of the country.[76] Again in 920 it was a Tarsus squadron of twenty-five ships which defeated a Fatimid force of 80 warships near Alexandria and balked an African conquest of Egypt, capturing the admiral of the invading fleet and carrying him back to Cilicia in triumph.[77]

Byzantium, weak on the sea under Leo the Wise, could do little against this maritime strength. In 902 Cyprus was apparently under Byzantine control again, and its governor and the Catapan of the Mardaites of Attalia had the special task of preventing communication between the Moslems of Crete and those of Syria.[78] How little they succeeded can be seen by the great raid of Leo of Tripoli against Salonika in 904. Yet they must have had some nuisance value, for in 912 Dimyana, Emir of Tyre and commander of the Syrian fleet, raided the island for not observing its traditional neutrality in Arab-Byzantine warfare.[79]

In general, then, despite conflicts in their own ranks, the Moslems of Tarsus, Syria, and even Egypt developed sufficient naval strength, particularly in the early tenth century, to supplement Crete's threat to Byzantium's sea routes. Not until Leo of Tripoli's fleet was destroyed in 923 did their warships cease to be a source of concern to the rulers of Constantinople. And even then ships from this same Cilician-Syrian coast were still powerful enough in 935 to thwart a third Fatimid attack on Egypt and enable Al-Ikshid, governor of Syria, to become ruler of the fertile Nile valley.[80]

Had these Moslem naval adversaries from Africa, Sicily, Crete, and Tarsus-Syria been the only ones with whom Byzantium had to contend in the century after 827, it would have been sufficient to explain her naval weakness in the Middle Sea. But in addition, this period saw the development of still another maritime foe who endangered her position in the Black Sea, an area which Constantinople had previously controlled without difficulty. This new danger came from the Varangian Rus from Kiev and South Russia. These Rus were Scandinavians, probably mainly Swedes, who had been drawn into this area by opportunities for commerce and

[76] Wiet, *op. cit.*, p. 95.
[77] *Al Kindi*, p. 276. Eutrychius *Annales* ed. *Pocock* II, 509-10.
[78] Const. Porphyr *De Ceremoniis*, pp. 656, 660.
[79] Masudi *Prairies d'Or* VIII, 282.
[80] Wiet *op. cit.*, p. 127-29. Lane-Poole *Egypt*, p. 82-91.

plunder along the Varangian trade route that stretched up Russian rivers from the Black and Caspian Seas. In these river trading towns they soon became the dominant ruling class, controlling the wealth that exports and imports brought to Kiev, Novgorod, and other such centers.[81]

Such trading activities gave them a knowledge of the wealth of Constantinople, or Tsargrad, which excited their cupidity. And so in 860 they launched a large-scale assault upon the city from the north with 200 ships. They chose a good time for their expedition. The main Byzantine fleet had just been badly mauled in 859 by the Aghlabids off Sicily, the Syrian Moslem fleet was attacking Attalia and the Cretans were active in the Aegean. Constantinople thus had little naval power to use against them. For ten months they besieged the city, until storms of winter drove them off.[82] Again in 907 they may have launched another assault on the city when, as in 860, Byzantine naval strength was at another low ebb after its loss of Taormina in the West in 902 and the sack of Salonika by Leo of Tripoli in 904. If so, they were beaten off without too much difficulty.[83] But the threat of their naval power in the Black Sea immensely complicated Constantinople's naval defense problems.

While Moslem naval power in the central and eastern Mediterranean was thus in the ascendency and the Russians were threatening the Byzantine control of the Euxine, what of the West and the Moslems of Spain? Here the Ommayid Spanish state showed at first much less interest in maritime strength than did other regions controlled by Islam in the Middle Sea. One reason lies in the fact that the rulers of Cordova continued their earlier policy of friendship with Constantinople and hostility to the Abbassids. Thus they took practically no part in the African Aghlabid assaults on Sicily and Italy. Only once, in 829, did a Spanish force assist the enemies of Byzantium. Then an expedition from Tortosa joined for a short

[81] Vernadsky *Ancient Russia*, p. 303-07. Byzantine aid in building the fortress of Sarkel for the Kazars was probably made necessary by Varangian Russian pressure in 833.

[82] For a full account of this attack see Vasiliev *The Russian Attack on Constantinople* (Cambridge, Mass. 1945).

[83] Many historians deny a Russian attack took place in 907, though it is mentioned in *The Primary Chronicle*. For this point of view see G. de Costa-Louillet "Y eut-il des invasions Russes dans l'Empire Byzantin avant 860" in *Byzantion* xv, 231-40. It seems to me more probable that some such attack did take place, hence the trade treaty of 911.

time in the attack on Sicily. It soon withdrew, however. Since the Carolingians were in 828 assisting Byzantium with an attack on Bone, this may have represented a temporary falling out between the old allies. Though individual Spanish freebooters may very well have joined pirate fleets and bands which ravaged Italian coasts and preyed on commerce from such Moslem strongholds as Garigliano, Tarentum, Bari, and Crete, relations between Spain and Byzantium remained friendly and cordial. To the court of Abd-ar-Rahman II, as well as that of Louis the Pious, in 839, the Emperor Theophilus sent envoys imploring help against his Moslem enemies in Sicily and Africa. His ambassadors were well received, and Cordova sent some in return to Constantinople, but little came of it except friendly words.[84]

But this cordial attitude was not in evidence in relations between the Spanish Ommayids and the Carolingians. Hostility between these two powers was constant and prolonged. Such naval power as Spain possessed in the early ninth century was concentrated along its northeastern coast from Tortosa to Valencia. And it was directed against the Carolingians by the all but independent Emir of Saragossa. Carolingian naval power disintegrated in the late years of Louis the Pious, as Tortosa and Barcelona were lost and control of Northern Italy weakened. Therefore the Spanish Moslems found they could raid Carolingian coastlines with impunity. They began in 838 by sending a fleet from Tarragona, with certain Balearic contingents, against Marseilles.[85] In 842 it was the turn of Arles and its environs.[86] In 846 Marseilles suffered again.[87] In 848 the Balearics accepted Ommayid overlordship and promised not to interfere with their shipping.[88] In that same year and again in 850 Arles was the object of attack once more.[89] Finally, resistance along the Southern French coast became so slight that Moslem pirates established themselves on the island of Camargue at the mouth of the Rhone in a semi-permanent base.[90] From here they

[84] Vasiliev *Byz. et les Arabes* I, 185-87.

[85] *ibid.*, p. 186. Condé *Historia de la Dominación de los Arabes en España* (Barcelona 1884) I, 227.

[86] Poupardin *Le Royaume de Provence sous les Carolingiens* (Paris 1901), p. 240.

[87] Masson, P. *De Massiliensibus Mercatoribus*, p. 129.

[88] Campaner y Fuertes *op. cit.*, p. 17-21.

[89] Masson *op. cit.*

[90] Duprat "La Provence dans le haut moyen âge" in *Bouches du Rhône, Encyclopédie Departementale* (Marseilles 1923) II, 33-36.

ranged inland and in 860 captured the Bishop of Arles.[91] Perhaps they established themselves in similar semi-permanent fashion further down the shore at or near ruined Maguelone. There the *gradus sarracenus* of later times testifies to their presence in this area.[92] Only a humiliating peace signed by Charles the Bald in 864 gave this part of France some relief from their depredations.

By the late years of the ninth century the crescendo of naval depredation seems to have quickened. In 888, in addition to such semi-permanent pirate bases as Camargue and Maguelone, the Moslems of Spain, perhaps reinforced by some from other regions, established a more permanent base at Fraxinetum on the coast of Provence. From it they proceeded to raid inland, as had been done earlier from Bari and Monte Garigliano. For 84 years most of Provence and the lower Rhone valley region suffered from their constant razzias. They even penetrated into the Alps and controlled the passes between France and Italy from Mont Cenis to the Mediterranean, making travel by these routes to the Po valley difficult if not impossible.[93] In addition, in 902, Spanish Moslems definitely occupied the Balearics and installed there a Moslem Wali or governor.[94] Though these islands had since 838 been under Islamic influence, the final annexation was delayed until this date, perhaps by Ommayid naval weakness.

This gradually growing Spanish border naval power was not in the ninth century backed up by much maritime strength in the rest of the peninsula. The Ommayids had no really organized fleet in this century at all, though the establishment of Fraxinetum and the occupation of the Balearics may mark a certain naval coming of age. Their naval weakness can be best seen in Spain's unpreparedness against Norse raids in the middle of the century. The first of these Viking attacks took place in 844, when a Scandinavian pirate fleet attacked Lisbon with 54 ships and then, joined by 26 others, went on to sack Seville and Necour on the African coast.[95]

[91] Ganshof "Note sur les ports de Provence," p. 32. There may be some confusion between these Moslem raiders and the Norse pirates who operated from this island base for two years in 859 and 860. *Annales Bertiniani* in *MGH Script.* I, 453. See also Vasiliev *Russian Attack*, p. 47-49.

[92] Arnaud de Verdale *Cat. Epis. Mag.* in *op. cit.*, p. 500.

[93] Poupardin *Le Royaume de Bourgogne (888-1038)* (Paris 1907), p. 86-112, 250-54. The fuller account is Patrucco "I Saraceni in Piemonte et nelle Alpi Orientale" in *Biblioteco della Società Storica Subalpini* (Pinerola 1908) xxxii.

[94] Campaner y Fuertes *op. cit.*, p. 40-56.

[95] Dozy *Recherches sur l'histoire et la litérature de l'Espagne* ii, 252-56.

Having no warships in the area, the Ommayid rulers were power-less to halt these attackers. Instead they sent an envoy to negotiate with the Viking's king. The envoy appears to have visited Jutland and to have been well received.[96]

But these diplomatic efforts did not assure the Ommayids any immunity from further raids. In 858 the Vikings launched an even greater assault upon Spain. In that year their vessels again ap-peared off Andalusia, plundered Algeciras and Necour, and then sailed into the Mediterranean. There they sacked Aribuela on the east coast and the islands of Majorca and Minorca, settling on the island of Camaria of the Rhone for two winters.[97] From there they raided far inland and included the cities of Luni and Pisa on the Italian coast among their victims. Some of them even sailed into the eastern Mediterranean and raided the Hellespont and perhaps Alexandria as well, before their return to their northern homes.[98] This daring Viking expedition not only reveals Spanish naval weakness but is significant in its revelation of the maritime position of the entire Mediterranean world in these years. The Norse pirates carefully avoided all areas with important war fleets which could interfere with their depredations. These were the Spanish coast between Denia and Tortosa, Aghlabid North Africa and Sicily, Southern Italy or the Syrian coast. Their victims, Southern Spain, Southern France, Northwest Italy, the Hellespont, and Egypt were just those areas where little or no naval power was to be found during these years.

This great raid may have given some pause to Cordova's rulers, but it is interesting to note that it did not result in a building up of any organized naval power of their own. This can be seen in 879, when an attempt was made to construct a fleet at Cordova to be used in a raid on Christian Galicia. The fleet was so badly put together, and its navigators were such poor seamen, that it foundered soon after it reached the ocean.[99] Not until the time of Abd-ar-Rahman III in the tenth century did a truly organized maritime force come into existence for Spain as a whole.

[96] *ibid.*, p. 267-78.
[97] *Al Bakri* (Algiers 1913), p. 184. *Ibn Idhari* II, 99.
[98] Vasiliev *Russian Attack*, p. 49-65. The idea that these Vikings mistook Luni for Rome is probably an error. Luni had been the only important port on the Ligurian coast of Italy since the seventh century and thus well worth attacking for booty. See Chs. III and IV on Luni's importance.
[99] *Ibn Idhari* II, 170.

But this early tenth-century Mediterranean world with Islamic peoples ensconced in the islands of the Balearics in the West, Sicily in the center, and Crete in the East—and with Sardinia and Cyprus neutralized—did not long endure. Both Byzantium in the East and Ommayid Spain in the West began to expand their naval power and disturb the naval equilibrium which existed. Both Romanus Lecapenus at Constantinople and Abd-ar-Rahman III turned their full attention to maritime affairs with important results.

Romanus Lecapenus, who had been admiral of the Byzantine fleet before his usurpation of power as Emperor, seems to have been the first ruler of Byzantium since Basil I who had a real appreciation of the importance of the fleet to his Empire. Under him there developed a renaissance in Constantinople's naval strength from the low point it had reached under Leo the Wise. In 923 his great victory over Leo of Tripoli's fleet freed the Aegean from piratical depredation for the first time in more than two decades. In 928 he sent units of the fleet to raid Egypt for the first time since 859.[100] Unfortunately a storm scattered this flotilla before it did much damage. By 941 Byzantium was strong enough on the seas to scatter and destroy a large Russian naval force of 1,000 ships under Prince Igor of Kiev which attacked Constantinople.[101] In 949 a large expedition was sent against Crete. Despite its size it failed to take Candia, the Moslem stronghold, and Crete remained in Islamic hands.[102] In 954, however, Byzantine corsairs felt bold enough to raid Farama on the Egyptian delta.[103] The new Byzantine fleet that Nicephorus Phocas was to use so effectively was already in being.

Nor was Byzantium inactive in Western waters. There was need for activity there as well as in the East. Once Fatimid power over Sicily had been reestablished in 917, its inhabitants, and those of Africa as well, turned to sea raids on Byzantine territory. In 918[104] and 924 Calabria was assaulted in the region about Reggio.[105] In 925 Orio was sacked.[106] The governor of Calabria found it wise to

[100] Theoph. Cont., p. 405.
[101] Liudprand Antapodesis, p. 137-40. Theoph. Cont., p. 423. Nestor, p. 33.
[102] Bury East. Rom. Empire, p. 231.   [103] Wiet op. cit., p. 147.
[104] Ibn Idhari i, 270.
[105] Cronica di Cambridge in Amari Biblio Arabo-Sicula i, 283.
[106] Chron. Barensis in Mur. Rer. Ital. Script. i, 31 and Lupus Prospatarios in op. cit., v, 38.

renew tribute payments of 11,000 gold pieces a year to secure immunity from these incursions.[107] Then the Fatimids turned their attention to other areas. In 928 Tarentum was attacked by 44 ships,[108] and at about this time Salerno and Naples found payment of tribute the better part of valor.

Perhaps it was this naval pressure from Africa and Sicily that caused substantial Byzantine naval forces to reappear in the Tyrrhenian Sea for the first time since 888. This fleet attacked with some success the pirate nest of Fraxinetum on the coast of Provence, which may have been interfering with the commerce of the Italian coastal cities of Amalfi, Gaeta, Naples, and Salerno. It was not able to accomplish its purpose because of the lack of land forces.[109] By 941, Byzantine diplomacy had gained Hugh, King of Italy, to its side. He promised to assault the Moslem stronghold on the land side, while Byzantium's fleet attacked from the sea. The naval assault was a success, but Hugh reneged on his side of the bargain. The Moslems continued to hold their base in Provence.[110]

The renewed naval strength of Byzantium in the Western Mediterranean seems to have alarmed the Fatimids. At any rate, in 935 they sent a full-fledged fleet to reassert their power in the Tyrrhenian Sea. It raided Sardinia, Corsica, and perhaps Genoa, and burned many ships.[111] This raid on Sardinia, the first in many years, may reflect a renewed Byzantine overlordship over this island, which had been all but autonomous for at least a century and which, like Cyprus, had a neutral position between Byzantium and the Moslems of Sicily and North Africa.[112] The Fatimids were, however, almost immediately paralyzed by a series of serious domestic difficulties. Following their third unsuccessful attack on Egypt in 936, Sicily revolted, and it took them from 937 to 940 to subdue the island's rebels, who were aided by Byzantium.[113] Then a few years later the even more serious revolt of the "Man on the

[107] Cedrenus II, 356-58.   [108] Ibn al Athir I, 317. Nuwairi II, 262.

[109] Luidprand op. cit., pp. 137, 139.   [110] ibid.

[111] Ibn al Athir I, 301. Ibn Idhari I, 301. Nuwairi II, 262.

[112] Sardinia was either autonomous or under Byzantine influence or control at this time. Besta La Sardegna Medioevale (Palermo 1908), I, 48-60. Carta-Raspi believes it was independent. Probably, like Venice and Naples, it was essentially autonomous. It was definitely not under Moslem rule. Besta also doubts that the Moslem raid of 934 was directed against Sardinia. Besta op. cit., p. 47. On Corsica we have no information. It, too, however, was probably autonomous under neither Byzantine nor Moslem control.

[113] Amari Storia II, 217-44.

Donkey" in North Africa threatened to destroy their whole African dominion.[114]

Not until 950 were they ready to turn their attention to Byzantine Italy. In that year they assaulted Calabria with a large land and sea armada. The Byzantines were unable to resist effectively and lost a Patrician and the strategos of the theme on the field of battle.[115] Only a renewal of the old tribute payments brought peace. Apparently Byzantine weakness, thus revealed, convinced the Neapolitans of the uselessness of their allegiance to Constantinople, which they proceeded to ignore. Constantinople's viceroys in the West, however, soon restored their power over the city in 956 by seizing it in a land and sea attack.[116] At about the same time diplomatic relations of a very friendly sort were reestablished with the Ommayids of Spain, the mortal enemies of the Fatimids.[117] This apparently broke the uneasy truce with Palermo, and raids and counter-raids on Calabria and Sicily troubled the last years of this period. Not until 961 was peace reestablished on the old basis of tribute from Calabria.[118] In the West, then, as in the East, these years saw a Byzantium more active and stronger than it had been since the early ninth century, and with sufficient naval forces to hold the Fatimids at bay, keep Naples in hand, reestablish diplomatic relations with Spain, and intervene in the waters off Southern France.

Ommayid Spain shared with Byzantium this new Western naval power. Probably the cause of Spain's maritime development lay in Abd-ar-Rahman's well-founded distrust of the intentions of his Fatimid neighbors in Africa. With their heretical Shiah beliefs and their wide ambitions against Idrissid and Rostemid territory in Algeria and Morocco, generally under Spanish influence, they were a menace to the security of the Ommayid dynasty in Spain.[119] It was against them, then, that Abd-ar-Rahman III constructed a well-organized fleet along the Spanish coast, and in 931 took over Ceuta on the African shore across from Gibraltar.[120] In 944 this same fleet proved its worth against another adversary. A Viking force ap-

[114] Marçais *Berbérie*, p. 147-53.
[115] *Ibn al Athir* I, 353-55. *Lupus Prospatarios* in *MGH Script.* v, 54.
[116] *Theoph. Cont.*, p. 453. *Cedrenus* II, 359.
[117] *Al Kairouani* trans. Pellesier et Remusat, p. 104. *Ibn Idhari* I, 382.
[118] *Theoph. Cont.*, p. 454-55. *Cedrenus* II, 359-60.
[119] Amari *Storia* II, 322-24. *Ibn Kallikan* trans. de Slane I, 340.
[120] *Ibn Idhari* II, 170.

peared off Andalusia in this year and plundered Cadiz, Medina, Sidonia, and Seville. At Seville the Spanish Moslem fleet attacked the intruders in force and destroyed most of the invading ships with fire. Few of the northern pirates escaped.[121]

Soon after this the Fatimids showed their hand. Triumphant over Sicily and African rebels, they turned their attention to the Caliphate of Cordova. In 954 the Fatimid ruler ordered the Emir of Palermo to ravage Spain. The latter sent his Sicilian fleet to the Spanish coast where Almeria, chief naval base of the Ommayids, was sacked and much booty and many prisoners carried back to Sicily.[122] In reprisal the Cordovan Caliph sent a Spanish flotilla of seventy vessels to ravage the coasts of Africa.[123] Raids and counter-raids continued with little respite during the next few years, while Gawhar, the able Fatimid general, led armies west which overwhelmed Rostemid and Idrissid rulers and established the power of his master over Sidjilmasa, Fez, and all interior Algeria and Morocco. Only Ceuta in 959 remained under Abd-ar-Rahman's power and unconquered by the Fatimids.[124] But the fleet which had been constructed by the ruler of Cordova remained powerful, a future danger to his Fatimid rivals of Medhia.

It might be well at this point to sum up the results of the naval action of this century and a quarter in the Mediterranean. From their positions along the coast from Syria to France the Moslems advanced into the center of the Middle Sea, beginning in 827. They established firm hold on Crete and parts of Sicily and from these centers set up advanced bases at Bari and Garigliano. In the West, a somewhat similar process was followed, though at a later date, with the Balearics playing the part of Crete and Sicily and Fraxinetum that of Bari and Garigliano. Sardinia and Cyprus were not so much occupied as neutralized by these events and played little part, except for brief periods, in this advance. The same can be said of Corsica, about which there is almost no information for this period.

The Carolingian state, which alone was affected by the Spanish Islamic advance, could not resist in any fashion. Its naval power had always been slight, and, as Charlemagne's Empire disinte-

121 Dozy Recherches II, 252-67.
122 Ibn Khaldun Hist. des Berbères II, 542. Ibn Idhari, II, 366.
123 Ibn Idhari II, 362 and 368-69.   124 Lane-Poole op. cit., p. 99-100.

grated at the end of the reign of Louis the Pious, even that slight maritime strength disappeared. Byzantium, better placed geographically, richer and better organized, resisted with more success. Its period of lowest ebb was probably about 860 when, after a great naval disaster off Sicily, Russians attacked Constantinople, Norse pirates the Hellespont, Syrians the coast of Asia Minor, and Cretans plundered widely in the Aegean.

Under Basil I, perhaps owing to a reorganization of the fleet at the time of Michael III, Constantinople enjoyed a period of resurgence on the sea. Cretans were beaten in the Aegean, and Cyprus was strongly reoccupied. With the help of Venice, Apulia was cleared of the Moslem invaders, and Nicephorus Phocas with a revived Byzantine Western fleet reestablished a firm rule over portions of Southern Italy.

This counteroffensive was stopped, however, by a great defeat off Milazzo in 888. Another period of naval decadence followed, reaching its nadir in the late years of Leo the Wise, when Taormina was lost, Salonika sacked, the Aegean in the hands of Leo of Tripoli, and perhaps there was even another assault on Constantinople by the Varangian Russians. Only the destruction of the pirate nest of Garigliano in 916, thanks largely to Fatimid internal troubles, redeemed this period from a Byzantine standpoint.

Finally, beginning at the time of Romanus Lecapenus, a thorough naval revival of Byzantium began to affect its power on the sea. Byzantine warships appeared in Western waters again in effective strength. The Aegean was cleared of Leo of Tripoli's pirate fleet, and Crete was assaulted in force in 949. The Russians were badly beaten in an attack they launched on the capital in 941. And raids on Egypt in 928 and 954 reasserted naval power in that quarter for the first time in many years. The fleet of Constantinople again became a major offensive force to be reckoned with.

While Byzantium was thus revived, the Ommayids of Spain became an important maritime power for the first time under the rule of Abd-ar-Rahman III. They not only controlled the Balearics and advance bases along the coasts of Southern France, but their naval power had to be considered by the Fatimids of Africa and Sicily as well.

The problem of just how this Moslem naval power was organized in the three major regions of its strength—Spain; North Africa and Sicily; or Crete, Syria and Egypt; remains a very difficult one to answer. Information is scanty, scattered and often confused. But at least the major outlines are apparent. In the first place, the Islamic border fleets, such as those under the Emirs of Saragossa, Tarsus, Crete and, in the early days, Palermo, seem to have been somewhat informal semi-pirate fleets manned very largely by Moslem adventurers or even Christian renegades whose primary interest was booty and plunder. Ibn Hawkal, in the late tenth century, has left a rather unflattering picture of these freebooters in his description of the quarter they inhabited at Palermo.[125] Maqrizi, similarly describing the reorganization of the Egyptian fleet after the Byzantine raid of 853, has painted a picture of ill-paid sailors who were recruited irregularly, and were looked down on by the more respectable members of the Islamic community.[126] Probably the organization of such border maritime forces was not much more formal than that of the land forces, who for centuries went on razzias into Christian territory along the Ebro frontier of Spain or the Taurus frontier of Byzantium. As late as the nineteenth century the pirate fleets of the Barbary coast followed a very similar pattern of organization.

This corsair character was even more pronounced in the role of such centers as Bari, Monte Garigliano and Fraxinetum. Each of these pirate nests was essentially autonomous, though Bari appears to have depended on Crete and perhaps Africa to some extent, Monte Garigliano on Sicily and Fraxinetum on Spain for support. These latter have much more in common with the buccaneers of the Caribbean in the seventeenth century than with fully organized maritime powers. The Soudan of Bari or even the Emir of Crete or Leo of Tripoli operated on the sea in a way that Henry Morgan of Port Royal eight centuries later would have thoroughly understood. The relationship of these pirates to the good Moslem merchants of Palermo, Alexandria, Tripoli, or Saragossa, or even to the Christian merchants of Naples, was not unlike that of Drake and Hawkins to those of Plymouth and Bristol, or Blackbeard to those of the Carolina ports of North America. In Fatimid times in North Africa there was even a government tax of one-tenth on the proceeds of buccaneering expeditions,[127] reminding one of Queen Elizabeth's system in sixteenth-century

[125] Ibn Hawkal *Description de Palermo* trans. Amari (Paris 1845), pp. 26 and 38.
[126] Bury *East. Rom. Empire*, p. 293-94.
[127] Marçais *Berbérie*, p. 142-43.

England. Raiding on the sea was a definite business and a prosperous one for the fortunate or the skillful.

But behind this screen of advance pirate fleets and bases, the Islamic Mediterranean world had a better naval organization of a more fixed and regular character. This seems to have been especially true of Aghlabid and Fatimid North Africa from the ninth century on, and of Sicily at least in the next century.[128] There fleets were constructed in regular arsenals, armed and manned by the government, commanded by a series of professional sailors from admirals down to captains, and were fully capable of taking on the Imperial Byzantine fleet in pitched naval battles. The victories gained by Sicilian and North African flotillas off Sicily in 859 and 888, dooming Byzantine hopes of holding this island, were by organized naval forces.

Concerning Spain's naval organization in the tenth century, there is a good deal of information, which probably can be applied to other Islamic areas as well. The admiral in charge of the Spanish Ommayid fleet was one of the four great officials of the Caliphate, and it was said he "divided in a certain fashion royal power with the Caliph. One reigned on the land, and the other on the sea." Almeria was the chief naval base, and there were located the most important naval arsenals from which the 200 ships that made up the regular navy were equipped. There were others apparently at Pechina, Algeciras, Silves, Alcacer do Sol, Alicante, Iviza, and Castella de Ampurias (Tortosa). Normally some ships were stationed at each of these bases, and in time of war would assemble at a certain fixed rendezvous, though most probably were to be found at Almeria and Pechina. Each ship had a captain or *caid* in charge of the fighting men and armament and a sailing master or *rais* who directed the sails and oars. A high official or Emir was in charge of each major naval expedition, unless the Lord High Admiral himself took charge.[129] That the Fatimids had a similar organization can be seen from their expedition against Egypt in 920 when an admiral was in charge and contingents from Tunisia,

---

[128] Both iron mines and other works were state-owned in Palermo and from them the Emirs provided materials for the state manned fleets of Sicily. Ibn Hawkal *op. cit.*, p. 28-9.

[129] Lévi-Provençal *L'Espagne Mussulmane au Xe Siècle* (Paris 1932), p. 85-86. Idrisi *Description de l'Afrique et de l'Espagne*, pp. 212, 217, 219, 237. *Ibn Idhari* III, 104. Ibn Khaldun *Prolegomènes* trans. de Slane II, 40-41.

Tripoli, and Sicily were represented.[130] Concerning the Eastern fleets of Syria and Egypt, weaker in this period, there is less information except that the Emir of Tyre seems to have been the naval commander of the Syrian flotillas.[131] The rendezvous point of joint Syrian-Egyptian expeditions against Byzantine territory was Cyprus, and the cost of a single expedition came to 100,000 dinars.[132] There was, then, a similar careful organization of eastern Moslem as well as African and Spanish Islamic flotillas.

Another interesting point about the Moslem naval forces of the period is that they were armed either with Greek fire or a naphtha compound very much like it. The *harraqas* used by the Aghlabids off Sicily in 835 were fire ships that threw a combustible substance at enemy vessels.[133] Leo of Tripoli used flame-throwing weapons in his attack on Salonika in 904.[134] The Fatimid fleet which raided in the Tyrrhenian Sea in 935 *burnt* the ships it attacked.[135] The Greek fire which was Byzantium's monopoly ceased, then, to be a terrible secret weapon as it had been in the preceding period. This may well help account for the lack of success enjoyed by Constantinople's maritime forces in much of this period. Without an advantage in their use of Greek fire, the Byzantines found control of the seas impossible to maintain. In armament, as in organization, they were little, if any, in advance of their Islamic adversaries.

There is slightly more information about Byzantium's maritime organization in this period than there is about that of the Islamic peoples. In a general way the old system of an Imperial fleet and various provincial or themal fleets continued to prevail—a system not too different from that on the Moslem side. But the disasters which dogged Constantinople on the sea after 827 caused a reorganization of her Eastern fleets about the middle of the ninth century. This probably started under Michael III, but the full effects of this reform were not apparent until the time of Basil I.[136]

[130] *Al Kindi*, p. 276-77.

[131] Masudi *Prairies d'Or* VIII, 282. Or perhaps the Emir of Tarsus was naval commander. Hill *Cyprus* I, 281-2.

[132] *Abu 'l Faraj* in De Goeje *Bibl. Geog. Arab.* VI, 195-8.

[133] Vasiliev *Byzance et les Arabes* I, 132.

[134] Schlumberger *Un Empereur Byzantin au Dixième Siècle, Nicephore Phocas* (Paris 1923), p. 27-30.

[135] Carta-Raspi *op. cit.*, p. 130-33.

[136] Bury "The Naval policy of the Roman Empire in relation to the Western provinces from the 7th to the 9th Century" in *Centenario della nascita di Michele Amari* (Palermo 1910) II. Bury is mistaken, however, in claiming the Isaurians

The Imperial fleet was entrusted to a new Lord High Admiral known as the "Drungarios of the Ploimen" who seems to have served as over-all naval commander as well. Detachments of this flotilla were stationed at the island of Mitylene guarding the entrance to the Hellespont. This became perhaps the most important naval base, a check to the activities of the Cretan pirates in the Aegean.[137] It was this fleet under Nicetas Ooryphos that crippled Cretan power in the Gulf of Corinth in 879.

Probably this same menace of pirate fleets from Candia caused another change in Byzantine maritime organization—a new naval theme in the Aegean. To the earlier maritime themes of Kibyrrhaeots and the Aegean was added a third, that of Samos.[138] Kibyrrhaeotic provincial fleets were responsible for protecting the south coast of Anatolia from Arab squadrons from Tarsus and Syria, as of old. The Aegean theme protected European Aegean coasts and Samos the Asia Minor Aegean shoreline from Cretan assaults. Other less important naval forces were maintained by the themes of Hellas, Peloponnesus, Cephallonia, and Pamplagonia.

There is less information about Byzantine naval power in the West in this period. Certainly it seems to have been relatively weaker than in the earlier period. Sicily's naval forces seem never to have recovered from the disaster of 827, and it was only when units of the Eastern and Imperial fleets were sent into Western waters that Sicilian governors were able to resist Islamic forces on the sea. This probably explains better than anything else their generally defensive policy. It may also help to give an explanation of the disobedience of the Campanian cities, which had little to fear from the Byzantine Western viceroys who had insufficient naval forces to enforce their demands upon them. Calabria, considered part of Sicily down to 902, apparently had a tiny themal fleet of ten vessels.[139] Apulia had no considerable naval strength. In fact the only considerable maritime forces in the West upon

---

neglected their navy until the *late* eighth or early ninth century. Bury *East. Roman Empire*, p. 299-330. See Ch. IV on this subject.

[137] Bury *The Imperial Administrative System in the Ninth Century* (London 1911), p. 108-10.

[138] *ibid.*

[139] See Bury "Naval Policy" on this subject. The Calabrian themal fleet of ten vessels is mentioned in 877 in the request of Pope John VIII to Gregory, Governor of Calabria, for naval assistance. Gasquet *Byz. Emp.*, p. 475-82. It is also mentioned in 848 when it raided Mondello in Sicily. *Ibn al Athir* VII, 4.

which Byzantium could rely were those of Venice, supplemented at times by some from the Dalmatian coast, both of them all but autonomous after 827. Venice apparently built warships after the naval disaster of 840, and it was largely thanks to her that Apulia was cleared of Moslems at the time of Basil I.[140] No doubt in a certain sense Venice's maritime strength can be considered as a sort of autonomous Western Byzantine themal fleet—particularly after Syracuse and Sicily were lost to the Moslems.

About the time of Romanus Lecapenus the Imperial fleet and the provincial fleets, both East and West, were considerably strengthened, perhaps by the construction of much larger, more powerful warships. The raids of these flotillas in the Western seas and off Egypt show this clearly. But during the earlier part of this period the most significant thing about Byzantine naval power lies in its generally defensive character. Only the Mardaites of the Anatolian coast, who were primarily corsairs and counterparts of the Tarsus fleet they opposed, showed that aggressiveness which was characteristic of Byzantium's Islamic opponents. A study of the naval portion of Leo's *Tactica* makes this very clear. This manual shows that Byzantine fleets were trained to avoid naval action except when absolutely necessary and that they were considered more as an adjunct to land forces than as a separate arm in their own right.[141] This defensive attitude and the caution it instilled into Constantinople's naval commanders may account as much as anything else for the poor showing of Byzantium on the seas in most of the period.

Another point of interest is how slight was the effect of land warfare upon naval power during this time. The battlegrounds between Islam and Christianity in the East as in the West remained relatively stable. In the West the frontier between Islamic and Christian Spain was approximately the same in 960 as it had been in 827. In the ninth century the Kings of Castile, Leon, and Navarre inched their way gradually southwards. In the tenth the strong military forces of the Ommayids drove them back and even established a sort of primacy over these northern Spanish kinglets.[142]

In the Orient along the Anatolian frontier between the Arabs

[140] Wiel, Althea *The Navy of Venice* (London 1910), p. 15-23.
[141] Leo *Tactica*, p. 989ff.
[142] Lévi-Provençal *Hist. de l'Espagne Mussulmane*, p. 304-22.

and Byzantium the same picture is apparent. The general frontier
lines of Ommayid and early Abbassid times remained. In the first
years of the ninth century Byzantium was very much on the defensive with the disaster of Amorium in 839 representing perhaps
the lowest ebb in Constantinople's fortunes.[143] Michael III's campaigns proved much more successful and redressed the military
balance.[144] By the time of Romanus Lecapenus the tide had definitely turned. Now Byzantium was encroaching on Armenia and
Cilicia, as the Abbassid state steadily fell into the hands of warring
provincial Moslem dynasties.[145] The stage was set for Nicephorus
Phocas and John Zimisces. Neither of these developments in Spain
and Asia Minor, however, affected naval power to any extent.

Elsewhere in the Mediterranean world the same thing is true.
Italy, which had presented a military as well as a naval problem
to Constantine V and Irene, was less threatened by land forces
under the Armenian and Macedonian dynasties. The hopes of Louis
II proved illusory, and one campaign of Nicephorus Phocas in
885-886 was sufficient to establish relatively firm land frontiers in
Southern Italy. The Ottos of Germany, who were to present Byzantine forces in Italy with the same sort of problem that they had
faced with Charlemagne, were still across the Alps in the first
Reich.

The most active land danger to Constantinople in the period
appears to have come from the Bulgars and those Asiatic nomad
peoples, the Cumans and Petcheneks, who followed them across
the steppes of South Russia into the lower Danube region. Added
to them should be the Varangian Russians. Byzantium had little
military success against Bulgar rulers in the late ninth and early
tenth centuries and, despite naval support, several Byzantine
armies paid the price of disputing the field of battle with Tsar
Simeon. But naval power and a diplomacy which incited barbarian
peoples in Bulgaria's rear to attack her kept this menace in check.
Bulgar armies, lacking naval power, could never seriously threaten
the city on the Golden Horn. By 960 the Bulgarian situation had
not got out of hand, nor had it affected Constantinople's basic
naval situation vitally.[146]

[143] Bury *East. Rom. Empire*, p. 253-71.
[144] *ibid.*, p. 282-84.
[145] Runciman *Romanus Lecapenus* has an excellent account of these years.
[146] Tsar Simeon of Bulgaria's attempt to gain an alliance with both the Fatimid
ruler of Africa and the Emir of Tarsus and thus gain the sea power he lacked and

In the Moslem world the same general picture prevailed. Under both Tulunids and Ikshids, temporary land successes united the naval forces of Tarsus, Syria, and Egypt under one ruler.[147] Also, thanks to the struggle of the Tulunids for Syria and Tarsus, Byzantine naval power was freed for a time from the threat of Eastern Moslem action, which explains much of Basil I's naval success. But despite this and Fatimid attacks on Egypt and the extinction of rival Rostemid and Idrissid dynasties in Western North Africa, up to 960 land warfare in the Islamic as in the Christian world had no serious naval consequences. Perhaps the most serious development for Islam was the rise in power of the bedouin Qaramathes of Arabia, whose raids into the Fertile Crescent and Syria were steadily weakening the effectiveness of Bagdad's control over the provinces nearest to the capital of the Abbassid Caliphs. But this was to be a development whose consequences affected the later rather than the earlier portion of the tenth century.

If land campaigns had little effect upon the destinies of the peoples who surrounded the Mediterranean and Black Seas, what of the effects of the changed naval situation in this period? The vital change was the passing of the important islands of the Mediterranean into Islamic hands. Control of Crete in the East, Sicily, Malta, and Pantelleria in the center, and the Balearics in the West, with a neutralization of Sardinia and Cyprus for most of this period, had important repercussions on naval power in the Mediterranean. Practically all the major international trade routes in this sea fell into Moslem hands. Only one route was clear of threat from Islamic land and island bases. That was the route leading from the Mediterranean up the Ionian and Adriatic Seas to Venice. For thirty years even that was stopped by the Moslem bases of Bari and Tarentum. But after 875 these naval centers were captured and the Adriatic cleared. Everywhere else the narrow seas of the Mediterranean were blocked by Islamic island and advance bases—the Aegean by Crete, the Tyrrhenian by Sicily and Monte Garigliano, the Gulf of Lyons by the Balearics and Fraxinetum. Byzantium preserved, it is true, until 902 and to some extent after-

---

needed was thwarted by the interception of the African envoys by Romanus Lecapenus. This episode reveals the role played by sea power in keeping Bulgaria from overwhelming Byzantium. This importance of sea power in this period has frequently been underestimated. *Cedrenus* II, 356. Vasiliev *Vizantiya i Arabya* II, 222.

[147] Wiet *op. cit.*, p. 88-95.

wards, a hold on the straits of Messina and thus a passage from Eastern to Western Mediterranean. But its grip on these straits was uncertain, as the cooperation of Naples, Gaeta, and Amalfi with Moslem powers proved over and over again. In general it seems fair to say that by 878 Islam had reversed the position it held vis-à-vis Byzantium in the period from 747 to 827. Now Islamic peoples were the masters of the Middle Sea and its international trade routes.

This, of course, is to view this process from the standpoint of its effects on the northern shores of the Mediterranean; Islam bottling up the Byzantine and Western Christian peoples in the narrow seas she did not control. But there is another aspect which should be considered. Moslem control of important island positions had a defensive object or at least result. Tarsus and neutralized Cyprus were a defense of the Syrian coast; Crete protected Egypt; Sicily, North Africa, and the Balearics protected Spain. In the late ninth century, for the first time since 645, these Moslem coasts were safe from hostile assault.

They could also feel they were relatively self-sufficient in the important materials needed for naval construction. Sicily had ample stores of ship timber and some iron.[148] North Africa, from Tunis west, had abundant timber and excellent iron deposits, and these were exploited in this period.[149] Spain, near Tortosa, had available stands of cedar and elsewhere much oak and abundant iron.[150] Cilicia's mountains furnished excellent wood for naval construction and Alexandretta was at this time an important port shipping timber to Egypt.[151] Perhaps Crete was not so severely deforested at this time as it became later, but even if it were, abundant supplies of cedar and cypress were available on the Anatolian coast nearby. True, the coast from Damietta to Sousse was treeless and produced no iron. But this lack could be made up not only by shipments from Syria and the Islamic West, but also by trade in these commodities from Adriatic Venice, which possessed ample ship timber and nearby iron from Northern Italy and the Tyrol.[152] Islamic shipping in the Mediterranean, as distin-

[148] Ibn Hawkal *Descript. Palerm.*, p. 29.

[149] Yaqubi, p. 74. *Baladuri*, p. 66.

[150] Yakut *Mu'gām al-buldan* I, 733. *Idrisi*, pp. 231, 237-38.

[151] *Al Istakhri*, p. 63.

[152] Schaube *Handelgeschichte der Romanischer Völker, des Mittelmeergebeite bis zum der Kreuzzuge* (Munich and Berlin 1910), p. 3-26.

guished from such shipping in the Indian Ocean, did not suffer at this time from lack of materials.

At this point it might be well to consider the economic effects of this new Moslem control of the Mediterranean, and how it compared with that of Byzantium in the previous century. In the first place, it must be recognized that the term Islamic control is only a vague generality. There could not be any system of common over-all control, except in a most general sense, because there was in this period no common political and naval unity in the Moslem lands that bordered the Middle Sea. The Dar-es-Islam was a valid concept, but not in the sense of an Empire comparable to that of Augustus, Justinian, or even Leo the Isaurian.

There were, as a matter of fact, three rather distinct naval centers of Islamic power in the Mediterranean throughout this period: one in the West, one in the Center, and one in the East. Of the three probably the most important was the central nexus of Sicily and North Africa under the Aghlabids until 909 and then controlled by their Fatimid successors. Perhaps the all but independent and short-lived Bari and Garigliano pirate nests should be considered as part of this Central Moslem naval power. West of the center was the Ommayid Spanish naval system, consisting in the ninth century of a border fleet under the Emir of Saragossa and Fraxinetum. In the tenth century this system broadened to include a well-organized Spanish fleet and control over the Balearic islands. The Eastern maritime system was the most amorphous, consisting of an independent Crete and all but autonomous Tarsus, Syrian, and Egyptian fleets. Twice, under the late Tulunids and under the Ikshids, these three flotillas were combined, and Crete appears always to have had close connections with Egypt. But not infrequently, as in 904 and 935, these maritime flotillas were not united but hostile to one another.

In general, though, there was little naval friction until the time of the Fatimids in the early tenth century. Then territorial ambitions caused the Fatimids to use their power on the sea against both Eastern and Western Islamic rivals. They attacked Egypt in 914, 920, and 935, and North African kinglets and Ommayid Spain in the 950's. Twice, in 913-917 and 937-940, their own Sicilian province revolted as well. That there were three Caliphates (Cordova, Medhia, and Bagdad) in this period is a proof of the disruptive forces at work in Islam. Therefore Islamic domination of the Mediterranean in this period was not anything approaching the Byzantine dominion of the Middle Sea. Though they broke Byzantine maritime supremacy, the Moslems did not set up—in fact could not set up—anything comparable to it.

It must be admitted, however, that Islamic naval control had immense repercussions on the economic life and trade of the entire Mediterranean-Black Sea area. The first and perhaps most important beneficiaries of this change, from an economic standpoint, were North Africa and Sicily, particularly the former in the ninth century. Thanks to Moslem control of the Mediterranean—particularly of the northern circle route to Egypt and Syria by way of Sicily, Crete, and Cyprus—the North Africans increased the importance of their role as middlemen in the commerce of the Middle Sea. They came to dominate the carrying trade between East and West, and it was principally their shipping that plied the Mediterranean to Syria and Egypt to bring the spices and luxury products of the Near and Far East to North Africa and the Moslem West.

The result was a startling new prosperity in the Magreb. Nothing is more striking than a comparison between this region in the late eighth and early ninth centuries and in the period we are considering. By late Aghlabid times Tunisia had become a rich agricultural land, its southern region covered with olive trees and vineyards, its central plain producing rich harvests of grain.[153] Its industries were hardly less developed than its agrarian riches. Near the present Tunisian-Algerian border was the city of "Majjana of the Mines"—a center which produced silver, antimony, iron, and lead.[154] The ores mined in this region were processed in the Magreb, mainly at the naval base of Sousse.[155] Glass was manufactured at Kairouan, and enamelled pottery of high quality was also produced.[156] Textiles had become an important industry, and the land was well known for both its fine carpets and its *tiraz* of fine woven stuff.[157] The Aghlabid state intervened directly in industrial and commercial life. Prices and standards of manufacture were super-

[153] *Yaqubi*, p. 212-13.
[154] Al Maliki *Riyad-en Nufus* in *Idris, Revue des Etudes Islamiques* (1935), p. 303.
[155] *ibid.*, p. 305.
[156] Abu 'l'Arab *Classes des Savants de l'Ifriquiya* trans. Ben Cheneb, I, 146.
[157] Ibn Khaldun *Prolegomenes* I, 366.

vised by the state by means of codes known as *hisbas* enforced by a public official known as a *muhtasib*.[158]

The most important commercial center was Kairouan, whence grain was exported to Alexandria, slaves from the Sudan were sent to the Eastern Mediterranean lands and perhaps Spain, and olive oil from Sahil and Tripolitania was imported for reexport to Sicily and Italy.[159] Tunis was another important commercial center, as were Madkoura, Gafsa, Beja, and Laribus.[160] Gabes, at the terminus of an important Saharan route, was also important.[161] So, too, were Sfax and Sousse. The former was a center of olive oil and fishing, while Sousse was a market for olive oil and the chief marine arsenal, closely connected with Sicily.[162] The proceeds of piracy, as well as trade and industry, increased the capital of the region, and everyone from the royal family on down speculated in commodities and trade.

Particularly impressive were the public works constructed in this period, such as the aqueducts of Raqqada and Kairouan and the walls of Sfax and Sousse. The city planning of these towns dates from Aghlabid, not Roman or Byzantine, times, though the style remained very similar.[163] Kairouan's intellectual eminence and position as a holy city for scholars was another result of this prosperity.

At the time of the Fatimids the wealth of the land increased in spite of heavy taxation levied by these rulers to fill their war chests. Certainly the great wealth expended by al-Moeizz in conquering Egypt came in large part from the flourishing state of the Magreb's trade and industry both internal and foreign.[164] So important had North Africa's commerce with Egypt become by the tenth century, for instance, that a large Berber population had come to settle in and about Alexandria.[165] Risings by this group had much to do with the preliminary successes that the Fatimids had in taking Alexandria in their expeditions of 914, 920, and 935. So confident were these same rulers of their control of the seas that they built their

[158] Marçais *Berbérie*, p. 80-82.
[159] *Nuwairi* in Ibn Khaldun *Hist. des Berbères* I, 453.
[160] Marçais *Berbérie*, p. 83-84.   [161] *ibid.*
[162] *Al Bakri* trans. de Slane 2nd Ed. (Algiers 1913), p. 59.
[163] Marçais *Berbérie*, p. 85-87.
[164] The Fatimid war chest gathered for the conquest of Egypt in 969 amounted to 24,000,000 dinars in gold—an immense amount. Lane-Poole *Egypt*, p. 101-02.
[165] Wiet *Egypte Arabe*, p. 127-29.

great fortress capital, Medhia, on the shores of the Mediterranean in 915; they were the first Islamic rulers to do so.[166] The introduction of Eastern plants, such as cotton and sugar cane and saffron, into the Magreb and perhaps Sicily at about this time shows the importance of the North African connection with the Near East.[167] So, too, does the carefully organized watch-tower system along the coast by which news could be relayed by beacon fires within one day from Alexandria to Ceuta.[168]

But North Africa did more than become a prosperous commercial, industrial and agricultural region in this period—far beyond anything it had been in Byzantine, Ommayid, or even Roman times. It also exploited its African hinterland in a way no previous possessors of this area had ever done. In Aghlabid and Fatimid times caravan routes were opened up across the Sahara to abundant gold supplies and slaves to be found in the Senegal, Niger, and Sudan regions. Sidjilmasa, founded by the Rostemid rulers of Tafilet in 758, was the most important caravan entry port for this commerce. In the tenth century taxes levied on this Sudan traffic alone amounted to 400,000 dinars a year.[169] There were actually three caravan routes that led to the gold of the Sudan; the one already mentioned through Sidjilmasa to the Senegal, a middle route through the oasis of Ouargla to the neck of the Niger, and an eastern one from Djerid or Tripoli through Ghadames to the Sudan proper. The two western routes were controlled up to the middle of the tenth century by the Rostemids of Tafilet, who were generally friendly to the Ommayids of Spain.[170] Gawhar, the Fatimid general, overwhelmed this kingdom, and after 958 Tunisian rulers got control of all three routes south, making sure to keep the bedouins in good order so they could not interfere with this lucrative commerce.[171] Thus the flow of Sudan gold fertilized the Magreb from the land side just as piracy, trade, and a middleman's position in Mediterranean commerce did from the seaside. It is

[166] *Al Bakri*, p. 65-68. *Ibn al Athir* I, 314-15.
[167] Mez *Renaissance of Islam*, p. 430-40.
[168] *Al Bakri*, p. 55.
[169] Lombard, M. "L'or Musulman du VIIe au XIe Siècle" in *Annales* (1947) II, p. 149.
[170] *ibid.*, p. 150. Gautier, E. F. "L'or du Sudan dans l'histoire" in *Ann. d'Hist. Econ. et Soc.* (1935) VII, 113-23. For sources see articles by Monteuil in *Bulletin de A.O.F.* (1928-9), XI, XII.
[171] Lombard *op. cit.*, p. 151. Ibn Khaldun *Hist. des Berbères* II, 10. *Ibn Hawkal*, p. 249. *Ibn Idhari* I, 244. *Abu 'l'Arab*, p. 235.

understandable that North Africa should have been so rich, so in-dustrial, and so powerful in this period. Nor should it be a matter of surprise that Magrebi dinars, coined from its rulers' rich stores of gold, were among the most important currency in the Mediter-ranean right down to the eleventh century.

What was true of North Africa was almost as true of Egypt. In 832, five years after the conquest of Crete, its last great Coptic revolt was put down, and over a century of internal disorder came to an end.[172] Soon the land began to recover the prosperity it had known in Byzantine and early Ommayid times. This increased stability is reflected in a renewal of Egyptian influence to the South. In 854 Egypt's neighbors, the Bagas of Nubia, repudiated their tribute, massacred miners and Egyptian officers in the Nubian mountains, and plundered Esne and Edfu. A large expedition sent up the Nile, aided by a force sent to the Red Sea port of Qaser, soon reduced this region to obedience.[173] With the Nubian gold workings rendered safe, their exploitation proceeded apace, and a golden stream flowed north into Egypt, as it did further west in North Africa. Commerce as well as gold also flowed in from the south. The Nile-Red Sea canal seems to have been reopened in this period, as Masudi mentions in the early tenth century that in ships at Crete he saw teak—which could have come only over this route.[174]

The Tulunids, who ruled Egypt in the late ninth century, show by their building of a separate merchant quarter in their own city near Fostat the concern with which Egyptian rulers viewed com-merce.[175] The wealth of the land is further emphasized by the great palace of Khormarawiah with its artificial trees gilded and silvered and its mercury lake. Tulunid expansion over nearby Syria and Tarsus similarly shows the strength of Egypt. A few financial figures from this period show the same wealth. In 870 Ibn Tulun, newly established in power, sent the Caliph of Bagdad 750,000 dinars in tribute.[176] Four years later this tribute amounted to 2,200,000 dinars.[177] During his reign the land tax rose from 800,000

[172] Mez *Renaissance of Islam*, p. 254.

[173] *Al Istakhri*, p. 288. Lombard claims tribute in gold from Egypt's Copts and from Pharaoh's tombs increased Egypt's liquid gold supply in this period. Lombard *op. cit.*, p. 148-49. Lane-Poole *op. cit.*, p. 41-42.

[174] Masudi *Prairies d'Or* III, 12. Wiet *op. cit.*, p. 168.

[175] Wiet *op. cit.*, p. 109-10.   [176] Lane-Poole *op. cit.*, p. 59-60.

[177] *ibid.*

to 4,300,000 dinars, an index of rising agricultural prosperity.[178]

By the tenth century, despite some disorders in its early years, Egypt seems even more prosperous. The Eastern trade to the Indian Ocean and Far East began apparently to desert the Persian Gulf-Mesopotamia route to Ormuz and Basra and turn back to the Red Sea and Egypt. According to Muqqadasi, Aden became in this century the chief entrepot of this lucrative commerce.[179] Bagdad definitely began to decay and lose population.[180] This may account in part for Ikhshid power, which from 935 to 968 included not just Egypt itself but Syria, Tarsus, and the Hijaz with its Holy cities of Mecca and Medina as well.

Egypt's prosperity was, however, based on more than agriculture, gold from Nubia, and the revival in importance of the international trade routes passing through it from the Mediterranean and Red Sea. It was also an important industrial country. Its abundant linen and flax were made into fine *tiraz* at Tinnis, Damietta, Shala, and Dabku.[181] Cloth of gold and silver were particular specialties and brought 20,000 to 30,000 dinars a year when exported to Iraq.[182] Crimson carpets were also an important manufacture. In this period paper also made its appearance in Egypt, replacing papyrus.[183] The first paper document of Egypt's governmental service dates from 912; the last dated papyrus was used in 935.[184] In addition, Egypt was at this time noted for its fine workmanship in gold, silver, jewelry, and armor.

But the land of the Nile differed from the Magreb in one important respect. It was essentially passive in commerce—trading with foreigners rather than trading with the outside world on its own account. Alexandria was the terminus of the Western Mediterranean trade, and to it came many Magreb merchants as well as some from Venice and perhaps Constantinople.[185] Farama was the port of entry for merchants from Syria and the Eastern Mediterranean regions.[186] Perhaps one reason for this passivity was

[178] *ibid.*, p. 60-64. This prosperity was maintained under the Ikhshids. Mez *Renaissance of Islam*, p. 29-30.
[179] Masudi *Prairies d'Or* III, 7 and 43-48 echoes these views. Wiet *op. cit.*, p. 169.
[180] LeStrange, G. *Bagdad under the Caliphs*, p. 77.
[181] *ibid.*, p. 173-74.   [182] Marqrizi *Kitat* I, 177.
[183] Mez *Renaissance of Islam*, p. 467-69.
[184] Marabecek *Mitteilungen aus den Papyrus Rainer* III, 98.
[185] Mez *op. cit.*, p. 118.
[186] *ibid.*, Also see Schaube *Handelgeschichte*, p. 149.

Egypt's lack of timber. Though she imported some from Alexandretta (Fort-el-Tinnis) and Venice and tried to use some special native substitutes, it is doubtful if her timber situation was ever really satisfactory in this period.[187]

Nearby Syria and Palestine shared in Egypt's prosperity, though portions of them appear to have been adversely affected by the struggle that took place between Abbassids, Tulunids, Ikhshids, and minor dynasties of Damascus, Aleppo, and Tarsus. Tripoli, Beirut, and Tyre and other ports along the coast were stimulated by the reopening of the sea to unrestricted Islamic commerce. Syrian traders took to the sea again, though their range of trade was more local than that of the Magrebi merchants, being confined primarily to Egypt and Constantinople.[188] The prosperity in both industry and trade of such centers as Aleppo, Damascus, and Jerusalem appears to have been great.[189] One financial figure emphasizes the wealth of the land. In 908 the revenues of Syria amounted to 38,000,000 dirhems (about 2,000,000 dinars) after salaries of officials had been paid.[190] This figure closely parallels Egypt's in Tulunid times.

Conditions quite similar to those prevailing in the Eastern and Central Mediterranean are found in the Islamic West. Spain in the late ninth and tenth centuries also began to enjoy agricultural, commercial and industrial prosperity. This was in startling contrast to her stagnation in late Visigothic and early Moslem times. Agriculture was still the main economic activity. Wheat was the most important crop, though olive oil, mainly for domestic consumption, was produced in vast amounts. Cattle, sheep, and goats were very numerous.[191] Fruit trees abounded, and wine was produced everywhere and openly consumed.[192] Rice and sugar cane were cultivated on well-irrigated lands on the lower Guadalquiver near Seville and in the vicinity of Malaga.[193] Linen, grown in the

---

[187] Egypt's rulers developed a type of synthetic timber from wood of the native acacia tree placed in water and the pieces swollen together. It was never too satisfactory and was very expensive. Maqrizi I, 204. Wiet op. cit., p. 174-75.

[188] On maritime Syria see Yaqubi Geography, p. 327. On Syrian trade to Constantinople see The Book of the Prefect v, 1-5.

[189] Heyd op. cit., p. 43. Mez op. cit., p. 508-09. Al Istakhri, p. 31. See somewhat later Muqqadasi Description of Syria trans. G. LeStrange, pp. 91-92, 167.

[190] Mez op. cit., p. 126.

[191] Yakut I, 733. Lévi-Provençal L'Espagne Mussulmane au Xᵉ Siècle, p. 162-64.

[192] ibid., p. 164-67.

[193] Yakut I, 316-18.

province of Elvira,[194] was exported, as was cotton (raised near Seville) that fetched high prices in North Africa.[195] Sericulture had made its way to the region near Jaen.[196]

Industry was not neglected, in contrast to the Visigothic era. Iron deposits were exploited between Seville and Cordova at Constantine and Firris (Castillo del Hierro);[197] mercury was produced at Almaden,[198] tin at Algarve,[199] lead near Cabra,[200] silver near Murcia.[201] Textiles also were an important industry. Wool cloth was manufactured at Bocarante,[202] carpets at Chincilla and Cirena,[203] linen stuffs at Saragossa,[204] and silk at Baza and Cordova.[205] This latter city was noted also for its fine ceramics, gold and silver work and leather.[206] Toledo was an important producer of swords. Even paper manufacturing seems to have come in from the East at about this time.[207]

Spain was in this period remarkably urban, even more so than the Magreb.[208] Cordova was, under Abd-ar-Rahman III, one of the great cities of the Islamic world, noted for its culture and learning as well as its wealth. Interestingly enough, the most advanced parts of the land were in the south and southeast facing the Mediterranean, which emphasizes the role the commerce of this sea played in Spain.[209] Perhaps Spain, like North Africa, was enriched by a good deal of the gold of the Sudan, particularly that which passed at the Western caravan route to Sidjilmasa and through Morocco.[210] At any rate, it was rich enough, according to Ibn Hawkal, to provide Abd-ar-Rahman III between 912 and 951 with revenues amounting to 20,000,000 gold dinars, or over 500,000 a year.[211] This was not public wealth which matched that of the Fatimids of North Africa, the Tulunids of Egypt, or Abbassid governors of Syria, but it was very considerable.

The effects, then, of Islamic naval control of the Middle Sea

---

[194] *ibid.*, I, 227; IV, 204.   [195] *Yakut* IV, 275.

[196] *Idrisi*, p. 209. Whether it was cultivated as early as the tenth century is a difficult problem. Probably it was.

[197] *Idrisi*, p. 256. *Yakut* III, 889-90.   [198] Al Makkari *Annalectes* I, 91.

[199] Lévi-Provençal *op. cit.*, p. 179.   [200] *ibid.*

[201] *ibid.*   [202] *Idrisi*, p. 234. Al Makkari, p. 122-23.

[203] *Idrisi*, p. 237.   [204] *Yakut* III, 79.

[205] Al Makkari, p. 123.   [206] Lévi-Provençal *op. cit.*, p. 185.

[207] *Idrisi*, p. 235.   [208] Lévi-Provençal *op. cit.*, p. 179-83.

[209] Al Makkari II, 198 on chief industrial cities of Spain.

[210] It was to safeguard this route that Abd-ar-Rahman III sent his fleet to take over Centa in 931. *Ibn Idhari* II, 170.

[211] *Ibn Hawkal*, p. 73.

..ère far-reaching and important. Not only did it result in a revived international commerce along the old international trade routes from West to Eastern Mediterranean, it also resulted in a revitalized Syria and Egypt and a newly prosperous Spain, Sicily and North Africa fed by sea commerce and the gold of the Sudan and Nubia. In the Western Islamic world there was one phenomenon of even greater importance—the industrialization of regions which had been mainly agricultural in late Roman, Byzantine and early Moslem times. In this "Renaissance of Islam," as Mez rightly called it, the West was the main gainer. Newly industrial, strong in naval power, monopolizing the international Mediterranean carrying trade to the Islamic East, the Moslems of the Magreb, Sicily and to a lesser extent Spain became the heirs of the Syrians, Greeks, and Jews of the late Roman and early Byzantine period.

A second significant change in the world of Islam lies in the field of finance. It is the spread of the gold dinar east and west, as the Moslem world from the Tagus to the Indies became welded by trade into a single economic unit. About 800 the gold dinar was confined to North Africa, Syria, Egypt, and parts of Italy. By 950 it had become the international currency par excellence of the Islamic world.[212] Abd-ar-Rahman III coined gold dinars in the early tenth century and put Spain on a gold standard in place of the silver one it had followed in late Visigothic and early Moslem times.[213] Even more striking is the expansion of the gold dinar in the East. In the late ninth and early tenth centuries the silver dirhem disappeared in Iraq, Persia, and the Indian Ocean from the Malabar Coast to Madagascar.[214] Silver continued to be used, it is true, but as a local and subsidiary medium of exchange and in trade with Russia and Western Europe.[215]

Even aside from this single gold standard, the economic unity of the Islamic world is revealed in this period by the wide use of

[212] Lombard op. cit., p. 152-53.

[213] Ibn Khaldun Hist. des Berbères I, 464. C. del Rivero La Moneda Arábigo-española (Madrid 1893).

[214] Kremer Ueber das Einnahmebudget das Abbasider-Reiches (Vienna 1887), p. 6. At the same time the tax receipts of Babylonia, Khuristan, Faris and Iran are shown only in coin instead of both coin and kind. This reflects the increased prosperity. Kremer op. cit., p. 309-23.

[215] Perhaps one of the reasons for the Varangian route and its silver coinage hoards lay in the necessity of Western Europeans' trading with like silver standard regions such as Moslem Persia, Iraq and Samarkand were up to the tenth century and thus bypassing dinar and byzant areas.

similar governmental and private economic practices from Spain to Turkestan. In Egypt the use of passports, a heritage of Ommayid times, continued under the Tulunids and Ikhshids and spread to Bagdad in the East.[216] So did careful state control of exports and imports. In general, foreign merchants paid 10 per cent on the goods they imported into the land of the Nile and received a pass or visa good for one year's residence in the country.[217] The Egyptian government kept its monopoly over the *tiraz* and other products.

Fatimid North Africa, where even pilgrims to Mecca and Medina were channeled through Kairouan and were required to pay special dues to the state, had a similar system.[218] The Moslem rulers of both the Magreb and Spain carefully regulated and supervised the industries of their urban centers.[219] They even set up certain state monopolies much on the Egyptian model. The coral fishing of La Calle in North Africa[220] and the iron mines near Palermo[221] are good examples of this. Ommayid Spain, in general, appears to have had less state control than Africa and Egypt, however. These regulations do not seem to have been for the purpose of shutting off trade or of using economic weapons in a warlike fashion, as Byzantium had done earlier in the Mediterranean Sea. They were to raise revenue. And there is little indication that trade was hampered by them. It seems, rather, to have increased steadily throughout this period.

Another indication of economic unity is in the development of techniques of international banking. Banking practices became very advanced in this period. The main bankers appear to have been Persians or Basrans from Iraq, though Jewish financiers were also powerful. Checks were widely used and had Persian names.[222] So, too, were letters of credit and bills of exchange. Ibn Hawkal found that drafts on Eastern bankers payable in the West were used in place of money in the Sudan in the tenth century.[223] Money and credit were cheaper than they had been in Justinian's time,

[216] De Goeje *Internationale Handelsverkeer in de Middeleeuwi, Verslagen in Medeelinger der K. Akad. Van* (Wetenschapen, 1909), p. 265. Mez *Renaissance of Islam*, p. 41.

[217] De Goeje *op. cit.*, p. 265-66. [218] *Ibn Idhari* i, 265.

[219] Marçais *Berbérie*, p. 80. Lévi-Provençal *L'Espagne Mussulmane*, p. 187-94.

[220] Ibn Hawkal *Geog.*, p. 182. [221] Ibn Hawkal *Desc. Paler.*, p. 28-29.

[222] Mez *Renaissance of Islam*, p. 476-78.

[223] Ibn Hawkal *Geog.*, pp. 42, 70.

when interest amounted to 12 per cent. In the Islamic world the standard discount on checks and bills of exchange was generally 10 per cent.[224] Some idea of the scope of this international finance can be seen in the distribution of Persians and Basrans, who were found in every commercial center; at Jiddah (terminus of the pilgrim route), Sidjilmasa in Morocco, Tripoli, Beirut, and Egypt.[225]

Another example of Islamic unity can be seen in the extensive spread of tropical and subtropical plants of economic value throughout the Dar-es-Islam, particularly into the Western Mediterranean. The citron and the orange were brought from India to Basra and Syria after 912. Within a few years they had become plentiful in Tarsus, Antioch, Palestine, and Egypt.[226] In this period, the silkworm made its way West—from Syria to Sicily and Spain— and perhaps the orange and lemon did also.[227] Sugar cane and cotton are also found at this time in the Magreb, Spain, and perhaps Sicily.[228] Rice and saffron began to be cultivated in domains of the Caliph of Cordova.[229] The movement of paper manufacturing along the same route is an instance of the same sort. The Arabs, even more than the Romans, were responsible for the introduction of such valuable plants to the Mediterranean world and their acclimatization to the soil of these regions.[230]

The Moslem control of the Middle Sea appears to have had little deleterious economic effect upon the Byzantine world to the north. There is little evidence that the Islamic peoples applied any trade blockade or control of commerce to and from the Byzantine Empire. Considering the political divisions within Islam, no common economic program toward Constantinople could have been applied anyway, but there is no evidence of any such attempt. Raids were launched with regularity upon Byzantine shores East and West, and Crete and Sicily were wrested from Constantinople's rulers, but there were long periods of peace between raids which permitted an active trade. Throughout this period there is no evidence that the Byzantine Empire suffered any economic decline. In fact, the evidence seems to point to quite an opposite

---

[224] *Yakut* I, 385, 399.　　　　　[225] Mez *op. cit.*, p. 478.

[226] Masudi *Prairies d'Or* II, 438. Makrizi *Khitat* I, 28.

[227] *Calendar of Cordova* ed. Dozy, pp. 25, 41, 91. *Chron. of Mora Rases* in *Mem. Acad. Madrid* VIII, 37-38, 56.

[228] Mez *op. cit.*, 435-36.　　　　　[229] *Yakut* I, 773; III, 316, 318.

[230] For the best summary of this subject see Hitti *History of the Arabs*, p. 528-29.

conclusion.[231] Constantinople was still, in the late ninth and e̶
tenth centuries, a rich and powerful city, still by far the grea̶
industrial and commercial center of the Mediterranean world. Its
gold currency remained abundant and of fine quality, the international medium of exchange for its Empire and the Balkan and
Russian peoples in Constantinople's sphere of influence.[232] Its
bankers or *trapezites* found abundant profits in the financial business that the prosperity of the capital made possible.[233]

Nor did Byzantium change the basic pattern of her trade practices in this period. Trebizond remained the trade gateway
whereby the silk, spices, perfumes, and Eastern wares of the Moslem lands of Iraq and Persia reached Byzantium.[234] Cherson in the
Crimea continued as the trade entry port for Russian products and
the terminus of the overland silk route to China that the Kazars
had so long controlled. There a tax of 10 per cent was levied on all
imports.[235] The Bulgars still traded with Constantinople and perhaps with Salonika under strict controls as to passports, length of
stay, and products which they could import and export. They were
confined to special quarters during their trading visits.[236]

One interesting change in trade to the north, however, was the
appearance of Varangian Russian merchants in Constantinople.
Soon after their unsuccessful descent on the capital, they began to
trade actively with golden Tsargrad to the south. Special trade
treaties in 911 and 944 carefully regulated the conditions of this
commerce.[237] Like the Bulgars, the Russians were closely supervised, given special quarters during their stay at the Golden Horn,
and required to leave at the expiration of a specified number of
months. The exports they carried away and the imports they
brought with them were carefully regulated.[238] The increased importance of such Russian trading centers as Kiev and Novgorod
along the Varangian route testify to the importance of this trade.

[231] Lombard *op. cit.*, p. 153.   [232] *ibid.*, p. 154.

[233] *Book of the Prefect* IX, 5; X, 4. Michwitz, G. "Byzance et l'économie de
l'occident" in *Ann. d'Hist. Econ. et Soc.* (1936) IX.

[234] *Masudi* II, 3. *Al Istakhri*, p. 462.

[235] Cross, S. H. *The Russian Primary Chronicle* (Cambridge 1930), p. 159-63.
Const. Porphyr. *De Admin. Imper.*, p. 71.

[236] Runciman *The First Bulgarian Empire* (London 1930), p. 144-48. *Book of
the Prefect* IX, 6. Const. Porphyr. *De Admin. Imp.* pp. 79, 177.

[237] Heyd *op. cit.*, p. 68-73.

[238] On treatment of Russian traders in Constantinople see Cross *Primary Chronicle*, p. 150-70.

The chief products that these Rus brought to Constantinople were furs and slaves, their exports to Russia being the spices and luxury products that this great metropolis provided.

Byzantium maintained its old contacts with the Latin West through such Italian trading cities as Venice, Amalfi, and others. Only those centers which still acknowledged Byzantine overlordship were allowed to export from Constantinople the spices, perfumes and silks available there, and some of the finest grades of silk were forbidden even these merchants and the nearby Bulgarians as well.[239] Probably Constantinople's balance of trade with the West was a favorable one, since Venetian ships late in the tenth century were paying import dues of 2 gold pieces per ship at Abydos and 15 gold pieces on their exports at the same place.[240] But it would be unwise to ascribe this state of affairs wholly to definite design on the part of the Imperial government. The West had little except gold to offer in trade that Constantinople needed. The timber, iron, and slaves which were the West's principal exports were just the products that Byzantium had in abundance, the former two within her own territory, the latter easily procurable from Russia.

With the Moslem world Byzantium's commerce was most active of all. She needed the spices, perfumes, and silk they had to offer. Though Trebizond remained, in theory at least, the only entry port for Islamic products into the Empire, in practice the Emperors of Constantinople modified their trade controls directed against Moslem merchants in the Mediterranean. A concerted effort appears to have been made to draw Moslem Mediterranean commerce to Constantinople.[241] Two guilds of the capital, the fine silk importers and the spice or perfume importers, owed their existence to this trade.[242] Moslem merchants were probably the best treated foreigners at the Golden Horn, and brought to it considerable amounts of silk and linen fabrics. Syrian merchants appear to have been especially favored and brought perfumes and Bagdadi stuffs to Constantinople.[243]

[239] Lopez "Silk Industry," p. 35-40. *Book of the Prefect* ix, 6. Runciman *op. cit.*, p. 148.

[240] Lombard *op. cit.*, p. 153-4.

[241] Lopez believes this was particularly true of *Western* Moslem merchants in this period. Lopez *op. cit.*, p. 29-31. Trebizond was still the trade center for *Eastern* Moslem merchants. *Al Istakhri*, p. 462. *Masudi* ii, 3.

[242] *Book of the Prefect* v, 1-2, 4-5; ix, 6; x, 2.

[243] *ibid.*, v, 1-5.

Whether Greek merchants in turn frequented Islamic ports in the Mediterranean in any considerable numbers is more difficult to answer. It is well, however, to note that there was a Greek merchant quarter—whether native or foreign it is impossible to say—in that portion of old Cairo built by the Tulunids.[244] And in 954 the Byzantine raid on the Delta of the Nile was followed by a popular massacre of all the Rum in Egypt.[245] Both of these suggest an active trade with the land of the Nile. In the early tenth century, when Byzantine naval power again became active in the Western Mediterranean, there is a mention of Greek merchants trading with Arles in 921.[246] Whether these were Eastern or Italian Greeks, however, is not made clear. In general, however, this period seems to have seen a somewhat freer trade allowed by Constantinople with the Moslem lands of the Middle Sea than was the case in the previous century.

There was, however, little relaxation of strict governmental economic controls. To a greater extent than was the case in Moslem Egypt and North Africa the Imperial Byzantine system called for strict regulation of industry. The *Book of the Prefect* reveals again and again the extent of this minute supervision. Mines, quarries and saltworks remained regalian rights.[247] The export of certain grades of fine silks and brocades and even their manufacture were under control of the government.[248] The sale of grain in the capital and perhaps other centers was carefully regulated.[249]

There seems little reason for assuming that Byzantium's trade balance with the Islamic world was unfavorable. Her silks, brocades, and fine industrial products were as prized in the East as in the West. But it does seem probable that her trade with Europe and Russia was more profitable to her than that with her Moslem neighbors. The richness of Constantinople in this period and the

---

[244] Wiet *Egypt Arabe*, p. 109.   [245] *ibid.*, p. 147-8.

[246] Ganshof "Les ports de Provence," p. 35-36. This is about the time that Byzantine naval forces were active off Fraxinetum, so it seems quite possible that Byzantine merchants were present in this area too. Dupont, A. *Les relations commerciales entre les cités maritimes de Languedoc et les cités d'Espagne et d'Italie* (Nimes 1942), p. 22.

[247] Andréadès "Byzance, Paradis de Monopole" in *Byzantion* ix, 171-81.

[248] *ibid.* On continuing Byzantine control of trade and persons into Moslem lands see the story of St. Elia of Castrogiovanni, who traveled freely in Moslem lands only to be arrested as a spy in Byzantine Italy, in *Acta Sanctorum* 17 Aug. Amari *Storia* i, 554-56.

[249] *Book of the Prefect* xviii, 24.

fullness of her treasury all point to a well ordered prosperity quite on a par with that enjoyed by Spain, Africa, Egypt, and Syria.

One of the most important things about the economic life of Byzantium at this time was its passive character from the standpoint of international commerce. Already strongly marked in the eighth century, the passivity of Constantinople and the Empire became even more marked in the ninth and early tenth centuries. Like Egypt, which it greatly resembled economically, it was an empire traded with rather than trading on its own account. Russians, Bulgars, Italians, and Arabs made the city of the Golden Horn the trade mart of the world, but they also controlled practically all its foreign commerce. Though the early years of the tenth century may have seen some revival of Byzantine merchant shipping, in general its mariners ceased to figure importantly in foreign trade. Even the Black Sea commerce, up to this period the private preserve of Greek shippers, was invaded by the Varangian Rus who carried their wares to Constantinople.[250]

It was this conservative, passive maritime tradition, fostered no doubt by the very strictness of the Imperial government's trade controls, which helps explain important changes in land holding in the Empire in the tenth century. The wealth which trade and industry brought into the Empire found few investment opportunities in trade and commerce. Therefore, there was a tendency for the rich, particularly the nobility, to invest their capital in land at a time when Moslems across the Middle Sea were following quite the reverse process.[251] The result was a steady encroachment upon the free holdings of the peasantry who formed the backbone of the army. Emperors like Constantine Porphyrogenitus and Roman Lecapenus tried by decree to halt this dangerous development and to protect the lands of free peasants from their richer neighbors and even grant the peasantry certain rights of preemption over the lands of the aristocracy.[252] In vain. More and more in the tenth century the peasantry lost their lands to the aristocracy

[250] Heyd op. cit., p. 52-6, has noticed that "in general the Byzantines were not interested in spreading their commerce into neighboring lands." Diehl has remarked on the same thing. Diehl Byzance Grandeur et Decadence, p. 96-99.

[251] For an excellent summary see Charanis "The Social Structure of Byzantium" in op. cit., p. 52-55. Also Neumann, C. Die Weitstellung des Byzantinischen Reiches aus den Kreuzzüge (Leipsig 1895). On the Arab aristocracy's speculations in North Africa see Nuwairi in Ibn Khaldun trans. de Slane I, 435-36.

[252] Jus Graeco-Romanum ed. von Lingenthal III, 246-47, 292-96.

by sale or force. Great estates of families like the Comneni and others began to cover Asia Minor.[253] Had there been investment possibilities in anything else but land, this development, which was to be so dangerous to the military security of Byzantium, might not have taken place.

Important regions of the Latin West, however, present at this time a very different economic picture from that of the rest of the Mediterranean world. In startling contrast to the humming cities and busy trade of Moslem Spain and North Africa, the Christian coastline from Barcelona to the Tiber was dead and all but deserted. Whatever trade and naval power had existed in these regions at the time of Charlemagne and Louis the Pious had by this time almost disappeared. Barcelona, Narbonne, Marseilles, Genoa, and even Pisa remained sparsely inhabited centers hardly able to protect themselves from the periodic raids of Moslems from Spain or from their advance base at Fraxinetum.[254] Almost equally unimportant, both agriculturally and commercially, were the islands of Sardinia and Corsica, which shared little in the prosperity enjoyed by nearby Sicily, the Balearics, and Spain.[255]

Undoubtedly Moslem attacks were partially responsible for this decadence, but it is hard to find in them a final explanation, which seems to lie in other causes. Perhaps the change in trade routes which occurred at the time of Byzantine domination continued after Moslem naval power replaced that of Constantinople. Cities like Amalfi, Gaeta, Salerno, and Naples on Italy's west coast, which had been important in the eighth century, continued so in the ninth and tenth. They not only maintained the advantage of their old Byzantine connection, which the other Western cities lacked, but were powerful enough to deal economically with the Moslems on relatively equal terms. The same is true of Venice in the Adriatic. Though this city supported Constantinople in clearing the entrance of the Adriatic of Moslem corsairs at the time of Basil I and continued to acknowledge Byzantine sovereignty and con-

[253] Nicephorus Phocas and Basil II repealed these laws of earlier rulers. *Jus Graeco-Romanum* III, 299, 303.

[254] On activities of Moslem pirates of Fraxinetum see Tyler, J. E. *Alpine Passes* (Oxford 1930), p. 55-56. On Languedoc's commercial unimportance in this period see Schaube *op. cit.*, p. 100 and Dupont *op. cit.*, p. 24; on the Ligurian coast of Italy see Lopez "Orig. du Capit. Gén.," p. 434-41.

[255] On the lack of importance of Sardinia at this time see Carta-Raspi *op. cit.*, p. 149-91. On Corsica, Cesari-Rocca and Villat *Histoire de la Corse* (Paris 1916), p. 39-41.

nections, her merchants were probably benefited by the Moslem sea supremacy.[256] Thanks to it, they were able to trade widely with Islamic lands undisturbed by Byzantine objections. The three products, iron, weapons, and timber, which they had in abundance for export, were particularly needed along Moslem coasts from Palestine to Medhia. In addition, the illicit slave trade brought their merchants huge profits in the Islamic slave marts from Cordova to Bagdad, where these human chattels were particularly valued in the harems and bodyguards of Moslem rulers.[257]

The Campanian cities like Naples were in even closer touch than Venice with their Islamic neighbors and more often than not in actual alliance with them. They protected and helped outfit Moslem pirates who preyed on their fellow Italians.[258] They also were nothing loth to serve as slavers, and they exchanged both slaves and textile products (produced at home or procured from Constantinople) for olive oil, eastern wares, and manufactured products available at Palermo, North Africa, and Spain.[259]

In the rest of Southern and Central Italy, Saracen pirates and adventurers did much damage on the coast and far inland between 840 and 886, but it is possible to overestimate the economic results of these devastations. By 876, when Apulia had been cleared of Islamic pirates, the Adriatic and east coasts of Italy ceased to be disturbed. And Nicephorus Phocas's campaigns in 885 and 886 ended the Moslem menace in all but the Garigliano region. Its liquidation finally cleared this region of Saracen depredations in 916.

The result was that Southern Italy fully recovered its prosperity by the tenth century. Trade was very active and both Moslem gold tarims and gold byzants circulated freely, particularly the former.[260] Even more significant was the economic development

---

[256] Diehl *Venise*, p. 18-21. Heyd *op. cit.*, p. 110-12.

[257] On the slave trade of Venice in the 8th century see *Liber Pont.* I, 443 and *Codex Carol.* ed. Gelzer epis. LXXV. In the ninth century, Muratori *Annalii d'Italia*, p. 960. In the tenth century, Schaube *op. cit.*, p. 8. Amari *Storia* II, 199-200. Mez *Ren. of Islam*, p. 159.

[258] *Chron. Salern.* in *MGH Script.* III, 526. Heyd *op. cit.*, p. 89-90. Gasquet *Byz. Emp.*, p. 420-23. Amari *Storia* II, 521-23.

[259] Gay *Italie Mer.*, p. 247-53.

[260] *Regii Neapolitani Monumenta* (Naples 1845), pp. 129, 143, 178. Monneret de Villard "La Moneta in Italia durant l'alto medio eva" in *Rev. Ital. di Num.* (1919-20) XXXII-XXXIII. Bloch, M. "Le problème d'or au moyen âge" in *Ann. d'Hist. Econ. et Soc.* (1933) V, 2-3.

of Venice and the Po Valley. Thanks to a special treaty with Lothair, Venice became in 840 the privileged supplier of this region with the wares of the East. She was given particular trading rights at Pavia and elsewhere in the upper Adriatic.[261] Every ruler of Northern Italy after this time renewed this charter with the city on the lagoons.[262] After Comacchio had been eliminated in the late ninth century, Venice had no commercial rivals in the international trade of this region.

From Pavia and other towns of Lombardy, the Eastern products that Venice and others supplied crossed the Alps to Germany and Northern France. The routes followed were the Alpine passes, principally the Septimer, Monte Cenis, and the Great St. Bernard.[263] In 911, during a visit of Conrad I to St. Gall, there was mention of silks imported from Italy.[264] In 949, Otto I sent Luitfred, a Mainz merchant, as his ambassador to Constantinople over this route and by way of Venice.[265] The extent of this commerce can be seen by tolls levied just south of the Great St. Bernard by Giso, Bishop of Aosta, in 960. They included taxes on many objects of trade— arms, swords and lances, shields and armor, salt, lead, tin, copper, hawks, and axes.[266] In 917, Ekhard of St. Gall mentions a retinue of merchants who passed his monastery returning from Italy to their homes.[267] And in 947 this traffic had become important enough for the abbot of this monastery to set up a market conveniently situated for this trade.[268] The abundant spices available at Cambrai and Mainz at this time probably travelled over these Alpine routes. The Brenner, easiest of the passes from Lombardy to Germany, seems to have been little used in this period because Hungarian interference made it impractical. Not until 955 did Otto's victory over the Hungarians clear this route.[269] Similarly, Moslem interference with traffic over the passes from Italy to

[261] Cessi "Pacta Veneta" in *Arch. Ven.* n. s. (1928-9) v-vi. Diehl *Venise*, p. 18. Cessi *Venezia*, I, 41-43.

[262] Solmi *L'amministrazione finanziaria del Regno Italico*, p. 80-110.

[263] Tyler *Alpine Passes*, p. 147-48. On blocking of commerce to France through the Alpine passes by Moslems of Fraxinetum see Tyler, *op. cit.*, p. 55-7. Sabbe "Importation des Tissus" in *Revue Belge* (1935) XIV, 813-23.

[264] Heyd *op. cit.*, p. 86. Schaube *op. cit.*, p. 89.

[265] Heyd *op. cit.*, p. 80. Luidprand *Antapodesis* trans. Wright, p. 207.

[266] Besson *Mémoires du Diocèse de Genève*, p. 473. Oehlman "Die Alpenpasse im Mittelalter" in *Jahrbuch für Schweiz geschichte* III, 248-9.

[267] Schaube *op. cit.*, p. 92.   [268] *ibid.*

[269] Tyler *op. cit.*, p. 144-5.

France limited severely the commerce passing over the passes in that region.[270] Thus it is apparent that some important trade did continue to flow into Europe from the Moslem and Byzantine East up to 960 by way of Venice and Alpine routes.

Perhaps this partly explains why Germany in the late ninth and early tenth centuries kept some form of order and government, and never suffered from the same sort of feudal anarchy that affected France. The Germans kept an important trade connection with the East through Italy, not to mention the Baltic, while France was less fortunate. Yet it must be admitted that the scope of this trade was severely limited. The Alpine routes might be satisfactory for luxury Eastern wares, such as silks, brocades, and spices, and over them arms and slaves could be shipped for export from Venice, but not for *bulk* export. Such commerce as this route provided might allow Venice and Lombardy to remain on the gold standard and enjoy some substantial prosperity, but it could not change the economic pattern of events in the rest of Western Europe. Not until easier and more accessible routes, like the Rhone Valley, were commercially practical again could Western Europe leave behind its agricultural localism and its Carolingian silver standard and become integrated economically with the more advanced Islamic and Byzantine worlds of the Mediterranean.

It must not be supposed, however, that the Adriatic-Alpine trade route was the only one whereby the West communicated with the East, though it was by far the most important one. Some commerce did follow the route to Southern France and up the Rhone Valley, though it was only a trickle. Verdun continued in this period to be a center of trade in eunuchs with Moslem Spain, and Jews continued to follow an overland route in the late ninth century that led down the Rhone Valley and through Languedoc to the Spanish border.[271] In the tenth century there was some stirring of commerce along the coasts of Northwestern Italy and Southern France. Arles apparently had some outside commerce in 921.[272] And the Fatimid raid of 935 in the Tyrrhenian destroyed

---

[270] *ibid.*, p. 154-57.

[271] It is interesting to note that the sea route to Spain was not used in this period in the slave trade. *Agob. Lugdun. Archepis. Epistolae* in *MGH Epis.* v, 185. *Mir St. Bert.* in *Acta Sanct. Bol.*, Sept. 1, p. 597. The same is true in the middle of the tenth century. *Vita Joh. Abb. Gor.* in *MGH Script.* iv, 369-75.

[272] Ganshof *op. cit.*, p. 35-6.

ships off Sardina and Corsica. Even Spain may have had a sea connection with northern Europe, as is suggested by the coinage of 2,000 *mancusi* by the English crown in 955.[273]

In general, however, the Moslems of North Africa and Spain appear to have traded very little with the Latin West, preferring to leave such commerce in the hands of the already established Italian cities and of the Jews who plied the roads from Northern France and Prague to the Spanish slave marts. The single Moslem traveler who visited Mainz in the early tenth century and described with surprise the wares exposed for sale there seems to have been an exception to the rule.[274] Perhaps the exploitation of Saharan and Eastern commerce took all the energies of the Islamic traders. Perhaps their own raids on Christian coasts and such pirate nests as Fraxinetum interfered with the possibilities of commerce in this direction.

Yet there is no evidence that the Moslems blockaded Latin Europe any more than they did Byzantium. This idea should be dismissed as a myth. If there is any doubt of this fact, it can be dispelled by an examination of the pilgrim traffic to the Holy Land in this period. It was uninterrupted by Islamic rulers and even increased in volume.[275] Even such a pirate ruler as the Soudan of Bari was eager to help a Western pilgrim on his way to Palestine by making available not only shipping but also a special pass to assist him in Egypt.[276]

In general, then, the years 827 to 960, those decades of Islamic control of the Middle Sea, saw many economic changes in Mediterranean trade and commerce take place. They saw a revitalizing of many older trade routes decadent in the period of Byzantine naval domination. They marked the coming of age of North Africa, Spain, and Sicily as important industrial areas tapping their mines, developing their manufacturing and agriculture and dominating

---

[273] *Lib. Monarch de Hyde* ed. Edwards in *Roll Series*, 154.

[274] Sabbe "Quelques Types de Marchands des IXe et Xe siècles" in *Revue Belge* (1934) XIII, p. 178-80.

[275] De Goeje *op. cit.*, p. 265. It must be admitted that both the hostilities between Spanish Ommayids and Carolingians, which did not end until 864, and the activities of the Moslem pirates of Fraxinetum from 888 throughout this period did interrupt commerce from Northwestern Italy and Southern France. So too did the fact that all the Arab world of the Mediterranean, including Spain after the early tenth century, was on a gold standard, while Western Europe (outside of southern Italy and the Po Valley) was on a silver standard. See Bloch "Problem d'Or," p. 7-9.

[276] Wiet *Egypt Arabe*, p. 86.

the Mediterranean trade to the East and the caravan routes to the gold of the Sudan. This period also saw Egypt and Syria again prosperous; and it saw a return of commerce to the Red Sea. It marked a great development of the whole Islamic world into a single economic unit with a common gold currency accepted from Persia to Spain. In this prosperity Byzantium shared fully, enlarging her own trade with Varangian Russia and reaching Europe through Venice and older Italian cities and the Black Sea-Baltic trade route.

In the Latin West most of Italy shared in this prosperity, selling perhaps more to the Arabs and buying more from Constantinople. Germany and to some extent Northern France and England were not unprosperous. Only Southern France, Northwestern coastal Italy, and the Western Islands of Sardinia and Corsica remained economically decadent. Lacking naval power and deficient in products wanted in either Islamic or Byzantine lands, these regions were to remain for almost a century more in the economic doldrums.

Yet this period was one of the most vital in the history of the Mediterranean world. The reversal of the older order of things and the transformation of the Islamic West into an industrial region, dominating in conjunction with the Italian cities the carrying trade of the Middle Sea, was the first step in the domination of this region by Western powers. It was a significant beginning for a future which was to see Western Europe the final arbiter of Mediterranean destiny.

6. The Age of Transition

In the last years of the tenth century and the first half of the eleventh, important changes took place in the pattern of maritime strength in the Mediterranean. The Fatimid Caliphs of Kairouan, after more than fifty years of unsuccessful attempts, finally managed to move East and take over most of the patrimony of the Ikhshids in Egypt, Syria and the Hijaz. They thus linked the naval power of the Moslem Eastern Mediterranean with the North African-Sicilian nexus in the center. At the same time Byzantium was also on the move. Emperors of Constantinople seized Crete, Cyprus, Tarsus, and Northern Syria, as well as other parts of Western Asia and the Balkans. Hence they confronted the Fatimids of Cairo with significant opposing maritime strength in the Eastern waters of the Middle Sea.

While these changes were affecting the East, the central Mediterranean did not stay static from a naval standpoint. When al-Moeizz left Kairouan for his new capital, Cairo, he split his Western domains into two main parts. He left the Kalbites as hereditary viceroys of Sicily and the Ziridites in the same position in North Africa. To these two were added in the early eleventh century two more, the Hammadites, who set themselves up as autonomous rulers in Algeria and another family who did the same in Tripoli. At first this subdivision of the Fatimid Western holdings and the internal disputes that followed had little effect on the character of Islamic maritime strength. By 1025, however, when Byzantium turned West from Syrian and Bulgarian wars, it was apparent that serious maritime weaknesses had developed for Islam in the central Mediterranean. Both Sicily and North Africa's naval power had declined dangerously—a point which was to be significant for the future.

In the West a similar situation came to prevail on the Moslem side. Ommayid Spain, so strong in the tenth century, after the death of Almansor rapidly collapsed into a series of petty quarreling Moslem principalities and lost its maritime strength. As this happened, the Latin West began to stir from the disorder and weakness it had known since the death of Charlemagne. The Ger-

[183]

man Emperors, Otto I, II, and III, at the head of Teutonic armies, crossed the Alps into Italy filled with grand designs and dreams of an Empire which would drive Arabs and Byzantines from Italy and Sicily. Their efforts proved abortive, as Charlemagne's had more than a century earlier. But they pointed the way of the future. At the same time in 972 the Moslem pirates of Fraxinetum on the shores of Provence and in the Alps were driven out, and this portion of Europe was freed from their depredations.

By the early eleventh century this new vigor was reflected in the West in the activities of Genoa and Pisa along the Northwest coast of Italy. Fleets from these cities put to sea for the first time in two centuries to dispute Western waters with Moslem maritime powers. The same drive is reflected in the increased naval strength of Venice in the Adriatic Sea. Italian mariners were beginning to claim their naval birthright. In addition to Italian naval initiative, other evidences of Western aggressiveness had become apparent. Bands of feudal adventurers from Normandy and France began to cross the Alps into Italy and the Pyrenees into Spain eager for booty and plunder at the expense of the older established Byzantines and Moslems.

It was, in short, an age of transition. Moslem control of the Mediterranean was not yet ended, though it was being disputed with renewed vigor by the Byzantines and the Italians of Venice, Genoa, and Pisa. The old order was passing, but the new had not yet come into being.

It was the Byzantine Empire—which, since 645, had never ceased to dispute the waters of the Middle Sea with the peoples of Islam—which began the new offensive against Moslem maritime power. Using the new fleet which had been steadily strengthened since the time of Romanus Lecapenus, the Imperial government of Constantinople launched a great assault in 960 upon the Moslem pirate stronghold of Crete. The naval expedition that protected and carried the army to Crete was a formidable one, numbering 2,000 warships and 1,360 supply ships. Some of the warships were of tremendous size, carrying 250 rowers and four banks of oars. Others were specially constructed landing craft which, like the LST's of World War II, were able to land on beaches and, using a sliding ramp, disembark heavily armed cavalry on the strand. The navy took care to protect the expedition carefully, and squadrons were dispatched to the East to guard against naval help from

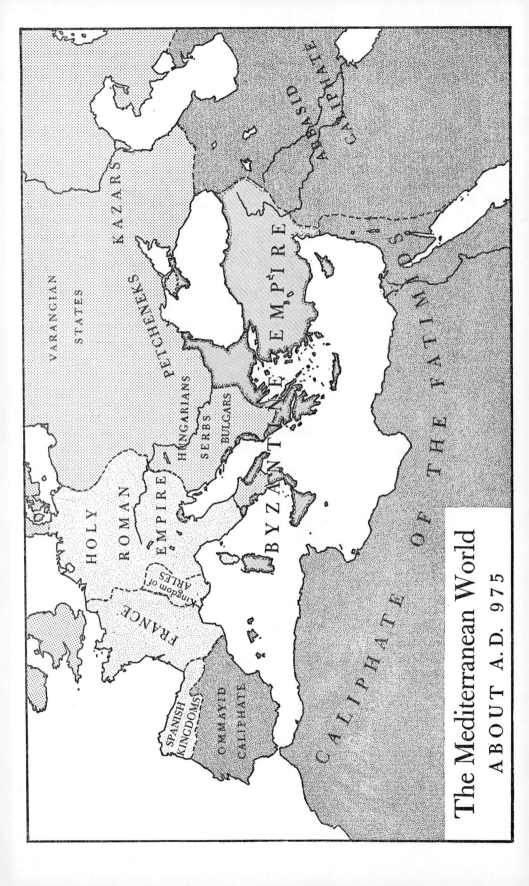

The Mediterranean World
ABOUT A.D. 975

Moslem Syria and Eastern fleets. There followed a sharp, hard struggle, but the generalship of Nicephorus Phocas proved brilliant, and in 961 Candia, the Moslem stronghold, fell to the invaders.[1] At last the Aegean was freed of its Islamic stopper.

The loss of Crete was keenly felt in the Islamic world, particularly Egypt. Kafar, the Ikhshid viceroy of the land, hastened to strengthen his naval forces with new additions. The hastily built Egyptian ships did not, however, prove very seaworthy, and anti-Christian massacres showed the temper of the Moslem population, who blamed the Christians for the poor construction of the craft.[2] A Byzantine flotilla appearing off Farama added to Egyptian fears. These fears proved justified, for in 963 Nicephorus Phocas, now Emperor, turned toward Tarsus and Cyprus with his army and fleet. An Egyptian squadron of 36 vessels was destroyed off the island and Cyprus, like Crete, came into full Byzantine possession.[3] The Egyptian fleet of the Ikhshids was apparently wiped out in this engagement and ceased to be a factor in the Mediterranean.

While Byzantium's sea power was thus active, her land power moved against Cilicia. By 965 Nicephorus Phocas's armies had occupied Tarsus, and this important maritime district was added to the Byzantine Empire.[4] The way to Syria lay open. By 968 Constantinople's armies had penetrated deep into the land. The interior cities of Hama and Homs submitted, as did the ports of Tortosa, Marakia, Djabala and Latakia. Only Tripoli held out, protected by immense walls.[5] In 969 Antioch fell, and Aleppo paid tribute.[6] North and coastal Syria seemed about to return to the allegiance they had thrown off more than three centuries previously. Within a decade the Eastern Moslem naval power of Crete, Tarsus, Egypt and much of the Syrian coast was eliminated.

Constantinople's naval efforts were not, however, confined to the East. In Western waters likewise Byzantium took the offensive. A serious Christian uprising on the island of Sicily gave opportunity for intervention. In 963 Taormina was recovered by Byzantine forces.[7] In 965 Rametta was occupied as well.[8] In that same year a large fleet sent by Constantinople appeared on the

---

[1] Schlumberger *Nicephore Phocas*, p. 41-49.
[2] Wiet *Egypte Arabe*, p. 147.
[3] *ibid.*, p. 148. Schlumberger *op. cit.*, p. 387-89.
[4] Schlumberger *op. cit.*, p. 390-412.   [5] *ibid.*, p. 580-609.
[6] Wiet *op. cit.*, p. 151-52. Michael the Syrian *Chron.* ii, 551.
[7] Schlumberger *op. cit.*, p. 354-56.   [8] *ibid.*

scene. It met a strong opposing Sicilian-African Fatimid squadron in the Straits of Messina. What followed proved that Constantinople's naval forces, though successful against Eastern Moslem fleets, were no match for Western Islamic navies. In this "Battle of the Straits," as in earlier engagements in these waters in 859 and 888, the Byzantines were disastrously defeated. Using something like Greek fire and huge grappling hooks, the Moslems battered the Byzantine flotilla and ended the attempt to seize control of the island of Sicily.[9] But peace was soon concluded between the two adversaries in 967.[10] The Fatimids were glad to conclude hostilities because al-Moeizz, Caliph of Kairouan, was preparing to move on Egypt. Thanks to Byzantine conquests in the East in Crete, Cyprus, Tarsus, and Syria, al-Moeizz realized that Egypt was ripe for the plucking. He wanted friendly Byzantine neutrality. Constantinople welcomed peace with the Fatimids because, in addition to her naval loss in 965, she had serious problems in other regions. Syrian campaigns were calling for her full attention, and Otto I, recently crowned Holy Roman Emperor in Rome, was beginning to cause serious concern with his pretensions in Italy.

The Fatimids made their great move east in 969 with a tremendous army and fleet under al-Moeizz's brilliant general Gawfar. Egypt fell with hardly a battle, and in addition Palestine, Southern Syria, and the Hijaz acknowledged Fatimid overlordship.[11] A Shiah Caliph finally controlled the holy cities of Mecca and Medina. Fatimid forces even pressed on to test Byzantine strength with an attack on Antioch, just recently taken by the forces of Constantinople. At this point troubles afflicted the victorious Fatimids. The bedouin Caramathes, Shiah in their religious beliefs, whose attacks on Ikhshid Syria had, along with Byzantine advances, prepared the way for the Fatimid victory of 969, turned against the Caliph of Cairo and Kairouan. They sent their forces into Syria in the rear of the Fatimid forces.[12] The Syrian coastal cities joined the Caramathes and defeated a Fatimid flotilla off Jaffa.[13] By 972 Syrian ships were attacking Tinnis on the Delta,[14]

[9] *Cedrenus* II, 353, 360. Ibn al Athir I, 363-66. Abu al Fida *Annales Moslemici* II, 448. Ibn Khaldun *Hist. des Fatamids* in de Slane *Hist. des Berbères* II, 529.

[10] *Nuwairi* II, 134. Amari *Storia* II, 318-22.

[11] Ibn Hammad *Hist. des rois Obaidites* ed. Vonderheyden, p. 64-68. Quatremère *Vie de Moeizz*, pp. 67, 82.

[12] Lane-Poole *Egypt*, p. 113.   [13] Wiet *op. cit.*, p. 180-2.

[14] *ibid.*, p. 183.

while Druze nomadic tribesmen swarmed across the Palestinian frontier into Egypt. Al-Moeizz quickly came East to take over personal command and landed in Egypt in 973. A third vast Caramathian host reached the outskirts of the new Fatimid capital of Cairo before it was turned back. It was pursued back into Arabia, by the victorious army of the Fatimids, and Syria and Palestine were recovered.[15]

Byzantium's naval forces did little against the Fatimids in this period because of the insecurity of her northern borders. Not only was the Fatimid attack on Antioch largely ignored, but John Zimisces, who succeeded Nicephorus Phocas as Emperor, hastened to make peace with the Ottos in Italy. He ignored their stabs into Calabria and attacks on Naples and Tarentum and married Theophano, a Byzantine princess, to Otto II in 970.[16] It was the Russian menace which alarmed Constantinople. A great expedition of Sviatoslav of Kiev had moved to the Danube. In 972 John Zimisces paraded Byzantine naval strength in the Golden Horn and sent it north against the Russians. Sailing up the Danube, it scattered Russian ships and blockaded their rear. The army blockaded the Russian host on the land side. After a long siege, the Varangians were forced to surrender, and Sviatoslav was killed by the Petcheneks at the Dnieper rapids while on his way back to Kiev.[17] The Russian menace ceased for almost two decades to concern Constantinople.

Then Zimisces turned to Syria. There was need of his presence there. The Fatimids had become more aggressive in their encroachments upon Byzantium's territory. In 975 Beirut had been retaken, and a Byzantine naval force badly defeated off Tripoli.[18] Zimisces's appearance changed things. With his army he swept through Syria all the way down into Palestine. Abu al Fida, the Arab historian, says that all maritime Syria, like the regions of the Euphrates, found itself without defenses against the Rum. Nobody defended the land. Even Damascus paid tribute.[19] Only Tripoli, defended by its walls and the Egyptian fleet, remained unconquered. But the submission of this portion of central and maritime Syria to Constantinople was but momentary. The valorous

[15] *ibid.*, p. 184-86. Schlumberger *John Zimisces* (Paris 1896), p. 222-25.

[16] *Chron. Salern.* in *MGH Script.* III, 556.

[17] Schlumberger *op. cit.*, p. 113-49.

[18] Lane-Poole *Egypt*, p. 114.   [19] Wiet *Egypte Arabe*, p. 191.

John Zimisces died in 976, and Fatimids and Caramathes came back into the land. By 978 all Southern Syria up to Antioch and Aleppo was under the rule of the Caliphs of Cairo, though Sunnite, anti-Shiah feeling and constant disorders made large sections of the land all but autonomous and free of effective Egyptian control.[20]

Byzantium's failure to follow up her earlier successes in Syria was due to more than the caliber of Moslem opposition. It was linked to domestic difficulties. The first years of Basil II's rule were not easy ones. They were marked by the terrible revolts of Bardas Skleros in 976 and of Bardas Phocas in 987 which shook the Empire to its foundations. These revolts were in large measure occasioned by attempts of Basil II to protect the free peasantry against the encroachments of the large landowners, who were more and more taking over their land and thus destroying the military strength upon which the Empire depended. They were in a sense, then, revolts of the border aristocracy, favored by Nicephorus Phocas and John Zimisces, against the central bureaucracy which was attempting to curb their power.[21] But it is interesting to note that there was another factor in these revolts—discontent in the provincial fleets. In both of these revolts the provincial Asiatic flotillas supported the rebels. As in 695, 727, and in the rising of Thomas the Slav in the early ninth century, the provincial fleets sailed on the capital.[22] The dissatisfaction of this portion of the navy had other causes than those which animated the large landholding aristocracy of Asia Minor. The clue is perhaps to be found in a decree by John Zimisces in which he forbade the Venetians in 971 to carry iron, arms, and ship timber to Moslem domains.[23] Byzantium was thus attempting, in its struggles with the Fatimids, to hamper its opponent's naval power by stopping essential maritime supplies from reaching their shores. There can be little doubt that the Venetians were not alone in receiving such orders, but that they were also applied to those regions of the Empire which the Emperors controlled more directly. The possession of Cyprus, Tarsus, and the north Syrian coast enabled the authorities at Constantinople to stop exports of timber to Egypt from the area. Further-

[20] *ibid.*, p. 192-93.
[21] Charanis "Soc. Struct. of the Later Roman Empire," p. 54-56.
[22] Schlumberger *Basil II*, i, 386-87.
[23] Tafel et Thomas *Fontes Rer. Austriae, Soc. de Venise* i, 25-28. Dandolo *Chron.*, pp. 167, 171.

more, recapture of these same places gave their naval forces a chance to control trade along the circle route to Syria and Egypt, the main pathway of commerce from the Western Mediterranean to the Near East. Just as similar decrees of Leo V had been followed by the revolt of the provincial fleets in support of Thomas the Slav, so one hundred and fifty years later similar prohibitions by John Zimisces saw the provincial fleets rise against Constantinople in the revolts of Bardas Skleros and Bardas Phocas. This cannot be mere coincidence. It seems to point to the fact that trade prohibitions enforced by Constantinople destroyed valuable markets in Moslem ports upon which depended the prosperity of the maritime districts which supported the themal fleets. They thus joined in rebellion against the government responsible for these policies.

Interestingly enough, the results were identical with those of 727 and 823. The themal fleets, particularly in 987, reached the Hellespont and besieged Abydos. As in the earlier revolts, however, the Imperial fleet at the Golden Horn stayed loyal and used Greek fire to scatter the rebellious provincial naval levies.[24] The revolts failed in their object, and by 989 Basil II was completely in control of his Empire again. But Byzantine naval strength along the vital Mediterranean coasts opposing Islam was seriously weakened by the losses of themal ships during these revolts. They could not be made good at once, and, until they were, Fatimid naval forces in Syria and Egypt had a definite advantage over their Byzantine maritime opponents.

The unfortunate effects of these revolts upon Byzantine naval strength were heightened by another circumstance—new difficulties in the Black Sea. Kiev, under its new ruler Vladimir, again became threatening. Constantinople had promised Anne, a Byzantine princess, to the Russian prince, but showed some reluctance in fulfilling the engagement to deliver the young lady. The impatient Vladimir, tired of waiting, decided in 989 to hasten the marriage by the seizure of the Crimea and Cherson, its important Byzantine port. The arrival of the Princess ended hostilities and ensured a long period of peace between Kiev and Byzantium, but naval forces in the Black Sea were necessary to make sure that the Varangian Rus remained friendly.[25]

[24] Schlumberger *op. cit.*, p. 395-6.
[25] *Cedrenus* II, 501.

Thus it was that the Fatimid Caliphs were not menaced on the sea or on the land in Syria during most of the period between 975 and 995. Despite their unpopularity in this province and difficulties caused by the raids of the Caramathes, they were able to maintain their position. This also explains why Byzantium's maritime strength in Western waters from 965 on remained so weak and unimportant.

The Fatimids were, however, not willing to count on a continuation of Byzantine naval inactivity off the Syrian coasts. So in 995 the Caliph al-Aziz ordered the building of a huge war fleet at new dockyards and arsenals at Maks. The objective was 600 new vessels—some of them certainly of very considerable size.[26] The Persian traveler, Nasir-i-Khusru, in the next century described one of the vessels of al-Moeizz, beached during the conquest of Egypt in 969, as measuring 275 feet in length by 110 feet in the beam.[27] But all did not go well in the construction of this new fleet. The arsenal of Maks and many of the ships were destroyed in 995 by a fire which was ascribed to the machinations of Byzantine agents. In reprisal one hundred Greek merchants were seized and executed.[28] Yet the building of the fleet went on, and some idea of Fatimid efficiency can be seen in the fact that in three months six new vessels of the first class were launched.[29] A strengthened fleet appeared on the waters of the Eastern Mediterranean carrying the ensigns of the Cairo Caliphate. It was more than needed. At last Basil had turned his attention to Syria in earnest. His troops besieged Tripoli, sacked Homs and Baalbec. But the Fatimid navy defeated Basil's maritime squadrons off Tyre in 998 and kept Tripoli supplied from the sea.[30] When a ten-year truce was negotiated between the two antagonists in 999, Byzantium kept what it had in Syria but little more. Maritime Syria remained Fatimid, and the Byzantines were forced to divide naval control of the Eastern Mediterranean with the powerful Egyptian navy.

In the next two decades, though there was considerable friction between Cairo and Constantinople, there were few naval encounters between the two Empires. Basil II used the full resources of the Empire and turned his own considerable military talents to Bulgarian affairs. For many years he bent all his efforts toward con-

[26] Lane-Poole *Egypt*, p. 112.
[28] Lane-Poole *op. cit.*, p. 120.
[30] Wiet *op. cit.*, p. 198-99.

[27] *Nasir Khusrau* ed. Schefer, p. 126.
[29] *ibid.*, p. 121.

quering these stubborn antagonists. Expedition after expedition was sent against the Bulgars, until in 1018 the country was finally subdued and annexed to Constantinople.[31] During this time the navy seems to have been relatively neglected.

This concern with Syrian, Russian, and Bulgarian wars on land and sea explains the naval situation in Western waters. Between 965 and 1025 almost no Byzantine naval strength was allotted to the protection of Constantinople's territories and interests in Italy. For sixty years the Italians were very largely left to fend for themselves. This was a serious matter because, despite Ziridite naval weakness in North Africa, the Kalbite Emirs of Palermo had some real naval strength which they could use against Southern Italy. When full-fledged hostilities broke out between Byzantium and the Fatimids, there were naval repercussions in the West. In 975 Moslem Sicilian squadrons appeared off Calabria and Apulia and sacked Gravina.[32] Two years later Calabria was again raided,[33] and attacks were made on Tarentum, Otranto, and Orio.[34] The assaults became almost regular annual affairs.

It is in light of these circumstances that the intervention of Otto II in Southern Italy should be viewed. Like Louis II before him, he had immense pretensions to power in Italy. Like that Carolingian monarch, he felt the need of protecting Italy against Moslem invaders. Married to a Byzantine princess, he perhaps believed that the traditions of both Charlemagne and Byzantium devolved upon him. But he was well aware of his own lack of naval power. He therefore attempted to gain control of Venice, which had the only considerable maritime strength available in Italian waters. His father, Otto I, had, after his coronation as Holy Roman Emperor in Rome, renewed Venice's privileges in Northern Italy in 962.[35] When Otto II came to power, this policy of friendship turned to hostility. Despite a confirmation of Venice's privileges in 977,[36] the German Emperor began to put pressure upon the city of the lagoons by economic measures against its mainland trade in Italy. Under these circumstances a large pro-German party in Venice took over control of the city, as had happened at the time of Charlemagne. Venice seemed a safe and loyal ally.[37]

[31] Runciman *Byzantine Civilization*, p. 49.
[32] *Ibn al Athir* i, 379-80. *Abu al Fida* ii, 524.
[33] Amari *Storia* ii, 368-70.   [34] *ibid.*, p. 370-71.
[35] Cessi *Venezia* i, 73.   [36] *ibid.*, p. 75.
[37] *ibid.*, p. 77-79.

When Otto II ventured south toward Calabria in a great expedition to expel the Saracens and add these Byzantine provinces to his domains, he had every reason to believe his expedition would be a success. But the Venetians deserted him at this critical moment. Still valuing their Byzantine connection, they gave no naval help. And Byzantium's viceroys apparently were equally hostile and cooperated with their old Islamic foes. Otto arrived with his army at Cape Stilo to find himself deserted on all sides and facing a strong Moslem force. What followed was a complete disaster. His army was cut to pieces, and he himself was lucky to escape north in a Byzantine ship which almost carried him off as a captive.[38] With his death in 983 his schemes collapsed with him. Venice remained outside the Ottonian orbit and carried west a Byzantine force which soon restored order to Calabria and Apulia under a new official known as a Catapan.[39] Otto III may have had his father's ambitions, but he never had an opportunity to carry them out. Before his death he had restored all of Venice's rights in Northern Italy and left Byzantine possessions in the south strictly to themselves.[40]

With the end of the Ottonian menace, however, the momentary cooperation of Byzantine and Moslem in Southern Italy soon collapsed. In 986 a Moslem force invaded Calabria again and sacked the town of Gerace.[41] In 987 it was Cosenza's turn.[42] In 988, 991, and 994 raids were made in the vicinity of Bari.[43] Then the Moslems increased their pressure, possibly because news of Byzantium's defeat by the Fatimid fleet off Syria reached them. In 1002 they began to penetrate the interior of Italy in large freebooting banks and sacked Beneventum.[44] In 1003 they occupied Bari, again in what appeared to be a permanent fashion.[45] It was this action which alarmed the Venetians. They had no desire to see a permanent Moslem settlement in this region commanding the entrance to the Adriatic. A naval expedition was therefore sent to Apulia in 1004, and the Moslems were expelled.[46]

[38] *Ibn al Athir* I, 389-91. *Abu al Fida* II, 446-48. Thietmar *Chron.* in *MGH Script.* III, 765-66. John Diac. *Chron. Ven.* in *MGH Script.* III, 27.
[39] Amari *Storia* II, 394-95.   [40] Cessi *op. cit.*, p. 79-80.
[41] *Lupus Prospatarios* in *MGH Script.* III, 556.
[42] Amari *Storia* II, 395.   [43] *ibid.*, p. 396.
[44] *Chron. Sancta Sophia Beneventum* in *MGH Script.* III, 177.
[45] Amari *Storia*, p. 397.
[46] John Diac. *Chron. Ven.*, p. 35. Dandolo *Chron.*, p. 233.

Checked on the Adriatic side, Islamic naval raiders continued their assaults on the Tyrrhenian shores of Italy. In 1004 Pisa was attacked,[47] an action which apparently caused the Pisans to react with an assault of their own in the following year on Moslems who had established themselves at Reggio.[48] This apparently checked Islamic assaults in this section of Italy for a moment, but in 1009 Calabria was again invaded and Cosenza taken.[49] With Otto III dead and Byzantium busy in Bulgarian wars, there was no power present to stop the invaders. Pisa was again raided in 1011, perhaps by Moslems from Spain.[50] Luni in the next year suffered Pisa's fate.[51] Other adventurers, in addition to Moslems, began to flock into the troubled region. In 1016, the Normans made their first appearance. In that year a band of them helped to drive off Moslem freebooters who were attacking Salerno.[52] As in the late ninth century, Southern Italy began to become the happy hunting ground of adventurers of all sorts.

Not until 1025 did Byzantium intervene. The pacification of Bulgaria was then complete. Moslem attacks, which were now extended to the Peloponnesus, may also have at last opened the eyes of Constantinople to the dangers from Sicilian-African flotillas. So Basil II mustered a huge army of Wallachian, Bulgarian, and Russian mercenaries which was sent to Southern Italy with an accompanying fleet. Landing in Calabria, this force soon reestablished Byzantine rule and then proceeded across the straits into Moslem Sicily.[53] Palermo was alarmed and asked for assistance. Fatimid Egypt, still recovering from the effects of al-Hakim's tyranny, did nothing to help. But the Ziridites of Medhia were of more assistance. Al-Moeizz, the Ziridite ruler, had just constructed a new fleet which he was using against nearby Tripoli. He hastened to send 400 vessels to assist the Sicilians. It was, however, largely destroyed by storms off Pantelleria and helped little.[54] Sicily was saved by outside events. The warlike Basil II died, and the more pacific Constantine VIII succeeded him. As a result, peace was concluded with Cairo in 1027, and the Italian expedition was withdrawn without accomplishing a great deal.[55]

[47] *Chron. Varia Pisan.* in *Mur. Rer. Ital. Script.* vi, 101.
[48] *ibid.*, pp. 107, 167.   [49] Amari *Storia*, ii, 398.
[50] *Marangone* in *Arch. Storica Italia* vi, part ii, 4.
[51] Amari *Storia* iii, 4.   [52] Amari *Storia* ii, 399-404.
[53] *Cedrenus* ii, 479. *Ibn al Athir* i, 450-51.
[54] Ibn al Athir *op. cit.*   [55] Wiet *op. cit.*, p. 226.

When Emperor Romanus Agryrus in 1030 ended this peace with the Fatimids by an attack on Syria, hostilities again were joined with the Arabs of Sicily and Africa. In 1031 Illyria was assaulted by the Moslems,[56] and in 1032 the coast and islands of Greece were the Islamic naval objective.[57] In 1035 the Cyclades and the islands off Greece were attacked.[58] These maritime raids were not, however, too successful. One Moslem naval force, which attacked the coast of Lycia, was completely wiped out in 1035 by a Byzantine provincial fleet.[59] On the Islamic side gradually there arose a desire for peace. Sicily, beset by domestic difficulties between Arabs and Berbers, was the first to end hostilities with Byzantium; in 1035 her Kalbite Emir acknowledged the suzerainty of Constantinople.[60] Apparently this was with the approval of the Fatimid faction on the island, but of not many others. A revolt, backed by the Ziridites of North Africa, unseated the pro-Byzantine Emir and placed his brother on the throne.[61] Cairo, however, proceeded to make peace in 1038 with her enemies to the north.[62] Perhaps the youth of the child Caliph al-Mustansir and the threat of economic blockade made such a course advisable. In this treaty the Fatimids showed their displeasure at recent events in Sicily by specifically promising not to assist Palermo if Byzantium chose to open hostilities against the island.[63]

Freed of the danger of Fatimid sea and land power assisting the Sicilians, Constantinople prepared a great expedition against the island under her most talented commander, George Maniaces. The fleet itself was unfortunately commanded by a certain incompetent, Stephen, who was in high favor with the dissolute court of Empress Zoe. At first all went well. In 1038 Maniaces landed with a huge mercenary force on the island. Syracuse and the entire eastern portion of Sicily were conquered, despite Moslem reinforcements sent in from Africa. But the fleet allowed Moslems to slip through the naval blockade and relieve Cefalu, and an attack on Malta proved abortive. Finally, Constantinople recalled its victorious general in 1040. Revolts of Norman mercenaries in Southern Italy further complicated the situation. Though George Maniaces returned, the campaign languished.[64] By 1043, angry

---

[56] *Cedrenus* II, 496. [57] *ibid.*, p. 497. [58] *ibid.*, p. 499-500.
[59] *ibid.* [60] *ibid.*
[61] *ibid.*, p. 503, 516-17. *Ibn al Athir* II, 270. *Nuwairi* II, 270.
[62] Wiet *op. cit.*, p. 230-31. [63] *ibid.*, p. 231-33.
[64] *Lupus Prospatarios* in *MGH Script.* v, 58. *Cedrenus* II, 520.

at lack of support, he revolted and marched at the head of his army on the capital. In Greece he was met by an Imperial army and defeated and killed.[65] With his death ended the attempt on Sicily and all real semblance of Byzantine dominion in Southern Italy. Under Constantine IX Monomachus, who became Emperor in 1042, a peace-at-any-price policy was pursued, and this had fatal results for the future of the Empire.

It is interesting to note that the gradual disintegration of Byzantine military and naval power under the successors of the great Basil II was matched by a similar decline in the lands of their Moslem opponents. The huge Fatimid fleet brought to Egypt by the Caliph al-Moeizz in 973 and strengthened by al-Aziz in the late years of the tenth century did not survive far into the eleventh century in any great strength. Perhaps al-Hakim's twenty-five years of tyranny marks the turning point, but there is no evidence of any considerable Fatimid naval strength being maintained by the time of al-Mustansir's accession in 1036. Though there remained a navy under Fatimid orders, it ceased to be a major factor in the Eastern Mediterranean by this time.

This might not have been so serious had North Africa continued navally strong. But, when the Fatimids left Kairouan for Cairo, they took their fleet with them. Their Ziridite viceroys had thus few ships to protect their Western domains from the strong Ommayid Spanish fleet of Almeria. There were still, however, great arsenals and dockyards at Medhia, where 200 keels could be laid down at one time. In 976 they began construction of a new fleet, but found difficulty in manning it. Before it left port, most of the sailors deserted.[66] Not until 1016, then, did the Ziridites really possess any considerable naval force. In that year al-Moeizz, the ruler of Medhia, began the construction of a powerful fleet, perhaps to use against his rivals in Tripoli and in the West.[67] It was this fleet which was largely wrecked going to the aid of Sicily in 1025. It may also have been units of this fleet which aided Sicily again between 1038 and 1043. But Ziridite flotillas never seem to have been as well organized or as strong as the earlier Fatimid and Aghlabid fleets.[68] Only Sicily kept some considerable naval

---

[65] *Cedrenus* II, 541-49. *Lupus Prospatarios* in *op. cit.*, pp. 54, 58.

[66] *Ibn al Athir* I, 378. *Ibn Idhari* II, 334.   [67] *Ibn Idhari* II, 403.

[68] It seems possible that the Fatimid Caliphs in Egypt deliberately keep the naval power of their Ziridite vassals in Tunisia weak to make revolt impossible. If so, it explains North Africa's mysterious naval decadence in this period.

strength in the central Mediterranean, and in the eleventh century she, too, appears to have neglected her navy.[69]

In the West a similar process was going on in Moslem Spain. The departure of the Fatimids and their fleet to Egypt, leaving a navally weak Ziridite ruler in Kairouan, appears to have lessened the need for a strong Ommayid navy, but there is little evidence of much decline in Spanish maritime strength under Hakam II and Almansor. Control of Ceuta was maintained, and Ommayid power was extended into the interior of Morocco as the Fatimid threat receded. When, in 966 and 971, Viking pirate fleets again tested Ommayid naval defenses, they found them still formidable. Their first assault off Silves, after an attack on Lisbon, was beaten off with little difficulty,[70] and their second, five years later, off Andalusia never even got started.[71] In 972 a Spanish naval expedition even sailed as far as the Palestine coast and the Aegean Sea, plundering as it went.[72] As late as 997 it was the Ommayid navy which made possible Almansor's greatest triumph by transporting his army by sea up the Atlantic coast to seize and plunder the great pilgrim shrine of Santiago de Compostela.[73]

But in the early eleventh century, as the Ommayid Spanish Caliphate disintegrated after Almansor's death, the fine naval organization of Abd-ar-Rahman III disappeared with it. The kinglets and adventurers who seized power in the confusion that ensued were little able to maintain respectable naval forces. There was only one exception, Mugahid, who made himself ruler of Denia. He organized a strong fleet and with it in 1014 expanded his power by adding the Balearics to his kingdom.[74] From his realms he sent his fleets out to ravage the Western Mediterranean. In 1015 with 120 ships he proceeded to attack and perhaps occupy Sardinia, taking enormous booty.[75] He also sailed to the Italian coast where he assaulted Luni and nearby coastal regions.[76] The Genoese and Pisans united against him and won a victory

[69] *Muqqadasi* ed. De Goeje (Leyden 1906), p. 15. Muqqadasi notes the naval strength of Palermo in this period.

[70] *Ibn Idhari* II, 403-04. *Al Makkari* I, 249.

[71] *Ibn Idhari* II, 405. Dozy *Recherches* II, 295-99.

[72] *Abraham ben David* in *Med. Jewish Chron.* I, 67.

[73] *Al Makkari* I, 270. Dozy *Recherches* I, 163-64.

[74] Ibn Khaldun *Prologomenes*, p. 455-66. *Nuwairi* I, 110.

[75] Dove *De Sardinia Insula* (Berlin 1866), pp. 50, 63. *Ibn al Athir* I, 195, 205.

[76] Amari *Storia* III, 5-8. Thietmar *Chron.* in *MGH Script.* III, 850.

over his fleet off Sardinia.[77] In the next year they proceeded to drive him from the island.[78] His fleets, however, continued to be a menace to Christian shores. In 1018 he raided the country of Barcelona,[79] and it was perhaps his pirate ships that attacked Narbonne in 1020.[80] He remained formidable until his death in 1044.

Despite Mugahid, however, the distinguishing new factor in the Western Mediterranean did not lie in Moslem sea power. It lay in the sudden naval renaissance of Pisa, Genoa, and the coastline of Northwest Italy. As early as 935 this area had possessed some shipping, though probably none of any particular importance.[81] By about the year 1000, the Italians along this coast began to take the sea in strength. Perhaps the clearing out of Fraxinetum's Moslem pirates in 972 by Count William of Provence was the turning point.[82] Perhaps the causes lie deep in the unknown of history. At any rate, after Pisa was attacked in 1004, she reacted with a successful counter-raid on Moslems at Reggio in 1005. After her second chastisement at Moslem hands in 1011 and the sack of nearby Luni, she became even more aggressive. By 1015 she and Genoa were strong enough navally to defeat the formidable Mugahid on the sea, and in the next year to drive him from Sardinia, whose valuable silver mines were a rich prize well worth possessing. By 1034 her maritime strength was great enough for her to attack the rich city of Bone on the North African coast.[83]

Now it would be a mistake to view this naval activity of Pisa and Genoa as being based on a desire to protect commerce from Moslem corsairs, though eventually this was perhaps the result of their naval power. Their action does not seem to have been founded at first so much on economic as on defensive motives. At first the inhabitants simply wished to drive away pirates who were attacking their coasts. Soon—how soon it is hard to say—they discovered there was rich booty to be gained on the sea as well. By 1034 they themselves had become corsairs, preying on Islamic commerce and coastal cities. Booty, not commerce, remained the

[77] *Marangone* in *MGH Script.* xix, 238. *Chron. Pisan et Brev.* in *Mur. Rer. Ital. Script.* vi, 106-7.
[78] Dove *op. cit.*, p. 65-7. Amari *Storia* iii, 8-9.
[79] *Ademar Chron.* in *MGH Script.* iv, 104-05.
[80] *ibid.*, p. 139.   [81] Amari *Storia* ii, 181-83.
[82] Syrius *Vita Maroli* in *MGH Script.* iv, 651-52.
[83] Amari *Storia* iii, 16-17.

primary driving force of the Pisan and Genoese fleets of the eleventh century.[84] Their opportunity came from the weakened state of Islamic sea power in the West. It was the neglect of their fleet by the Ziridites, the collapse of Ommayid Spain, and the weakened state of Moslem Sicilian flotillas which gave these cities their maritime opportunity. By 1043 they were already making the most of it.

The case of Venice on the east coast of Italy was of quite a different character from that of the mariners from the Ligurian and Tuscan coastal cities. Venice had always been, and was at this time, primarily interested in trade and commerce, not buccaneering. She did, however, develop considerable naval strength in the Adriatic in the late tenth century. This was probably because the lack of Byzantine naval power in these waters forced her to protect her commerce from raids by Croatian pirates along the Illyrian coast. This had long been a problem for the Venetians, but at about 1000 she felt strong enough to take matters into her own hands and conquer these pirate centers, which were also, incidentally, commercial competitors as well. In that year, Doge Peter II Orseoli, with a large fleet, reduced Zara, Veglia, Arbe, Trau, Curzola, Lagosta, and Ragusa to the status of dependencies.[85] From 1002 the Doges referred to themselves as Dukes of Venice and Dalmatia.[86] In 1004 they showed their naval strength further by expelling the Moslems from Bari and Apulia.[87]

It must not be thought, however, that the Venetians used this new naval power to make themselves independent of Byzantium. Though they were, in fact, strong enough to stand alone, they valued the commercial advantages that the Byzantine connection brought to them. In 971 they complied, at least for a time, with John Zimisces's injunction not to trade with Moslem ports in such commodities as ship timber, iron, and weapons.[88] After a period of wavering, they deserted the cause of Otto II to keep on the right side of the rulers of Constantinople. They agreed, in return for commercial privileges in Eastern Byzantine waters, to transport

---

[84] Lopez "Orig. du Capit Gén.," p. 445-51. For an excellent account of the forces behind this sudden blossoming of Western Europe's offensive power see Munro, D. C. and Strayer, J. R. *The Middle Ages* (New York 1942), p. 158-88.

[85] Diehl *Venise*, p. 25-27. On ninth and tenth century Venetian control of trade of this region see Cessi *Venezia* I, 88-90.

[86] Dandolo *Chron.*, p. 228-31.   [87] *ibid.*, p. 232. Cessi *op. cit.*, p. 90.

[88] *Taf. et Thom.* I, 25-30.

Constantinople's armies to Italy, and they served as carriers of important mail and envoys between the West and the city on the Golden Horn.[89] They were still, in the early eleventh century, connected with the Byzantine Empire by a sort of dominion status. But their maritime, like their commercial strength, had grown considerably. Already they were becoming a great Mediterranean as well as an important Adriatic naval power.

To summarize naval developments between 960 and 1043 is to note some important changes. First and perhaps most important, the late tenth century was one in which a revived Byzantine navy took to the sea, recaptured Crete and Cyprus, and wiped out Moslem naval strength in Tarsus and Northern Syria by annexing these regions to the Empire. In so doing, it destroyed a major part of Islam's naval strength in the Eastern Mediterranean. It was, however, checked by Fatimid naval forces in the West in 965 and in the East by the Egyptian fleet of Cairo's new Caliphs in 975. After a period of civil war, which seriously affected its naval strength, it took to the offensive again only to meet defeat in 998 off Tyre at the hands of a newly constructed Fatimid armada. There followed a long interval in which naval forces were neglected or used to supplement land campaigns against Bulgaria. Not until 1025 did the Byzantine navy become a factor again, this time in an attack on Sicily. Then, after some sparring against raids by the Moslems in the Aegean, in 1038 the navy was sent West again to take part in the last great attack on Sicily. When that failed, it was used only once more against Russian forces which assaulted the Empire in 1043.[90] Then like all Byzantine forces, the fleet was allowed to decay as the Empire slipped into pacifistic ineptitude.

On the Moslem side, the period saw the Fatimids of North Africa, profiting by Byzantium's destruction of possible naval rivals, seize Egypt in 969 and with their fleet check Byzantine naval forces in 975 and 998 off Syria. They left their vassals, the Ziridites in Kairouan, navally weak, though the Kalbites of Palermo still had considerable naval strength which they used in raids on Italy. By the early eleventh century Fatimid naval power in Egypt had declined and the Ziridites, despite real efforts, had not

[89] ibid., 35-39. MGH Const. et Acta I, 45-50.

[90] Neumann, C. Die Weitselling des Byzantinischen Reiches aus den Kreuzzuge (Leipsig 1895) is the best account of the causes of the decline of Byzantium's fleet in this period.

achieved any considerable maritime strength. Even Palermo began to weaken upon the seas; hence Byzantine successes in 1025 and 1038. The third great center of Islamic naval power, Moslem Spain, also declined in the period. Powerful up to the death of Almansor, it lost its maritime organization with the breakup of the Ommayid Caliphate. Only the pirate king of Denia, Mugahid, kept alive the traditions of Spanish Moslem naval strength in the Western Mediterranean until his death in 1044.

These weaknesses in Moslem Spain, North Africa, and Sicily, not to mention the weakness of Byzantium in Western waters, afforded Western Europe her naval opportunity. Provence expelled its Moslem invaders, and Genoa and Pisa took to the sea, defeating Mugahid. Then, discovering the profits of piracy, they pushed their naval expeditions across the Mediterranean to raid Moslem coasts. At the same time Venice, on the other side of Italy, transformed the Adriatic into a Venetian lake by clearing Apulia of Moslem pirates and conquering the cities of the Dalmatian coast. By 1043 these Italians had the only really aggressive naval forces in the Mediterranean. To them the naval future of the sea was to belong.

There remains the question of the influence which land campaigns had on maritime strength in the Middle Sea in this period. In contrast to the preceding period, sea power was much influenced by land power between 960 and 1043. Both the Fatimid and Byzantine navies, for instance, were much affected by the activities of their soldiers. It was the armies of Nicephorus Phocas and John Zimisces which made possible the conquest of Cilicia and Northern Syria and thus destroyed centers of Eastern Moslem naval power. It was the activities of the raiding Caramathes and of rebellious Syrian interior cities like Damascus which forced the Fatimids to pay attention to land power and so limited the effect of their naval victories over Byzantium in 975 and 998. It was Basil II's army, not his fleet, that forced the Caliphs of Cairo to accept grudgingly Byzantine control of Antioch and Aleppo. It was likewise the military weakness of the shadowy Abbassid Caliphs which prevented them from interfering.

Most important, however, was the effect of Basil II's preoccupation, during the height of his power, with Bulgarian affairs. It was the Bulgarian war to which for two decades he bent every effort. In so doing he spent the Empire's substance on his army and neglected the fleet. Had even a portion of the effort, spent upon the land in two decades of constant struggle, been used in strengthening Byzantium's naval forces and proceeding against Sicily, the entire history of the Mediterranean might have been different.[91] Not until almost too late, in 1025, just before his death, did Basil turn to the neglected West and send his ships and his soldiery against this island. His death robbed the Empire of the directing hand it needed and, though in 1038 another attempt on Sicily was made, the incompetence of Constantinople's rulers did not permit its success. In forgetting what Justinian, Leo III, and Romanus Lecapenus had known almost instinctively—that Byzantium was essentially a naval, not a land, Empire—Basil II neglected his great opportunity. In doing so he dug the Empire's grave. From this insistence on army priority, from this preoccupation with land campaigns that culminated in the costly Bulgarian War, came the evils which led to the disaster of Manzikert and the fatal weakening of Byzantium.

Interestingly enough, in Italy and Spain land campaigns also affected sea power to a great extent. The Ottos in Italy, with their Teutonic land armies, were no more able than Charlemagne or Louis II to cope with Moslem or Byzantine sea power. They failed in their attempts on Venice, Calabria, Apulia, and the cities of the Campanian coast. Yet they did seriously weaken Byzantium's position in Southern Italy and made possible a chaos which the Normans were to exploit to the fullest a few decades later. Italy did not recover that balance between native Italian principalities and Byzantine-held themes which Nicephorus Phocas had set up in the late ninth century. For this the Ottos were perhaps as much to blame as Basil II himself.[92]

In Spain, in a somewhat different way, it was the military policies of Almansor which ultimately destroyed the Ommayid Caliphate and Spanish Moslem naval power with it. Almansor was a military commander of great ability, as were his Byzantine contemporaries, John Zimisces and Basil II. But like them, his policies of land expansion brought disaster to his state. To assure success

[91] It is interesting to note that Toynbee dates the real breakdown of Byzantine civilization from the time of Basil II's Bulgarian wars, though for a different reason. Toynbee, A. J. A Study of History (London 1939) IV, 601-16.

[92] Amari does not, I believe, sufficiently appreciate the disruptive role exercised by the Ottos in destroying the Byzantine organized balance of power in Italy. Amari Storia II, 377-84.

in his wars with the Christian kingdoms in Northern Spain, he changed the character of the Ommayid army. He employed large numbers of slaves and mercenaries as crack troops in place of the Arab *jound* and border levies who had been the main reliance of the state prior to the tenth century. These slaves and mercenaries were either savage Berbers from Africa or Christian adventurers and slaves. As long as he lived, this army ensured him internal peace and foreign success. But it had two dangers. Its use meant that the Spanish-Arab aristocracy ceased to interest itself in military matters and got the habit of hiring others to do their fighting for them. And, even more important, after his death these slave and mercenary troops got out of hand. They turned against the Spanish civilian population they were organized to defend. The sheepdogs murdered their sheep. And both the Caliphate of Cordova and the naval organization built up by Abd-ar-Rahman III disappeared in the resulting chaos.[93]

The effects, then, of changes in naval strength and land campaigns resulted in a very different Mediterranean world in the middle of the eleventh century from that which had existed a century previously. The most important difference lay in the fact that Byzantium's conquest of Crete, Cyprus, Cilicia, and Northern Syria reversed the basic maritime picture in the Eastern Mediterranean. The naval protection which possession of these islands and regions had given Moslem Syria and Egypt was now gone. The only completely safe maritime route between the Moslem East and West now lay along the dangerous North African coast from Alexandria to Sousse. Two contemporary tenth-century Moslem observers accurately describe the changed situation. In 972 Ibn Hawkal complained that the Rum offended the Moslems with all manner of attacks on the shores of this sea (the Mediterranean). They seized ships and oppressed merchants.[94] Muqqadasi wrote fifteen years later in similar vein. He explained that Cyprus protected Syria, Crete protected Egypt, and Sicily protected North Africa. After Byzantine naval victories, however, the Rum (by which he may mean Italians as well as Byzantines) frequented the sea and only the Sicilians and Spaniards could keep them in their own confines and gulfs.[95]

[93] Lévi-Provençal *Hist. de l'Espagne Mussulmane*, p. 457-504.
[94] *Ibn Hawkal* trans. in *Biblia Arabo-Sic.* ed. Amari ɪ, 27.
[95] *Muqqadasi*, p. 15.

Obviously, then, by the late tenth century the Eastern Mediterranean had ceased to be an Islamic sea. The Western portion, however, continued so until about the middle of the eleventh century. As long as Sicily and the Balearics remained in Moslem hands and Sardinia continued neutralized, Africa and Spain had a protection that Egypt and Syria had ceased to enjoy. The Pisan and Genoese fleets which drove Mugahid from Sardinia (though final occupation did not take place until 1050) and the Byzantine attacks on Sicily in 1025 and 1038-1043 gave a foretaste of the future. Already in the West, as in the East, the naval initiative was passing out of the hands of Islamic peoples into those of the Christian Byzantines and Latins who inhabited the northern shores of the sea. And in this change geography favored the latter, as at the time of the Ommayid naval efforts between 645 and 752. The series of protected gulfs and bays, noted by Muqqadasi, lay on the north shore of the Mediterranean. Constantinople at the head of the Aegean, Venice at the head of the Adriatic, and Genoa and Pisa at the top of the Tyrrhenian had a protection that was lacking on the Moslem coasts. By the late tenth and early eleventh centuries an aggressive Latin West and Byzantine East began to capitalize on these geographical advantages.

But more than geography lay behind the change in Islamic maritime strength by the early eleventh century. It was perhaps the very prosperity of the Islamic world which lay behind the decay of Islamic fleets. In the late tenth century, Ibn Hawkal, viewing Sicily, which remained still aggressive on the sea at this time, reveals a contempt for those Moslem pirate freebooters who had been the advance guard of Islamic naval strength in earlier periods.[96] Prosperous and respectable, the Islamic world apparently began to forget its maritime freebooting past. The attitude of Ibn Hawkal toward the piratical Rum was, as a matter of fact, not, unlike that of Englishmen, who, forgetful of Drake and Hawkins, excoriated the operations of John Paul Jones in the waters off Britain during the Revolutionary War. So, too, did New England, forgetting its privateering past, view the activities of the *Alabama* in the Civil War. It reveals perhaps a most significant change in Moslem naval aggressiveness and maritime attitude. It helps explain why Moslem powers allowed Byzantine and Western European reactions to strip away the protective screen of pirate advance

[96] Ibn Hawkal *Desc. Pal.*, p. 26, 38.

fleets without giving these border forces much assistance. True, the wiping out of Bari and Monte Garigliano took place in the period of Islamic Mediterranean ascendancy, but most losses of border maritime strength occurred at this time. Crete, Tarsus, and Fraxinetum were lost without any help being given by Moslem coasts they protected. And while the Emirs of Palermo and Mugahid's pirate fleet continued older aggressive Islamic maritime policies until the middle of the eleventh century, they too had already failed by 1043 to halt the advance of Genoa and Pisa in the Western Seas and Venice in the Adriatic. By 1043 the loss of advance positions and the weaknesses of Moslem organized fleets in Fatimid Egypt, Ziridite North Africa, and divided Moslem Spain presaged the end of Islamic control of the Mediterranean.

Yet it must be admitted that up to 1043 the Mediterranean was still largely Moslem, despite weakening Islamic strength. The Fatimid fleet of Egypt, the aggressive raids of Sicilian and African pirates on Southern Italy and even the Aegean, the Balearic-based fleet of Mugahid, all assured a large measure of Islamic control. In a general way the situation still resembled that which had lasted from the middle of the tenth century, though it was obvious that this situation could not long prevail.

In naval organization, however, the period saw few important changes. Byzantium's maritime strength was still based on that system of Imperial and provincial fleets as it had been reorganized in the late ninth century. As her conquest on land and sea advanced her power south, she merely moved her principal bases in the same direction. Cyprus thus became a principal naval base for the Kibyrrhaeotic themal fleet after 965.[97] Perhaps Crete, likewise, became an advance base for the Aegean provincial flotillas. The Fatimid, Ziridite, Sicilian, and Ommayid fleets continued to be organized in the same way that they had been in the earlier period. Venice, also, seems to have had a war fleet similarly well organized at this time. Even pirate flotillas, whether they were based on Palermo, Denia, Zara, or Genoa and Pisa differ little in this period from those described earlier.

The main significant change lies in the increased size of some classes of warships used by both the Moslems and their Byzantine opponents, a subject that deserves more study than it can receive in these pages. It was perhaps Constantinople which began first

[97] Schlumberger *Nicephore Phocas*, p. 387-9.

to build large galleys in place of the smaller *chelandias* and *dromons* of earlier periods. Some of them were present in the assault on Crete,[98] and there is mention of "great ships" used by Byzantium in the "Battle of the Straits" in 965.[99] Moslem naval builders similarly went in for similar huge warships, as is deduced from the dimensions of some of the Fatimid ships used by al-Moeizz in the conquest of Egypt in 969.[100] Probably only advanced states could afford such vessels, which may have limited them to the fleets of the Fatimids, Ommayids, and Byzantines, though an increase in the size of Venetian warships may actually date from this period.[101]

What was the effect of the somewhat changed naval situation upon the economic life and trade of the Mediterranean-Black Sea world? Did Byzantine and Western European naval resurgence, Ommayid Spanish collapse, and the eastward movement of the Fatimids adversely affect the prosperity of the peoples of the Middle Sea? In general, the answer seems to be in the negative, for the period was one of continuing and rising economic prosperity for all concerned.

Let us first examine the Moslem world. Egypt, already prosperous in Tulunid and Ikhshid times, seems to have increased her high level of economic activity under early Fatimid rulers. Cairo, the newly established capital of the Caliphs on the Nile, was in 987 already reported by Muqqadasi as the largest and most important metropolis of the Moslem East.[102] About the middle of the eleventh century a Persian traveler, Nasir-i-Khusru, was even more impressed by the city. He speaks of its 20,000 shops—all owned by the government, and of the important fine pottery and glass that were produced there.[103]

Egypt continued to be an important agricultural and industrial country. Sugar and honey were produced in large quantities,[104] and at Assiut opium was grown as well.[105] This city was also a center for the manufacture of linen cloth.[106] So, too, was Tinnis,

[98] *ibid.*, p. 41-3.

[99] *Ibn al Athir* I, 363-66. *Abu al Fida* II, 448. *Nuwairi* II, 266. Ibn Khaldun *Hist. des Fatamids* in de Slane *Hist. des Berbères* II, 529.

[100] *Nasir Khusrau*, p. 126.

[101] Hazlitt *op. cit.*, p. 140-46, has an account of the huge castellated galleys used by Venice against Robert Guiscard in 1084.

[102] *Muqqadasi*, p. 47.   [103] Wiet *op. cit.*, p. 303-04.

[104] *ibid.*, p. 306-07.   [105] *ibid.*, p. 305.

[106] *ibid.*

where, in addition colored linen textiles, scissors and cutlery were produced in large amounts.[107] Egypt's *tiraz*, as of old, remained a source of wealth, and the state factories continued to turn out the valuable cloth-of-gold, taby, and other luxury products. Workers in such establishments appear to have been well paid and contented.[108]

The Fatimids of Egypt also continued and perhaps increased the state controls over Egyptian economic life which had been so noticeable a feature of the land since Ptolemaic times. They continued the passport system. They rigidly supervised and taxed the state markets in which all goods had to be displayed.[109] They organized gangs of slaves to exploit the gold diggings of Nubia.[110] They also appear to have intervened in maritime affairs. Just as they increased the strength of Egypt's navy, so, too, they owned and operated a portion of Egypt's merchant fleet, which they sent on trading expeditions throughout the Mediterranean.[111] They thus attempted, perhaps, to change the passive nature of Egypt's foreign commerce, though with what success it is difficult to say.[112]

Nearby Syria and Palestine, also under Fatimid influence, despite civil disturbances and foreign invasions, appear to have shared some of the high level of prosperity that Egypt enjoyed. Both agriculture and industry were highly developed. Sugar cane, newly introduced from the East, was cultivated in Galilee and near Tyre.[113] Nablus and much of Syria produced a superior grade of olive oil.[114] Damascus was renowned for its copper ware and its textiles.[115] Both Ramle and Tiberias produced a *tiraz* of colored stuff.[116] Paper was manufactured at Damascus and other cities in Syria.[117]

The trade of this region with the South and East was thriving. Aden was a main port for the entire Indian Ocean trade to India and China.[118] From the Red Sea, traders were active to Abyssinia

---

[107] *ibid.*, p. 304. Quatremère *Mémoir sur Egypte*, pp. 377, 380.

[108] *ibid.*, p. 305.

[109] *Muqqadasi* trans. G. LeStrange, pp. 91-92, 104, 167.

[110] Lombard *op. cit.*, p. 150.   [111] Wiet *op. cit.*, p. 305.

[112] This Egyptian mercantilism may be one reason for the decline of North Africa's commerce with Egypt so noticeable toward the middle of the 11th century, as well as the growing Ziridite-Fatimid hostility. See Chapter VII.

[113] *Muqqadasi*, pp. 162, 180.   [114] *ibid.*, p. 174.

[115] *Al Istakhri*, p. 31. Quatremère *op. cit.*, pp. 377, 380.

[116] Wustenfeld *Geschichte der Fátimid Kalifen*, p. 162-64.

[117] *Muqqadasi*, p. 12. Nasir Khusrau, p. 12.   [118] Wiet *op. cit.*, p. 169.

and Zanzibar.[119] Apparently this route was also followed by many Moslem pilgrims going by sea to Jiddah on their way to the holy cities of Mecca and Medina. There is no evidence that the Red Sea-Nile canal was in operation at this time, and the chief trade and pilgrim route went through Aidhab and by land to Assouan and then down the Nile to Cairo and Alexandria.[120] Commerce with Nubia up the Nile was well developed and important.

Mediterranean trade from Egypt and Syria was also flourishing. Alexandria had commercial relations with Sicily and Constantinople,[121] and Tripoli was frequented by foreign merchants from Byzantium, Moslem Spain, Sicily, and Western Europe.[122] From this port sailed the Caliph of Cairo's own merchant fleet which traded with Constantinople, Sicily, and North Africa.[123] The Venetians and Amalfitans appear to have been the Western European traders who were most active in their commerce with the Fatimids, with Venice supplying ship timber, iron, and arms (particularly lacking in this region), and carrying back spices, textiles, and other luxury products.[124]

Trade was also active with Iraq and Persia, probably principally from Syria. Turbans of linen made in Tinnis were, however, exported to Persian markets,[125] and *tiraz* of the state factories, sent to Iraq, sold for large sums until the Fatimids forbade this trade as part of their economic warfare against their Abbassid rivals in Bagdad.[126]

The many splendid buildings constructed by the Fatimid Caliphs, and the fabulous wealth contained in the treasure of Caliph Mustansir, before its destruction in the troubles that afflicted Cairo in 1067, emphasize how wealthy Egypt was in this period.[127] So, too, do the head-taxes levied on the Christian population of the land. In the ninth century they amounted to ½ dinar a head and caused much murmuring, as at Tinnis in 815. By the year 1000 they had been raised to 1½ dinars per head and provoked little complaint.[128]

[119] *ibid.*, p. 306.   [120] *ibid.*, p. 307.   [121] *ibid.*, p. 308.
[122] *ibid.*, *Muqqadasi* ed. De Goeje, p. 15.
[123] Wiet *op. cit.*, p. 308.
[124] John Diac. *Chron. Ven.*, p. 27. Dandolo *Chron.*, p. 223. Diehl *Venise*, p. 19-21.
[125] Maqrizi *Kitat* I, 177.
[126] Mez *Renaissance of Islam*, p. 160-64.
[127] Lane-Poole *Egypt*, p. 147-48.
[128] *Michael the Syrian* II, 516. *Muqqadasi* trans. LeStrange, p. 213.

The picture presented by Ziridite North Africa differs little from that of Egypt. Ibn Khaldun says that "never was there a kingdom among the Berbers vaster, richer or more flourishing than that of the Ziridites."[129] Evidence from Ibn Hawkal in the late tenth century and from Al-Bakri in the eleventh fully bears out his assertion.

Agriculturally, North Africa in this period remained very productive. Grain continued to be the main crop produced in the north about Beja, and on the plains west of Kairouan olive trees covered the land from Sfax to Tunis, and Kairouan itself lay in the center of olive groves.[130] Dates and sugar cane were important crops in the oasis of Djerid in the south.[131] Bananas and sugar were cultivated at Gabes.[132] Cotton was grown at Hodna, Msila, and elsewhere.[133] Indigo was produced at Sabob and saffron at Carthage and in the interior.[134]

In industry there was even more development than in agriculture in this period. Such centers as Gabes, Sfax, Sousse, and Kairouan were particularly renowned for their textiles.[135] Gabes, for instance, wove high quality silk produced by silkworms in the vicinity.[136] Sfax's cloth, copied after that of Alexandria, was considered to surpass the original in quality.[137] The fine cloth woven at Kairouan was apparently finished at Sousse, whence brocades of cloth-of-gold were sent as presents by North Africa's rulers to their overlords, the Caliphs of Cairo.[138] Near Gafsa was manufactured a special cloth known as *ksa toraqi* which was exported to Egypt.[139] In addition, the land produced other manufactured wares besides textiles. Tunis produced excellent pottery.[140] Zawila, Cabra, and Bougie were centers for glass manufacturing.[141] Copperware was also made in many localities.[142]

Kairouan was the main commercial, as well as the most important industrial, metropolis. Muqqadasi listed it as outstanding in the Islamic world, along with Barca, Cyrene, and Sidjilmasa.[143] Each day 26,000 dirhems in levies on goods were collected at the

[129] Ibn Khaldun *Hist. des Berbères* II, 19.
[130] *Al Bakri*, pp. 46, 56, 99, 116, 120.
[131] *ibid.*, p. 41. Ibn Hawkal *Descr. of Africa* in *Journ. Asiat.* (1842) I, 178, 215.
[132] *Al Bakri*, p. 41.　　　[133] *ibid.*, p. 60.　　　[134] *Ibn Hawkal*, p. 223.
[135] Marçais *Berbérie*, p. 179.　　　[136] *ibid.*
[137] *Al Bakri*, p. 46-47.　　　[138] *ibid.*, p. 78.　　　[139] *ibid.*, p. 101.
[140] *ibid.*, p. 88.　　　[141] Marçais *op. cit.*, p. 180.　　　[142] *ibid.*
[143] *Muqqadasi*, p. 47.

gates of this city. Tunis, Sousse, Sfax and Gabes were also important as trade centers.[144] Sfax, for instance, sent its olive oil to Egypt, Sicily, Europe, and other parts of North Africa.[145] Medhia traded extensively with Egypt and Syria.[146] Tripoli, at the head of one of the Sudan routes, was a center of the trade in Negro and European slaves who were exported to Eastern Islamic markets.[147] Barca was filled with the merchandise of both East and West.[148] Bone was visited by Spanish merchants,[149] and Oran and Tennis traded actively with Andalusia.[150] Coral fishing made Tennis, as well as distant Ceuta, important ports.[151] Monastir was the site of a great annual fair which brought merchants from overseas.[152]

Trade with the Sudan to the south was as active as that with lands about the Mediterranean. The Caliph al-Moeizz, upon leaving North Africa for Egypt, ordered his Ziridite viceroy to continue his policy of heavy taxation and stern measures to keep the bedouin tribesmen of the interior from interfering with the caravan routes. This apparently was done, for in 992 elephants and giraffes were brought from the Sudan as presents for the Ziridite rulers.[153] During the course of the tenth century, Sidjilmasa came again, like Morocco, under Ommayid influence, but the other two caravan routes to the gold of Sudan and the Niger remained in the hands of the rulers of Kairouan. Over them came steady streams of gold and slaves to enrich the coffers of both the merchants and monarchs of North Africa.

Some idea of the wealth of the land can be gained by a few figures. Customs levies at Sousse, Medhia, Sfax, and Tunis, not counting entry and exit dues, enriched the public treasury to the tune of 80,000 dinars a year in this period.[154] The revenue of Bone, which reached the private treasury of the sovereign, amounted to 20,000 dinars annually.[155] Well might the sandals used at the Ziridite palace be made of precious wood of India fastened together with golden nails.[156] And it is understandable how al-Moeizz in the early eleventh century could afford to spend 1,000,000

---

[144] Marçais *Berbérie*, p. 181. *Ibn Idhari* I, 318. *Al Bakri*, p. 58.

[145] *Al Bakri*, p. 79.   [146] *ibid.*, p. 25.   [147] Amari *Storia* II, 419.

[148] *Ibn Hawkal*, p. 161.   [149] *Al Bakri*, p. 122.   [150] Amari *Storia* II, 419.

[151] *Ibn Hawkal*, p. 362.   [152] *Al Bakri*, p. 79.   [153] *Ibn Idhari* I, 256-8.

[154] Ibn Khaldun *Hist. des Berbères* II, 19-20. *Al Bakri*, p. 78.

[155] *Al Bakri*, p. 70.

[156] *Ibn Idhari* I, 249-84.

dinars on his sister's wedding and 100,000 dinars on his mother's funeral.[157]

Sicily in this period, if not earlier, had come to share in North Africa's wealth and prosperity. Muqqadasi listed it as one of Islam's chief centers of commerce.[158] Its agriculture and industries were in flourishing condition. On the island cotton, saffron, and hemp were widely grown. Oranges, lemons, sugar cane, and silkworms were probably introduced at this time.[159] Sal amonica was produced in quantity in the Aetna region and other places.[160] Silver, iron, lead, mercury, sulphur, and naphtha were other products which the island had in some quantity.[161] Nor were textiles neglected. Fine cloth was woven. Some of the robes of the children of al-Moeizz of Egypt were of Sicilian origin.[162] Silk weavers were already important in Sicily at this time. Trade with Africa was brisk, and frequent voyages were made by merchants to Medhia, Sousse, and Clipea.[163] Olive oil was imported from Sfax, and trade with distant Syria and Egypt was important.[164] Palermo, with a whole quarter devoted to merchants and filled with moneychangers, tailors, armorers, and leather workers, was the island's principal metropolis and one of the Mediterranean's main Moslem cities.[165]

Spain shared in this same prosperity. Its wealth seems to have increased after Abd-ar-Rahman's death, since the revenues of the Caliph Hakam II were double those of his father.[166] The gold of the Sudan, flowing through Morocco to Ceuta, fertilized Spain's economic life as it did that of nearby Ziridite North Africa. Trade with coastal Africa and the Eastern Mediterranean was also important. The importance of Spain, from an economic standpoint, does not even appear to have been much compromised by the

---

[157] Ibn Khaldun *Hist. des Berbères* II, 19-20. Also note the merchant who was wealthy enough in 976 to pay a tax of 400,000 dirhems to the Ziridite government. Mas Latrie *Traités de Paix*, p. 13.

[158] *Muqqadasi*, p. 47.

[159] Pirro *Sicilia Sacra.*, p. 770. *Yakut* in *Biblio. Arab-Sic.* I, 190-91, 201. Amari *Storia* II, 509-10.

[160] *Yakut* I, 204. *Muqqadasi*, p. 239-40.

[161] *Yakut* I, 201, 206. Amari *Storia* II, 507.

[162] Al Mahasin in ed. *Cairo* IV, 193. *Maqrizi*, p. 410. This Moslem Sicilian industrialism is in sharp contrast to the overwhelmingly agrarian character of the island in Roman and Byzantine times. Amari *Storia* I, 331-32.

[163] *Al Bakri*, p. 67, 68.   [164] *ibid.*, p. 46.

[165] Ibn Hawkal *Desc. Palerm.*, p. 24.

[166] Lévi-Provençal *L'Espagne Mussulmane au Dixième Siècle*, p. 72-73.

disorders which accompanied the fall of the Caliphate of Cordova in the early eleventh century. Its Moslem kinglets remained rich and cultured.[167] Even nearby Morocco felt the strong influence of Andalusia. Up to the eleventh century Fez and other Moroccan centers appear to have been chiefly influenced in architecture and coinage by Tunis. But in this century it was Spain which provided the models.[168] The great libraries of Cordova, the intellectual vigor of Spain's scholars, and the cultivated poetry of her Arab upper classes, despite the constant civil strife, testify to the continuing prosperity of this rich land.

From an economic standpoint, then, this period in the whole Moslem Mediterranean from Lisbon to Damascus, represented a continuation of the preceding period from 827 to 960, even an expansion and fulfillment of earlier developments. Despite growing naval weaknesses, Byzantine and Western maritime resurgence and political subdivision in Spain and North Africa, this section of the Mediterranean enjoyed a prosperity unknown even in Roman times. An increased industrialization in Africa, Sicily and Spain, wide cultivation of Eastern agricultural products, extensive trade, and a common use of the gold dinar continued, despite storm clouds on the horizon, to make this period a sort of golden age for Islam—one that Ibn Khaldun, in the twilight of the fourteenth century, viewed with nostalgia.

The Byzantine Empire shared even more fully in the prosperity of the Islamic world in this period than it had in the years previous to it. Partly, no doubt, this was due to her expansion south and east at the expense of Islam. Now, with Crete and Cyprus firmly in her hands, Byzantium was in a position again to share in the profits of the great international circle route from Syria and Egypt by way of these islands to the West. Few merchant ships could sail westward from the Eastern Mediterranean without paying tribute to Constantinople, unless they used the dangerous North African coastal route. In addition, Constantinople's expansion into Northern Syria and her conquest of Antioch and control over Aleppo gave her additional trade advantages, reinforced by her power in

[167] On the flourishing state of Spain and particularly her agriculture in the eleventh century see Ibn al-awan *Le Livre de l'agriculture* trans. J. J. Clement-Mullet (Paris 1864-7), 3 vols.

[168] Marçais *Berbérie*, p. 129.

Northern Mesopotamia. For the first time since the seventh century the best route from Iraq and the Persian Gulf to the Mediterranean was in her hands. Though probably much commerce from the East came to the Mediterranean by way of Aden and the Red Sea controlled by the Fatimids, the old Sassanian routes still remained important. The trade treaty of the late tenth century between Constantinople and the Moslem rulers of Aleppo reveals the importance of this commerce. By its provisions Byzantine officials in this city levied a tax of 10 per cent on all imports of raw silk, brocades, precious metals, and jewels, while the local rulers levied dues on garments, linen, cattle and other wares imported from Byzantine territory.[169]

Aleppo thus became one of the chief trade gateways of Byzantium with the Arab world to the East. So important was it that Basil II, when he banned trade with Fatimid Egypt at the time of al-Hakim's Christian persecutions in 1015, specifically exempted Aleppo.[170] It seems probable, too, that this city replaced Trebizond in large measure as the most important trading center with Persia and the East. The route to Aleppo and Antioch was easier than that through the mountains of Armenia to the Black Sea. Belief in this change of trade terminus is strengthened when one considers the fate of Armenia, which had been the great intermediary between Mesopotamia and Constantinople and had reaped a rich reward in wealth and power in the process. With the establishment of a Byzantine Northern Syria, Armenia lost its political and economic importance and was overrun by Byzantium and annexed to the Empire in the eleventh century.[171] The Armenians themselves apparently followed the changed trade routes south, and by the late eleventh century had established themselves in the cities of Southern Anatolia and Northern Mesopotamia from Edessa to Adana, a region which became known in crusading times as Lesser Armenia.[172] Another indication of the wealth this route brought is to be found in the case of Cyprus. This island, so unimportant and underpopulated from the time of Justinian II on,

---

[169] *Yahya Ibn Said* ed. and trans. Kratchkovsky and Vasiliev in *Patrologia Orientalis* XVIII, 823-4. *Kemal al Din* ed. and trans. Freytag, G. W. *Regierung des Saad-Alduala Zu Aleppo* (Bonn 1828), p. 10-15.

[170] Wiet *Egypte Arabe*, p. 230-33.

[171] Der Nersessian *Armenia and the Byzantine Empire*, p. 11.

[172] *ibid.*, p. 11-12.

suddenly blossomed into a wealthy center of commerce with new cities and important merchant trading population.[173]

Constantinople itself probably reached the highest level of prosperity it had known since the time of Justinian. This was, as Schlumberger points out, the apogee of Byzantium. Liudprand of Cremona's evidence concerning the riches of the Imperial palace and the size and wealth of the city on the Golden Horn are enough to convince one of this fact.[174] The great treasure which Basil II, despite his wars, left to his unworthy successors was fully as large as that of the Fatimids of Egypt or the Ziridites of North Africa. The renaissance in art, the intellectual vigor of such a man as Psellus, the scope and character of Byzantine writings, all attest to the vigor of Constantinople's Orthodox civilization in this period.[175]

One of the major noticeable elements in Byzantium's economic life, her passivity in the field of foreign trade, became even more emphasized, however, during these years. Certainly in the tenth century the old trade controls governing commerce continued in force. During certain periods, as in 971, Byzantium's rulers attempted to halt shipments of timber, iron, and weapons to their Moslem enemies. Between 1015 and 1027 a general trade ban forbidding commerce with the Fatimids was in force.[176] Nevertheless trade with the Islamic world was never abandoned for long, and Byzantine merchants in some numbers frequented Syrian and Egyptian ports. But by and large, as in the years previous, it was the Moslem trader who carried his wares to Constantinople and exported the products Byzantium afforded in return. Certainly by the eleventh century Constantinople's merchant marine carried a very small proportion of her foreign trade to even the Islamic world.

This is even more true of the Empire's commerce with the Latin West. Venice, after a short period between 978 and 983 (in which she deserted Byzantium for the Ottos) returned to the fold. She received in 992 very important customs privileges at Constantinople which made her in fact the favored trader with the city on the Golden Horn.[177] Already she was, in Liudprand's time, evading regulations by shipping out forbidden silks through the

---

[173] Hill Cyprus, I, 257-60.

[174] Liudprand "The Embassy to Constantinople" in The Works of Liudprand of Cremona (trans. Wright), p. 235-77.

[175] Runciman Byzantine Civilization, pp. 226-39, 244-53, 271-76.

[176] Lopez "Silk Industry," p. 31.   [177] Taf. et Thom. I, 25-30.

connivance of customs officials.[178] After 992 her trade position there became all but unassailable. The older regulations, which governed residence of foreign merchants and limited the time they could stay in the city, were not enforced against either the Venetians or their fellow Italian Amalfitans. By the middle of the eleventh century merchants from both cities were living in Constantinople in definite quarters as permanent residents. They and other Italian traders already had what amounted to a monopoly of all Western trade with Byzantium.[179] In addition, they were apparently in the process by this time of gaining a similar position in Byzantium's city of Antioch, where Amalfitan merchants were particularly active.[180] They were thus already bypassing Constantinople itself in carrying valuable Eastern products from the shores of Syria to Western markets.

In one respect the Byzantine naval and land resurgence in the East after 960 benefited Italian merchants immensely. Protected by their Byzantine suzerainty and the activities of Constantinople's fleet, they could now reach both Constantinople and Antioch undisturbed by Moslem pirate interference. They could also follow this same route to Egypt and Syria without being molested, as Moslem merchants might be, by Byzantine commercial blockade or depredations. They were, in fact, the chief beneficiaries, from an economic standpoint, of the victories of Nicephorus Phocas, John Zimisces, and Basil II. They were in the lucky position of being able to gain all the benefits of Byzantine naval protection with none of the responsibilities—except when exasperated Byzantium, as in 971, demanded that they cease supplying Moslem ports with materials used against Constantinople. They, like colonial New England, had all the benefits of Empire protection and few of the burdens.

There was still a third group of foreigners who benefited from an important trade with Byzantium in this period—the Varangian Russians. Though their encroachments on the Crimea and other sections of the Empire caused John Zimisces and Basil II to resist them with armed force at various times, they traded actively with Constantinople. Cherson ceased at this time to be of any importance; Kazaria fell apart under Russian and nomad attacks. As

[178] Liudprand op. cit., p. 267-69.
[179] Heyd op. cit., p. 56. Schaube op. cit., p. 3-30.
[180] Diehl Venise, p. 20-21.

a result, the Black Sea trade fell almost entirely into Russian hands. Trading with Constantinople under the provisions of early tenth-century trade treaties, as well as furnishing excellent mercenaries for the Byzantine armed forces, Russia became an important and rich economic region in the late tenth and early eleventh centuries. The Varangian route, leading from the Black Sea through Kiev and other cities to the Baltic, became an important link between Western Europe and the wares of the East. Russia itself adopted Greek Orthodox Christianity and Byzantine culture at the time of Vladimir. The trade of Kiev with golden Tsargrad to the South was mainly in slaves and furs, both of which were probably in some measure relayed on to Arab merchants putting in at Constantinople. In return, Russian traders bought textiles, spices, and other Eastern wares and carried them back to Kiev and beyond. The richness of Vladimir's capital city of Kiev, and the fact that he coined gold in this period, are testimony to the importance of this commerce.[181]

Byzantium, then, shared in the expanding wealth of the Islamic Mediterranean and extended this prosperity through trade far into Russia. But it is possible that her economic passivity had already begun seriously to compromise a continuance of this state of affairs by the middle of the eleventh century. The growing hold of Italian merchants upon her Mediterranean trade may already have changed her economic relationship vis-à-vis Western Europe. The presence of gold byzants in the West suggests that by this time the balance of trade had swung against her—that her trade advantage over the West was ending.[182] Though Moslem and Russian trade seems to have been still profitable, this change was to be significant.

Similarly, the growing Italian trade monopoly further emphasized the already dangerous strength of the military landholding aristocracy who invested money and effort in land rather than in trade and commerce. Both John Zimisces and Nicephorus Phocas, members of this group themselves, had encouraged this process, reversing earlier trends. Basil II, after two serious revolts, attempted, with little success, to break up the estates and protect the free peasantry.[183] By 1043 the situation was dangerous indeed. Trade

---

[181] Lombard *op. cit.*, p. 157-58.
[182] Bloch "Le problem de l'Or," p. 14-15.
[183] *Jus Graeco-Romanum* iii, 299, 303.

was in the hands of foreigners, and armed strength in the hands of an aristocracy which could neither be trusted nor dispensed with. Byzantium, despite her apparent wealth and power, was approaching the disaster which Manzikert was to bring upon her.

There remains the Latin West. In this region the economic changes in this period were the most significant and far-reaching. In general, however, it was by way of the older Italian centers of commerce—Venice and Bari on the east coast and Amalfi, Gaeta, Salerno, and Naples on the Tyrrhenian Sea—that Western Europe felt the effects of the economic prosperity of the rest of the Mediterranean-Black Sea world. In this sense this period marks no break with the eighth, ninth, and early tenth centuries. Venice was in many ways unique among Western trade centers and deserves special attention. It began to enjoy in the late tenth century, under its Orseoli Doges, an economic power and prosperity far above what it had known before it came of age.

The first basis of Venice's wealth lay in its trade connections in the Byzantine Empire. These were of long standing, but in 992 they were increased by Basil II's grant of such low customs duties at the Golden Horn that she had an actual trade advantage over all other Westerners trafficking within the Empire. But these privileges were not extended without a *quid pro quo*. Venice bound herself in return not to extend her privilege of low customs duties to the goods of Amalfitan, Barian, and Jewish merchandise carried on Venetian ships. She also agreed to put her merchant vessels at the disposal of Constantinople when the latter wished to send troops to Italy. And she continued to use her shipping to carry couriers and messages of a diplomatic and official nature to and from the Adriatic and Byzantium.[184] Her smuggling of forbidden silks shows she was not above abusing her privileged position, however, even in Liudprand's time.

By the late tenth century she came to enjoy as privileged a position in Northern Italy and the Adriatic as she did in the Byzantine East. All the cities of the Dalmatian coast were by 1000 reduced to obedience to the city of the lagoons and paid tribute to Venice.[185] In Northern Italy also she enjoyed great privileges, which in large part went back to the time of Charlemagne and Lothair. Otto II, however, eager to control this rich city, revoked many of her trading rights in the Po Valley and applied economic

[184] *Taf. et Thom.* I, 21, 35-39. [185] Cessi *op. cit.*, p. 89.

measures to force her into submission. By 983 Otto had realized how impossible his attempt was, and he grudgingly renewed Venetian trading privileges, subject to certain payments to the Imperial treasury.[186] By 996 Otto III changed his father's policy. He wooed the city with additional commercial advantages in his realm. He not only forced the hostile Bishop of Belluno, who controlled certain valuable timber preserves, to make peace on terms advantageous to Venice, but he also removed the tribute payment of cloth-of-gold required of the city. He confirmed Venetian hunting and fishing rights in Lombardy. He returned to them property confiscated by his father in Lombardy, and he granted legal extra-territoriality to Venetians within his Italian domains. These actions all but gave a monopoly of the eastern trade of Northern Italy to the Venetians.[187]

It is, however, important to note that these rights were not extended beyond the Alps. Venetian wares were exposed for sale in Pavia, Ferrara, and several other centers and there only. Henry II, for instance, in his confirmation of Venetian privileges in Italy in the early eleventh century, actually forbade merchants of the city to sell their wares anywhere within his kingdom except at Pavia and two other centers.[188] German merchants, carrying these wares back across the Alps into Germany, were thus protected from any Venetian competition in this period. Subject to this limitation, however, Venice's trade position in Northern Italy was immensely important, and she had no rivals. So profitable did commerce become that in this period her old noble families, depending upon estates, joined the merchant class and became absorbed into the economic trade life of the city.[189]

Venice's commercial advantages in Constantinople and the Adriatic did not, however, mark the full extent or range of her commercial connections. By this time she had a trade network extending to all important Moslem centers of the Mediterranean world. Doge Peter II, architect of much of Venice's greatness in the late tenth century, sent ambassadors to all the Saracen princes of the Mediterranean. Venice thus traded with the Moslems of

[186] ibid., p. 78. [187] ibid., p. 82-83.
[188] John Diac. Chron. Ven., p. 38.
[189] Luzzatto, G. "Les noblesses, les activités économiques du patriciat vénitien" in Ann. d'Hist. Écon. et Soc. (1937) IX, 25-27. This was in startling contrast to Byzantium, whose nobility were steadily becoming more agrarian.

Sicily, North Africa, Egypt, and Syria.[190] So extensive was her commerce with Moslem ports in timber, iron, and arms that John Zimisces in 971 felt it necessary to take action against it and ordered it to cease. Slaves also were an important Venetian export in this period, bringing periodic protests from such monarchs as Otto I and ineffective regulations by the Doges.[191]

Amalfi, on Italy's west coast, appears to have been Venice's main trade rival in the Byzantine and Moslem East, though Bari's merchant shipping also ventured to Constantinople.[192] The Amalfitans, too, were settled in their own quarter in the capital city on the Golden Horn. They also smuggled out prohibited silks from the city.[193] In their large ships they also ventured to Antioch, where their trade was particularly active and had close relations with the Fatimids in Egypt and Syria, including certain special rights and a church in Jerusalem itself.[194]

The other Campanian centers, such as Naples, Gaeta, and Salerno, were equally active commercially and equally wealthy, but their trade seems to have been more confined to Sicily and the Moslem West and did not extend, as did Venice's and Amalfi's, to Byzantium, Syria, and Egypt. Ibn Hawkal noted in the late tenth century that Neapolitan textiles were sold in Palermo.[195] Arab money was coined in Salerno in the eleventh century.[196] The industrial nature of Sicily, North Africa, and Spain, with their wide imports of Eastern spices, made them, as a matter of fact, as good sources of luxury products as Constantinople, Cairo, or Alexandria. Hence the Campanian cities were able to obtain all the wares they could dispose of at a profit. To emphasize the close connection between Moslem ports and these cities it is worth noting that from 965 to 1025, when Byzantine maritime strength was all but lacking in Western waters, none of these cities was subject to Moslem raids. These were concentrated on Byzantine Calabria and Apulia and the Tuscan and Ligurian coasts.

To sum up, then, the trade of Southern Italy and the Po Valley increased in this period with both Islamic and Byzantine ports.

[190] John Diac. *Chron. Ven.*, p. 29.

[191] Schaube *op. cit.*, p. 6. Amari *Storia* II, 200.

[192] *Taf. et Thom.* I, 38. Heyd *op. cit.*, p. 95-7.

[193] Lopez "Silk Industry," p. 40-41. *Jus Graeco-Romanum* I, 261-62. Liudprand *op. cit.*, p. 268.

[194] *Gesta Roberti Wiscardi* in *MGH Script.* IX, 275. Heyd *op. cit.*, p. 108-09.

[195] Amari *Storia* II, 515.   [196] *ibid.*, p. 523-24.

This marks a continuation of earlier develepments already noted. The significance lies not in the trade of these areas, but in the growth of trade in the late tenth and early eleventh centuries, with Venice and Amalfi gaining a constantly larger share of it, thanks to their Eastern trade connections. Most of Italy, like the rest of the Mediterranean, shared, then, in the general prosperity of the period.

So far, the parts of Italy dealt with are just those parts which since the eighth century had gradually increased their share of the international commerce of the Mediterranean, those areas which had an old Byzantine connection and yet were far enough away from Constantinople's control to be able to trade freely with the Moslems as well. But another quite different process was going on in Italy at this time—the naval rise of Genoa and Pisa—and with this a maritime renaissance of the old Carolingian coast from the Ebro to the Tiber.

This new maritime activity had no connection with Byzantine naval victories or trade connections with the Islamic world. It was a new process related to the internal changes which had taken place in Western European society[197] and the weakness of the Moslems in the West. One might date its genesis from the expansion of the Ottos across the Alps in 962 or the expulsion of the Moslem freebooters of Fraxinetum in 972. Actually there is more connection between these two events than appears on the surface. Otto I as early as 953 sent an embassy to Abd-ar-Rahman III requesting withdrawal of this base,[198] and in 968 actually planned a campaign against it.[199]

But whatever the genesis of this movement, by the year 1000 it was definitely in motion. And already its most characteristic feature was that it was primarily a military rather than an economic affair. It represented a common effort of nobility and others to expel the Moslems from the positions they had on land and sea. If it had an economic basis, it was one of booty—not of trade. And added to these military and freebooting motives there soon was a third, the religious—lacking in most of the previous encounters with the Islamic world up to the eleventh century. Just where and when this religious motive entered the picture it is difficult to say.

[197] Munro and Strayer op. cit., p. 158-96.
[198] Vita John Abb. Gor. in MGH Script. III, 375.
[199] Wikukind in MGH Script. IV, 464.

Perhaps it was a secular echo of the Chuniac reform movement. Perhaps it resulted from Almansor's plundering of Compostela and al-Hakim's destruction of the Holy Sepulcher—news of both of which events was brought back to Western Europe by the pilgrims who flocked in this period to both shrines. The importance of this religious motivation is difficult to assess, but it undoubtedly existed.[200]

Many groups in Western Europe played a part in this offensive. The Normans, already present in Southern Italy in 1016 at Salerno and active as mercenaries in George Maniaces' army invading Sicily in 1038 and as robber barons in Apulia in his rear; the Norman and French adventurers, who in 1018 fought for the Count of Barcelona against Mugahid;[201] the Pisans and Genoese, who battled the same Moslem pirate king off Italy in 1015 and Sardinia in 1016—all were part of the same movement, a mysterious expansion of Western Europe south into the Mediterranean. The movement was to culminate in the Crusades.

The opportunities afforded adventurers in the early eleventh century on land and sea in the Western Mediterranean were immense. In Spain, for instance, the disorganized state of the land and the reluctance of the Arab aristocracy to do their own fighting put a premium on Christian mercenary soldiers, whether of native Spanish extraction or of northern European origin. They were used in the armies of both the Moslem kinglets and the Christian monarchs. As a matter of fact, they had, under Almansor, already been the backbone of the Ommayid army.[202] Under his successors in Seville, Granada, Beja, and Valencia they became the terrors of the land. The Cid was simply a later and very successful example of this type—neither more nor less cruel, greedy, and warlike than any number of others. The Kings of Christian Spanish realms differed from him only in their legitimate character, not in their methods, ideals and interests.[203]

The Genoese and Pisans were very similar to their Spanish land counterparts or the Normans in Southern Italy. Their naval struggle with Mugahid gave them a taste for booty. By 1034, with the sacking of Bone, they had turned to large-scale freebooting. Piracy

[200] Munro and Strayer *op. cit.*, p. 159-66.
[201] *Chron. Ademar* in *MGH Script.* iv, 104-05.
[202] Lévi-Provençal *Hist. de l'Espagne Mussulmane*, p. 458.
[203] Dozy *Recherches* ii, p. 103-96.

on the sea, like similar activities on the land in Southern Italy and Spain, gave organized and not overscrupulous fighting men a chance to gain valuable gold and plunder.

Already as early as 1043 this expansion south on land and sea began to have important economic results for this section of Western Europe. Most important, it resulted in the accumulation of capital in gold, up to this time relatively scarce in these regions, which had been largely agrarian and on a silver Carolingian standard.[204] The results of this process have been most carefully studied in Genoa.[205] But in general the same process was going on all along the coast from Barcelona to Pisa. Gold from Moslem Spain, seized on the sea or as a result of plunderings in the fertile lands of Byzantine and Italian provinces in Southern Italy, flowed back into parts of Western Europe which to a great extent had been economically stagnant up to this time. Thus had Aghlabid North Africa gained much of the capital which had transformed it into a wealthy, prosperous region in the late ninth century. So, too, did Elizabethan England and Revolutionary New England accumulate much of the gold and silver they used later in maritime trade expansion. To view this process as a reaction against Moslem piracy or an Islamic blockade is to miss the point. Though it started, perhaps, in this fashion, it soon became a method of gaining wealth. And upon this wealth later economic growth largely depended. Pirate gold built Genoa and Pisa as surely as it did Palermo, Medhia, Plymouth, Bristol, Salem, and a hundred other ports.

This development began soon to have an effect on trade and commerce. With the Western coasts clearer of Moslem pirates than they had been for centuries and capital in gold available, raiding began gradually to change to trading. Already by 1043 there were signs of economic stirrings along the entrance to the Rhone Valley route into Western Europe at Montpellier and Marseilles, still faint but certainly apparent.[206] Wares began to follow this ancient trade route again.

The same thing is true of other trade routes from the Mediterranean into the heart of Western Europe. As the Moslems were

[204] Braudel, F. "Monnaies et civilizations. De l'or du Sudan à l'argent d'Amérique" in *Annales* (1946) I, 11.

[205] Lopez "Orig. du Capit. Gén." in *op. cit.*

[206] Arnaud de Verdale *Cat. Epis. Mag.* in *op. cit.*, pp. 508, 510. This tells of tolls on ships landing goods near Montpellier about the middle of the eleventh century.

cleared from Fraxinetum and the Alpine passes and the
garians were driven east, more routes for merchandise beca'
sible from the Po Valley to Germany and France. The *!*
the pass most used by German Emperors going south into Italy,
began to hum with new life. In the early eleventh century it appears to have carried an increasing amount of Italian wares north
and German goods south. In 1017 Thietmar of Merseburg noted
in his chronicle the wreck of four Venetian galleys carrying spices
to Venice, thus showing how closely tied this area was with Italy.[207]
Conrad II in 1028 felt the route was important enough to grant
the right to levy tolls at Saben to the Bishop of Brixen.[208] Slaves
from Prague and metals from eastern Germany went south in
large amounts over Brenner, Plocken, and Pontebba routes.[209]
Trade between Italy and France increased as well, thanks to open
Alpine routes. Not only did the Kingdom of Burgundy fall into
the hands of the German rulers, but in 1037 Conrad II granted
to the merchants of Asti freedom from all tolls within the
Empire.[210]

There are other indications of the increase in commerce over
the Alpine passes in this period. The increase of Byzantine gold
coins in Germany,[211] the luxury of the Ottonian court, the influence
of Byzantine art motifs in German Romanesque architecture—all
these point to the close connections with the East that increased
trade along Adriatic-Lombardy-Germany routes made possible.
The very movement of the Ottos south into Italy probably reflects
the increased interest in the sources of this trade wealth. It was
not just desire to control the Church, vital as this agency was to
Ottonian government, that dictated Otto I's decision to take over
Northern Italy in 962 and assume the crown of Holy Roman Emperor. He and his successors wished to gain the riches that Italy,
through its trade, had to offer, and to control the beginning as well
as the end of the trade routes bringing wealth into their Empire.

There was still a long path that had to be travelled before
Western Europe, beyond Italy, became fully integrated into the
gold-based, international worlds of Mediterranean Islam and
Byzantium. But by the middle of the eleventh century in Germany
and Southern France a beginning was definitely being made. The

[207] Thietmar *Chron.*, p. 238.
[208] Tyler *Alpine Passes*, p. 156.
[209] Schaube *op. cit.*, p. 94.
[210] *ibid.*, p. 91.
[211] Bloch "Le problème d'or," p. 14.

best sign of this growing integration is perhaps to be seen in the pilgrim trade to the Holy Land. It steadily increased in the period under discussion—despite the persecutions of al-Hakim. By 1027 there is record of a party of 700 pilgrims, of which Richard de St. Vanne was a member, making this long voyage in a body.[212] Already, then, large numbers of Latin Westerners were becoming acquainted with Eastern Mediterranean regions they were to control a century later.

To sum up, by 1043 weakening Moslem naval control of the Mediterranean, marked by Byzantine maritime resurgence and the turning to the sea on the part of the Genoese, Pisans and other Westerners, already foreshadowed the future. This change in naval strength did not, however, adversely affect the economic level of prosperity of the Mediterranean-Black Sea area. Rather it continued to increase in wealth and trade. Moslems, Byzantines, and Varangians of South Russia, as well as most of Italy, fully shared in this prosperity, with such Italian centers as Venice and Amalfi showing the greatest development in the expansion of their commerce and carrying trade in the Mediterranean. Western Europe, too, began at last to be affected and drawn into this international commercial system, as Genoese and Pisan fleets helped open up the Rhone Valley route and the Alpine passes carried larger amounts of goods to and from Central Europe. The Latin West, losing its agrarian localism and throwing off its weaknesses, began to claim its share in the commerce of the Middle Sea so long dominated by Byzantium and Islam.

[212] *Hugonis Chron.* in *MGH Script.* viii, 393. *Gesta Epis. Verdun* in *MGH Script.* viii, 394.

7. The Triumph of the West

The last fifty years of the eleventh century witnessed the triumph of Western European Italian fleets over the older Islamic and Byzantine sea power which had so long ruled the waters of the Middle Sea. By 1100 Western Europeans were masters of Corsica, Sardinia, Sicily, Southern Italy, and the coasts of Palestine and Syria. They controlled the great international maritime trade routes between the East and the West.

This change was made possible by the disasters which overwhelmed the older centers of trade and commerce about the Mediterranean and Black Seas. Byzantium, for instance, already weakened by internal disputes, was attacked in 1071 by the Seljuk Turks. These Central Asian nomads, after their victory at Manzikert, overran the interior of the rich province of Asia Minor, never to be ejected. Syria, too, felt the impact of Turkish attacks, which all but destroyed effective Fatimid control there. Russia's Kievan kingdom began to lose contact with the Black Sea and Byzantium, as the savage Turkish Uzes, on the heels of equally barbarous Petcheneks and Cumans, cut through her Dnieper defenses and occupied the steppes of South Russia. Egypt suffered two decades of disorders as Negro, Turkish, and Berber slave and mercenary troops got out of hand and plundered the land. Ziridite North Africa, breaking with its Fatimid overlords of Cairo, found itself devastated by the great Hilalian nomadic invasion. Moslem Spain, all but crushed by the pressure of the Christians to the north, saved herself only by calling in even more savage Berber nomads, the Almoravids of Saharan Morocco.

It was, in short, a period in which, with the exception of Western Europe, every important area about the Mediterranean and Black Seas was thoroughly disorganized by the appearance and pressure of outside nomadic peoples. Petcheneks, Seljuk Turks, Hilalian Arabs, and Almoravids had this in common: they were all nomads, driven from their desert homes by political, economic or climatic conditions, with little respect for the highly evolved political and economic systems they found in the lands which they invaded. They were essentially destroyers of settled civilization. It is not surprising, then, that Western Europeans so easily entered into the naval and trade heritage of Byzantium and Islam during this period. Only in Spain did they meet a definite check, and then at the hands of the nomad Almoravids, not the settled native Spanish Moslems. Elsewhere they won in large part by default. Normans, Venetians, Pisans, Genoese, and French feudal knights and adventurers were attacking peoples and regions fatally weakened by nomad pressure. The First Crusade was thus not the cause of Western Europe's entry into its heritage of Mediterranean dominance, it was the end of a process—the final step already foreshadowed by Western aggressiveness for almost a century in a world in which both Islam and Byzantium were steadily declining.

Perhaps the most important development in this period was the breakup of the Fatimid North African Empire and its results. This breakup had already been foreshadowed in the growing coolness between Cairo and Kairouan after the accession of the Ziridite ruler, al-Moeizz. It became even more noticeable when Sicily, at the time of its invasion by Byzantium in 1038, received aid from Ziridite Africa, but none from Fatimid Egypt.[1] Henceforth Sicily's Emirs looked no longer to Cairo's Shiah Caliphs for assistance and became all but independent. Kairouan was not slow to follow Palermo's lead. The first step was a massacre, unpunished by the Ziridites, of all the Shiahs in their capital city.[2] This was followed, in 1041, by a recognition of the Abbassid Caliph of Bagdad, rather than the Fatimid Caliph of Cairo, as spiritual head.[3] In 1049 rugs and cloth with Shiah formulas thereon were burnt, and the circulation of Fatimid coinage was forbidden.[4] Finally in 1051 the white garments, emblematic of the Fatimids, distributed to the people of the Ziridite court and religious leaders, were dyed black, the Abbassid color.[5] The break was now complete. But the breakup of Moslem Africa proceeded even beyond Ziridite and Kalbite independence. Both Tripoli and the Hammadites of western Tunisia and Algeria, already autonomous, hastened to declare their independence of Kairouan. Not only was Fatimid allegiance repudiated in this area, but four distinct Moslem principalities, Tripoli, Tunisia, Hammadite Algeria, and Sicily emerged

[1] Wiet *Egypte Arabe*, p. 130-33.
[2] *At Tigani* in *Journ. Asiat.* (1852) II, 91.
[3] Ibn Khaldun *Hist. des Berbères* I, 31. *Ibn Idhari* I, 411. *Ibn al Athir* I, 454-55.
[4] Marçais *Berbérie*, p. 168-71.   [5] *Ibn Idhari* I, 418.

from the ruins of Cairo's authority in the Magreb. North Africa became as divided and chaotic as Spain was after the fall of the Ommayid Caliphate.[6]

What followed was even more serious. Fatimid Egypt, ruled by the weak and incompetent Caliph Mustansir, was unable to take any direct retaliatory action against this rebellion in her Western domains. Instead, two large Arab bedouin tribes, the Beni Hilal and the Beni Solaim, whose presence nearby endangered Egypt's security, were directed west against the Ziridites. In 1052 they reached Tunisia. Kairouan's ruler, al-Moeizz, met them with an army near Gabes to bar their entry into the land.[7] His forces were utterly routed. The Arab nomads then moved into the rich countryside, sacking unprotected cities and destroying the settled agricultural population—joined apparently by native Berber bedouin tribesmen always willing to raid the farming and city populations.[8]

Only Kairouan and its nearby suburb of Mançouriya, surrounded by high walls, was able to resist. But as, year after year, the nomads continued to stay in the countryside, devouring its substance like a swarm of locusts, the resistance of the Ziridites weakened. In 1059 they withdrew from their capital of Kairouan to the security of their seacoast citadel of Medhia.[9] Mançouriya with its great palaces was sacked and utterly destroyed. Many inhabitants of the land fled to Sicily and Spain.[10] Anarchy reigned throughout the interior, and with the inability of the Ziridites to maintain order local magnates and adventurers seized independent power in Gabes, Sfax, Gafsa, Bizerte, Laribus, and Tunis. Effective central government disappeared.[11]

The domains of the Hammadites further to the West were, at first, little disturbed by these Arab nomads. In fact, Hammadite rulers appear to have welcomed the opportunity these invasions gave them to dispose of their Ziridite rivals. In 1064 en-Naçir, the Hammadite prince, led an army into Tunisia against the Ziridites. His attempt ended in failure. He was as badly defeated at Shiba

[6] *Ibn Khaldun* i, 17, 44. Amari *Storia* ii, 415.

[7] Marçais *Berbérie*, p. 194-6.

[8] *Ibn Khaldun* i, 44; ii, 29, 39. Gautier *Les Siècles Obscurs du Magreb*, p. 385-94.

[9] *Ibn Khaldun* ii, 31.

[10] Al Marrakeshi *Hist. des Almohades* trans. Fagnan (Alger 1893), p. 385.

[11] *Ibn Khaldun* ii, 33-39. *Ibn al Athir* i, 470. *Ibn Idhari* i, 445. Marçais *op. cit.*, p. 196-98.

as al-Moeizz had been at Gabes a decade before.[12] So weakened
was he by this defeat that his realm in turn lay open to nomadic
infiltration. Within a few years he was forced to abandon both his
capital, Qala, in the interior and the plain of Bone and retire west
to Bougie. This port city, which had been founded in 1067 and
was surrounded by hills, soon became the central nexus of Hammadite power.[13] Refugees from the interior of Tunisia and Algeria,
seeking the security of these relatively peaceful domains, soon
made it an important center. In fact, this Hammadite principality
and the hills of Little Kabylie were the only areas of Tunisia and
Algeria, with the exception of coastal cities like Tunis and Medhia,
which escaped being overrun and ravaged by the bedouins. The
hinterland, and particularly the flat lands in southern and central
Tunisia, were terribly devastated.

Meanwhile to the west another bedouin people, the Saharan
Berber Almoravids, were also on the move against settled agricultural regions. They, like the Beni Hilal and the Beni Solaim, started
in the year 1052. By 1063 they had taken Fez and overrun a whole
series of petty Moroccan principalities. They then swept west into
Algeria as far as Algiers.[14] By 1086 they had founded a bedouin state
(much better organized than that of the Arab nomads to the west
of them, who seemed incapable of any government at all) between
the Hammadites of Bougie and the Atlantic. In that year they
were summoned across the straits of Gibraltar into Spain by the
Moslem kinglets, who were becoming alarmed by the advance
south of their northern Christian foes. In Spain, Almoravid arms
proved capable of halting the Christians, but they did not then
return to Morocco as the Spanish Moslems desired. Instead, they
founded a kingdom in Spain that lasted well into the next century.[15] Fiercely proud and puritanical at first, they were soon
debased and softened by the luxury of Andalusia, which pandered
to their bedouin vices and destroyed their virtues. By the time
their state fell to the Almohads, there was little left of the religious
enthusiasm and vigor which had at first characterized their movement.[16]

---

[12] Marçais *op. cit.*, p. 199-200.   [13] *Ibn al Athir*, p. 472. *Al Bakri*, p. 105.
[14] *Ibn Khaldun* II, 75. Roudh al Kaitas *Hist. des souverains du Magreb et Annales
de la Ville de Fez*, trans. Paumier, p. 199.
[15] Mas Latrie *Traités de Paix*, p. 26. Burke *A History of Spain* 2nd Ed. (London
1920), p. 202-03.
[16] Burke *op. cit.*, p. 203-05.

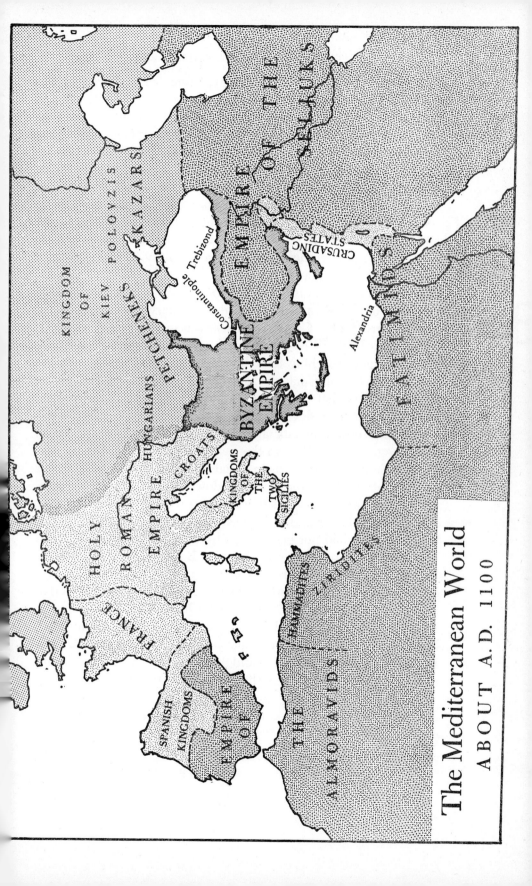

The Mediterranean World
ABOUT A.D. 1100

In the East, the situation of Egypt and Syria proved in this period equally unfortunate. Relations between Fatimid Egypt and Syria and Byzantium after the peace of 1038 were at first harmonious. In 1055, however, war broke out over Constantinople's failure to send Cairo grain promised in 1052.[17] The short war on land and sea proved rather inconclusive, though the Fatimids showed little ability on either element. Shortly thereafter hostilities ended, and Byzantium ceased to threaten Egypt's position in serious fashion. Despite loss of Ziridite Africa and Sicily, Egypt and Syria seem to have been rather prosperous, particularly as Dizbiri, Syria's governor, showed a real ability in keeping order and suppressing brigandage.

In 1060, however, disaster fell upon the land. Its cause was the rebellion of the Fatimid slave and mercenary troops whom the weak government of Caliph Mustansir was unable to keep in order. For seventeen years Negro, Turkish, and Berber soldiery devastated the land, reaching their height of destructiveness with the sack of the Caliph's palaces at Cairo in 1067.[18] So serious were these disorders that famine stalked this rich agricultural region. Syria, left to its own devices, fell into the control of local dynasties who seized power in city after city, while the nomadic Seljuk Turks began to invade from the east.[19] Only the fact that the Byzantine Empire nearby was in equal disorder, thanks to civil war and the attempts of the great landowners to seize power, prevented the Fatimids from suffering even worse disasters.

Caliph Mustansir and his dynasty would probably have disappeared if they had not been saved by outside assistance. In 1073 the government of Cairo sent a certain Badr to Syria as governor. By his ability he soon brought order out of chaos there and re-established Fatimid authority. Then, with 100 vessels of the Syrian fleet, he sailed on Egypt.[20] By 1077 he had restored order in the Delta and pacified the land. From then on until his death he ruled, like Almansor of Spain a century before, as a military dictator. Under his stern regime Egypt and Syria recovered a large measure of prosperity. Unable and perhaps unwilling to attempt to restore

[17] Wiet op. cit., p. 225-29. Egypt's negotiations to procure grain from Byzantium were the result of a severe famine in Egypt. This may be the cause of the many nomadic movements in all directions in this period. See Lane-Poole Egypt, p. 142-43.

[18] Wiet op. cit., p. 238-40. Lane-Poole op. cit., p. 147-48.

[19] Wiet op. cit., p. 242-45.   [20] ibid., p. 246-48.

Fatimid rule over North Africa, he at least brought some measure of order to the state.[21] All this ended with his death and that of the Caliph he served so well, al-Mustansir, in 1094. He left no worthy successors. Egypt sank again into the weakness and futility from which it was not aroused again until the coming of Saladin in the next century.

Meanwhile in the nearby Byzantine Empire very much the same pattern of events was unfolding. The aged Constantine IX Monomachus, who ruled as Emperor from 1042 to 1055, had inherited the problem of a landholding, warrior aristocracy which had grown much too rich and powerful on its large Asia Minor estates. His answer to the problem, one apparently supported by the civil bureaucracy, was to eliminate the power of this group by curbing the military establishment which gave them their authority and influence. Thus he not only pursued a pacific foreign policy in the East and abandoned Byzantine Italy to its fate, but definitely scaled down the army and navy.[22] There might have been some merit in such a policy if it had not been for the fact that new and dangerous enemies were appearing in 1044 along the Eastern frontiers—the Seljuk Turks. They were, however, no particular threat until after 1056 when the Macedonian line of Emperors came to an end.

Then the Empire, already weakened by the economies in the military establishment instituted by Constantine IX, and more and more coming under the commercial domination of Western Italian merchants who were monopolizing its trade, fell into disorder. There followed civil wars and a series of short-lived Emperors, each striving to found a new and permanent dynasty on the throne. One of these was, in 1071, unwise enough to lead an unprepared army far into Armenia and there challenge the might of the Seljuks. The battle of Manzikert which followed ended in complete disaster for Byzantium. The army was destroyed, and the Emperor Romanus IV himself made captive. Asia Minor lay open to invasion.[23] The Turks swarmed in, sacking cities and in nomad fashion destroying the settled agricultural population. Like the Hilalian Arabs in North Africa, they reduced the land to beg-

[21] *ibid.*, p. 248-54.

[22] Zonarius *Epist. Hist.* ed. Bonn (1897) III, 627, 653. Psellsus *Chron.* I, 151-53. On the decay of the fleet see Neuman, C. "Die Byzantinische Marine; Ihre Verfassung und ihr Verfall" in *Hist. Zeit.* (1898) XLV.

[23] Runciman *Byz. Civ.*, p. 147.

gary. One by one the largely undefended Anatolian themes fell to Turkish bands, and a Seljuk Sultan made Iconium his Anatolian capital. By 1076 the Turks had reached the sea in various places, and at Smyrna one adventurer, Tzaches, even organized a fleet whose piratical raids in the Aegean threatened the capital itself.[24] When Alexius Comnenus became Emperor in Constantinople in 1081, he found a disorganized Empire. Turks were in control of most of Anatolia. Naval and military forces were thoroughly disorganized. And Petcheneks and Cumans were swarming across the Danube into his Balkan domains in the West as well.[25]

Kievan Russian proved equally weak. Partly this was the result of the disappearance of the Kazar kingdom, a buffer state which guarded the South Russian steppes just as Armenia protected Byzantine Asia Minor. Russian moves against Kazaria proved as unwise as Byzantine occupation of Armenia.[26] In each case it was nomadic Turkish peoples who benefited. When the princes of the Russian cities quarreled among themselves in the course of the eleventh century, the Uzes, Petcheneks and Cumans were able, with little difficulty, to overwhelm Varangian fortresses guarding the Dnieper route. Firm contact with the Black Sea and Byzantium was thus lost. Though Russian principalities kept some measure of prosperity and strength until the coming of the Mongols in the thirteenth century, by the late eleventh century they had already lost the wealth and vigor which had distinguished the kingdoms of Sviatoslav and Vladimir.[27]

It is against the background of such developments that the activities of the Western European peoples must be considered. A North Africa, Spain, Egypt, Byzantium and Russia in chaos and weakness gave great opportunities to aggressive Westerners to encroach upon all parts of the Mediterranean world.

The mariners of Genoa and Pisa were among the first to take advantage of this situation. In 1050 they joined together again, urged by Pope Leo IX, to expel Spanish Moslem pirates from Sardinia.[28] Apparently their quarrels had permitted Ali, Mugahid of Denia's son, to reoccupy the island after their earlier victory in 1016. About the same time they also established some sort of authority

[24] Vasiliev *Byzantine Empire* II, 23-25.

[25] *Cedrenus* II, 652, 668-74.

[26] Vernadsky *Kievan Russia* (New Haven 1948), pp. 22, 42-47. Der Nersessian *Armenia and the Byzantine Empire*, p. 11.

[27] Vernadsky *op. cit.*, p. 118.   [28] *Al Makkari* II, 257.

over nearby Corsica.[29] In 1063 Pisa widened her range of activities by launching a great assault on the Moslem maritime center of Palermo and took much booty.[30] These activities in the Tyrrhenian alarmed some of the Campanian cities, which had long had close commercial ties with the Saracens, and under Gisulf of Salerno (1052-1077) this city seized Genoese and Pisan ships passing along the coast.[31]

By 1087, however, so strong had the naval power of Genoa and Pisa become that they launched their most important raid of all. This was a naval expedition of 400 ships, including Amalfitan contingents and a large number of troops supplied by the Pope. Its objective was the Ziridite stronghold of Medhia on the coast of Tunisia. It proved very successful. The Italians landed their forces, seized the harbor and town, and gained immense booty and plunder. Only the citadel held out, and Tamin, the Ziridite Sultan, was forced to pay, as the price of withdrawal, an immense ransom and to promise not to interfere with the shipping of the Italian cities in African waters. The importance of this raid was very great.[32] Not only does it mark the first appearance of Genoese and Pisan ships in any strength beyond the Western Mediterranean, but their interest in commerce is marked by the agreement extorted from Tamin not to interfere with Italian shipping. This may reflect, on the other hand, Amalfitan interests rather than those of the Ligurian and Tuscan cities. Amalfi had had great commercial interests in Eastern waters for many years—more than any other Italian city except Venice.

Meanwhile the situation in the Spanish peninsula was also such that it gave Italian mariners ample opportunities for profitable intervention. Northern adventurers and Spanish Christian soldiers of fortune, both urged on by an aggressive Church as well as their own cupidity, were up to 1086 finding the Spanish Moorish kingdoms profitable sources of booty and plunder. The King of Castile in 1085 had occupied Toledo and extended his frontiers south.[33] He was forcing the Moslem ruler of Seville, strongest of the Islamic

[29] Mas Latrie *op. cit.*, p. 8-9.

[30] Marangone *Ann. Pisa* in *MGH Script.* xix, 238. *Chron. Var. Pisa* in *Mur. Rer. Ital. Script.* vi, 161.

[31] *Gauf. Malaterra* in *op. cit.* v, 569, 590.

[32] *Ibn Khaldun* ii, 24. *Ibn al Athir* i, 487-88. *Marangone*, p. 239. *Malaterra*, p. 590.

[33] *Al Makkari* i, 228.

princelings, to make heavy tribute payments as Castilian troops penetrated far south into Andalusia.[34] The same principles of penetration and extortion were being followed by the Cid in Valencia.[35] The Italian cities joined in this pursuit from the sea, sharing in the booty. On Almeria they levied a ransom amounting to 113,000 gold maraboutins, and they forced Valencia to pay 20,000 dinars to escape sack.[36] Already the Balearics, to be seized in the early twelfth century, were suffering piratical raids at their hands. Bari, Monte Garigliano, and Fraxinetum were being amply avenged upon weakening Islamic shores.

While these developments were taking place, Sicily, long the protective bastion of Islam in the Western Mediterranean, was losing its strength and defensive importance. There was a continuation of the internal schisms and struggles between Moslem Berber and Arab inhabitants which had almost permitted Byzantium to capture the island between 1038 and 1043. In 1052 a fleet which al-Moeizz, Ziridite ruler of Africa, sent to bolster the defenses of Palermo, was wrecked off the island of Pantelleria.[37] Then, with Hilalian Arab invasion, African assistance was limited by need of every effort being made at home, and Sicily was left to fend for itself.

Its peril, which was great, came not so much from the maritime revival along the Ligurian and Tuscan coasts of Italy (though Palermo did feel the fury of Pisan assault in 1063) as from a new and ruthless enemy—the Normans of Southern Italy. The Normans had made their appearance in this region as early as 1016. By 1040 they had already built up a freebooting principality in Northern Apulia, and their activities in Italy behind the advancing troops of Maniaces had been one reason for his failure in 1038-1043. After 1040 leadership of the most aggressive Norman bands in Italy came to be exercised by Robert Guiscard of the prolific and able Hauteville family.[38] Gradually he built up a strong state in Apulia and Beneventum at the expense of local Italian princes and Byzantine authorities. In 1059 his position was regularized by

[34] Hitti *History of the Arabs*, p. 540.

[35] Dozy *Recherches* ii, 35.

[36] Lopez "Orig. du Capit Génois," p. 445-47.

[37] *Ibn al Athir* i, 502.

[38] Amari *Storia* iii, 30-41. Haskins *The Normans in European History* (New York 1915), p. 200-1.

the Pope, who made him a papal vassal for his assistance against German troops at Rome threatening Papal independence.[39]

Meanwhile Roger, younger brother of Robert, had appeared in Southern Italy, and was put in charge of certain Norman bands and conquests in Calabria. Like Robert, Roger was a man of real ability and soon had built up a Norman state in Calabria, largely at the expense of Byzantine authorities in this region.[40] Papal recognition of the Guiscards in 1059 had included a promise to them of control of Moslem Sicily if they could capture it. By 1061 Roger was ready to start. In that year he led a force across the straits and seized Messina—a step made possible by ships furnished by conquered Reggio and by certain *dromons* that Robert made available from conquered cities in Apulia to the east.[41] Then the Normans pressed inland and defeated a Moslem Sicilian force near Castrogiovanni.[42] Roger was unable to follow up this victory at once. Affairs in Italy demanded his attention, and he withdrew from the island, leaving his conquests in the hands of trustworthy lieutenants.

The invasion and successes of Roger Guiscard and the Pisan raid on Palermo in 1063 apparently frightened the Moslems of Sicily. They appealed to Medhia for assistance. Tamin, who had succeeded his father al-Moeizz in 1062 and had just won a victory over his Hammadite rivals at Shiba, responded with some help in 1064.[43] For four years African forces were on the island. Their presence there seems to have caused friction with the Sicilian Moslems, who came to hate them. Angered by Sicilian opposition, the Ziridites withdrew their forces in 1068, taking many Moslem notables of the island with them.[44] Sicily was left alone to face the Norman storm, launched by the Guiscards.

It was not long in breaking upon the island. Robert Guiscard had captured Bari in 1071, and that was the last Byzantine holding in Italy. Thus Robert's fleet was available for duty against Sicily.[45] With this naval force, numbering 56 vessels, and an ample land army, Roger launched an assault on Palermo, the Moslem capital. The city was soon invested by land and sea. Unable to get naval assistance from Africa, it fell to the Normans, to become

[39] Amari *Storia* III, 50-54. Haskins *op. cit.*, p. 203-04.

[40] Haskins *op. cit.*, p. 202, 206-07.   [41] Amari *Storia* III, 55-75.

[42] *ibid.*, p. 79-81.   [43] Ibn al Athir I, 503. *Nuwairi* II, 273.

[44] Amari *Storia* III, 112.

[45] Malaterra *op. cit.* in Caruso *Bib. Sic.* I, 159, 198-99.

their major island base.[46] In fact, so little did Tamin of Medhia desire to meddle in Sicilian affairs that he concluded a treaty of alliance and friendship with Roger in 1075, which remained in force for many years.[47]

There followed a slow but steady conquest and consolidation of Norman power in Sicily. In 1077 Trapani fell,[48] and in 1078 Taormina was in Norman hands.[49] In 1081 conquest paused as Roger found it necessary to relieve his brother Robert's forces holding Messina with his own troops, probably because of the latter's need for them in his plans and projects in the Adriatic. The Norman advance continued in 1086. In that year Girgenti was taken,[50] and in 1087 Syracuse, last major city in Moslem hands, fell to the Normans.[51] By 1090 Roger had completed the island's conquest less than thirty years after he had begun it.

The Norman Guiscards then pressed on in 1090 to seize Malta, probably rendered indefensible by the great Italian naval expedition against Medhia in 1087.[52] With its fall, Western Europe gained control of the vital straits between Africa and Sicily as well as the island of Sicily itself. Interestingly enough, the Normans received no assistance from the Italian cities of Genoa and Pisa in their conquest of Sicily, and none from the Campanian maritime centers except indirectly. As soon as they had established their rule over the island, however, the Italian merchants reaped much of the advantage that accrued. The Venetians, the Amalfitans, and later the Genoese—all were given extensive commercial privileges in Sicily which allowed them to share in the trade and industry that the older Islamic possessors of this land had so carefully built up for several centuries.[53]

This conquest of Calabria and Sicily by Roger Guiscard was also accompanied by similar expansion to the north along the Tyrrhenian Sea. Before Sicily was finally conquered, the Campanian cities of Naples, Gaeta, Salerno, and Amalfi also submitted to the Guiscards; Amalfi accepted Norman suzerainty in 1076, and the last independent Norman bands near Salerno were absorbed into

[46] Amari Storia III, 120-33.
[47] Mas Latrie op. cit., p. 28-29 for provisions of this treaty.
[48] Amari Storia III, 149-51.   [49] ibid., p. 152-53.
[50] ibid., p. 161-67.   [51] ibid., p. 168-76.
[52] ibid., p. 180-83. On the unsuccessful attempt of Byzantium to take Malta in 1040 see Amari Storia II, 485.
[53] Taf. et Thom. I, 135-38, 171-76. Annal. Jan. in MGH Script. XVIII, 108.

their forces at about the same time. From Rome south to Reggio all was Norman.[54]

While Roger was thus building Norman power on the west coast of Italy and Sicily, his older brother Robert was equally active on the east coast. It has already been noted that by 1071 he had occupied Bari, the last Byzantine holding in Apulia. But this did not satisfy his ambitions. Realizing Byzantine weakness, much increased with the disaster of Manzikert, he turned his ambitions to the other side of the Adriatic. In 1075 his fleet was active off Dalmatia.[55] Venice, alarmed, sent a naval force which expelled his vessels and forced the cities of Spalato, Trau, and Zara to promise not to call in the Normans again.[56]

Checked here by Venetian strength, Robert turned his attention to Byzantine territory further south. In 1081 his fleet, reinforced by Ragusan contingents, assisted his armed forces in laying siege to Durazzo, across the straits from Bari.[57] This move again alarmed the Venetians. They had little desire to have Norman power firmly established on both sides of the entrance to the Adriatic. Therefore a fleet of 63 ships was sent to the relief of this Byzantine city. It drove off the Norman flotillas, but only temporarily.[58] In the next year treachery delivered it into Guiscard's hands. With this as a base, Robert continued his assaults on Byzantium's western Greek territory. Venice, firmly allied with Constantinople, continued her naval opposition. In 1084, for instance, a Venetian fleet of 70 sail, including nine huge castellated galleys, twice defeated a Norman force of 120 vessels off these shores, only to lose badly late in the year when some naval strength was withdrawn to the city of the lagoons.[59] Despite Venice's hostility, the fierce Norman ruler continued his attacks, until his death in 1085 removed the threat of Norman aggression from Alexius Comnenus and Venice alike. But the Kingdom of the Two Sicilies established in Southern Italy and Sicily remained a potent new maritime power to be reckoned with in the Central Mediterranean.

While it is true that Venice had ample reason to oppose Robert Guiscard's Adriatic ambitions on her own account, she was careful to make Alexius Comnenus pay a steep price for the naval assist-

[54] Haskins, *op. cit.*, pp. 204, 213.   [55] Dandolo *Chron.*, p. 248.
[56] *Taf. et Thom.* I, 41, 43.   [57] Vasiliev *Byzantine Empire* II, 17-18.
[58] Anna Comnena *Alexiad* trans. Corsi, p. 150. Cessi *op. cit.*, p. 124-26.
[59] Dandolo *Chron.*, p. 24-28. Yewdale, R. B. *Bohemond I, Prince of Antioch* (Princeton 1924), p. 18-24.

ance she rendered him in these years. Nothing better illustrates the naval weakness of Byzantium in this period than the fact that the Emperor of Constantinople had to depend completely upon Venetian naval strength to defend his Empire from Norman assaults. The *quid pro quo* was the Golden Bull he granted Venice in 1082. In it he gave Venice complete freedom from all customs dues and duties in all ports of the Empire in the Aegean and Mediterranean, except those of Cyprus and Crete. In addition the Amalfitan colony in Constantinople was made subject to Venice. This completely destroyed most of the remnants of Imperial control of foreign merchant shipping in the Byzantine state and gave the Venetians what amounted to a monopoly of commerce.[60] The provisions which relegated the Amalfitans to a position of dependence upon Venice may, however, have been a form of revenge against them for submitting to Constantinople's Norman enemies in 1076 rather than any particular concession to the city on the lagoons.

Too much attention has been given to this treaty by some historians without enough analysis. While it did grant Venice an extraordinarily privileged position in the economic life of the Empire at the expense of both other Italian merchants and the traders of the Byzantine state as well, it still contained important reservations. In the first place, Venetian merchants were excluded from the Black Sea ports, which the Comneni maintained as an exclusive preserve for Byzantine commerce. And secondly, Crete and Cyprus were not thrown open to Venetian traders without payment of customs dues, as were other localities along Byzantine coasts. This ensured that these two important island positions would remain under full fiscal and strategic control of Constantinople's authorities. Since Cyprus controlled East-West trade to Syria and Crete controlled that to Egypt, this reflects the determination of Byzantium to maintain some measure of control over this circle route, despite concessions to Venice's traders. But granting these reservations, it must be admitted that the Golden Bull of 1082 marks the official end of Byzantine policies of long standing, the conclusion of efforts to control foreign traders in the Empire, and the turning over of most of her Mediterranean trade to the Venetians. It was the logical end of that gradual growth of Venice's power in Byzantine waters which had begun in the eighth century.

[60] *Taf. et Thom.* I, 51-54.

The aggressiveness of the Normans in Italy, Sicily, and the Adriatic, of the Pisans and Genoese on the sea in the western Mediterranean, of French feudal adventurers in Spain, of Venice in Byzantine waters, added to Papal and Cluniac encouragement of a general assault upon the heathen Moslems for religious reasons, and the piety which was sending thousands of Western Christians on pilgrimage to the Holy Land—all these tendencies merged to form that movement we call the First Crusade. In other words, the First Crusade represented a complex amalgamation of forces already active in the Mediterranean West—religious sentiment, lust for booty on the part of Italian mariners and feudal adventurers, and desire for commercial and trade advantages.[61]

The immediate causes of this movement are easier to understand. They were two in number: First there was the appeal of Alexius Comnenus to the Pope asking for military assistance against the Seljuk Turks.[62] And second, there was the conquest of Jerusalem by the Turks, and the consequent stories of mistreatment of Western pilgrims by these fanatical Moslem nomads.[63] Alexius's appeal was for some Western knights who would buttress his land armies in Anatolia—probably much on the order of the mercenary Varangians who had for a century served Constantinople well. But Pope Urban II chose instead to emphasize not the plight of Constantinople, but the more popular religious appeal of a rescue of the Holy Land from the pagan Turkish troops of the Seljuk. At two great conclaves, one in Northern Italy and one in Southern France, his appeal for a Crusade roused tremendous enthusiasm among all classes of Western European society.[64]

What followed alarmed Byzantium. In 1096 a horde of disorganized Western crusaders under Peter the Hermit and Walter the Penniless marched through Hungary and Bulgaria and arrived at Constantinople. They were useless as soldiers, and their thievery alarmed the city's inhabitants. Alexius ferried them across into Asia Minor as swiftly as possible. There the Seljuks annihilated

[61] Munro, D. C. The Kingdom of the Crusaders (New York, 1936), p. 30-35.
[62] Munro, op. cit., p. 32. Krey, A. C. "Urban's Crusade—Success or Failure" Amer. Hist. Rev. (1948) LIII.
[63] ibid., p. 33.
[64] Urban cleverly shifted the ground from the saving of Constantinople to the conquest of Jerusalem at these conclaves, particularly that in France. See Munro op. cit., p. 32-34. Krey op. cit., Charanis, P., "A Greek Source on the Origin of the First Crusade" Speculum (1949) XXIV.

them in one battle. If this first horde alarmed Constantinople's Emperor, the second group of crusaders who arrived seemed even more menacing. They were well led, well disciplined Western feudal forces under Bohemond and Tancred, Raymond of Toulouse, Robert of Flanders, and Godfrey de Bouillon. They represented three rather distinct groups of Western European feudalism. Bohemond and Tancred's followers were typical of those Normans of Southern Italy who had long been Byzantium's most aggressive enemies. The forces of Raymond of Toulouse represented those Southern French nobles who had long been battling the Moslems in Spain. Robert and Godfrey's followers were representative of Northern French feudal adventurers.[65] Alexius suspected that their presence in the East, particularly that of Bohemond, Tancred, and Raymond, was but slightly connected with religious zeal. He furthermore recognized his own military weakness. Therefore, after making them swear an ill-humored fealty to him for their future conquests, he promptly ferried them into Asia Minor.[66]

Cooperation between Byzantines and Westerners proved short-lived. It ended when Alexius received Nicea's surrender secretly and thus cheated the crusaders out of the sack of the city. Relations became even more strained when, after the crusaders defeated a Turkish Seljuk army in central Anatolia, Byzantine forces stayed behind the Western army as it regained lost areas of Asia Minor. By the time the crusaders reached Antioch, they hated the Byzantines. The leaders also quarreled amongst themselves. Bohemond's trickery at Antioch, Raymond's ambitions, revealed in his establishment of his county of Tripoli, the success of Baldwin at Edessa, and the final conquest of Jerusalem established by 1100 a whole series of Western feudal principalities in Syria and Palestine.[67]

But the success of the crusaders was less dependent on the abilities of the various leaders and the military prowess of their troops than it was on two other factors. First in importance was the arrival of Italian naval power on the coasts of Syria, bringing reinforcements and naval assistance needed to reduce the Syrian Moslem coastal cities. Secondly, there was the failure of the Fatimid Egyptian fleet to intervene in these waters against the crusaders.

[65] Cahen, C. *La Syrie du Nord au Temps des Croisades* (Paris 1940), p. 201-04.
[66] *ibid.*, p. 207.   [67] *ibid.*, p. 209-26.

Of the two events, the appearance of Italian fleets off the Syrian-Palestinian coasts was the most interesting. It was a Genoese fleet at Antioch which made possible the final success of the crusaders there, and from that time on the progress of the crusading army down the coast was immeasurably assisted by sea support.[68] Even Venice in 1099 sent an Adriatic flotilla, which aided in the capture of Jaffa in the next year.[69] The interesting feature of this naval support lies in the lateness of its appearance. The routes used by the crusading armies to reach their rendezvous point, Constantinople, were almost entirely by land. Bohemond and Tancred marched across Greece. Raymond of Toulouse along the Dalmatian coast, and Robert and Godfrey down the Danube. From Constantinople they also followed a land route to Syria across Asia Minor. Not until arrival at Antioch did naval support reach them, and then at first from western Italian coasts, not Venice. This seems to suggest that the Venetians, whose naval power was the strongest of all the Italians in Byzantine and Eastern waters, had little initial enthusiasm for this enterprise and intervened with some naval assistance only when the conquest of Antioch assured success. Then their fleet appeared on the Palestinian coast more to safeguard their trade interests from the possible competition of Genoese, Pisan, and Amalfitan merchants than from any crusading zeal. With their intervention, however, the naval and trade elements of Western expansion joined the feudal and religious in the East. The conquered Syrian ports provided the Italian fleets with fabulous booty in spices and Eastern wares, and they soon established permanent factories there to control the trade and pilgrim traffic from this region to the West.[70]

The failure of the Fatimid fleet to intervene, despite pleas of the Syrian maritime coast for assistance, is much more difficult to understand. The Fatimid fleet was not inconsiderable at this time. In the late eleventh century it had included 75 galleys, 10 transports and 10 galleases under a Lord High Admiral with bases at Alexandria, Damietta, Ascalon, and other Syrian ports.[71] Perhaps it had decayed with the death of Badr in 1094. But the failure to use it at all was more probably the reflection of the weakness and

---

[68] Also of Greek, English and Flemish ships. *ibid.*, pp. 208, 211, 219, 221, 223.
[69] Hazlitt *Venice* I, 145-46.   [70] Munro *op. cit.*, p. 21-24.
[71] Al Kalkashandi *Die Geographie und Verwaltung von Aegypten* trans. Wustenfeld (Berlin 1879), p. 171-72.

passivity of the last Fatimids. And it doomed Moslem resistance to the crusaders in Syria and Palestine.[72]

To sum up, then, by 1100 Western Europeans were in control of most of the Western Mediterranean, firmly established on the islands of Corsica, Sardinia, Sicily, and Malta and in Southern Italy and pressing hard against the Balearics. Their fleets were raiding the Moslem coasts of Africa and Spain. Thanks to the crusaders they were equally dominant on the Palestine-Syrian coasts. Through Venice they controlled most of the waters of Byzantium in the Aegean and along the coasts of Greece and southern Asia Minor. Both ends of the important circle route between East and West in the Mediterranean were firmly in their hands. From a naval standpoint they controlled most of the crucial strategic naval positions in the Mediterranean, and almost all the shipping that plied these waters now had to pay them tribute. They were in control of the international routes of the Middle Sea which Byzantium and Islam had so long dominated. Particularly significant was Western control of the passages between Eastern and Western Mediterranean, thanks to Norman conquest of Malta, Sicily, and Southern Italy. Henceforth Western Islam was separated from its Eastern strongholds in Egypt and the Near East. Likewise the crusading principalities had the effect of separating Byzantium from the Moslem East except through Seljuk intermediaries.

There remains the problem of the economic life and trade of the Mediterranean-Black Sea world during this period of transition, violent change and disorder. Perhaps Moslem North Africa was most severely affected. The break between the Fatimids and Ziridites had certain immediate economic consequences, not the least important being the decree of the rulers of Kairouan in 1049 which forbade circulation of Fatimid coinage in their domains.[73] This may have adversely affected trade between Egypt and Sousse, Sfax and Medhia, as well as causing some diminution in the role of Magrebi merchants as middlemen in the international trade of the Mediterranean. But if so, the Hammadites of Bougie at first appear to have profited most. Trade moved to their domains. In 1067 al-Bakri noted that merchandise from Iraq, Hijaz, Egypt, and all parts of the Magreb was coming to this kingdom.[74]

[72] Munro *op. cit.*, p. 83-85. On Egyptian neutrality see Cahen *op. cit.*, p. 213-14, 221-22.

[73] Marçais *Berbérie*, p. 170-71.   [74] *Al Bakri*, p. 105.

After 1054 the North African trade picture became more somber. The Hilalian Arab invasion brought ruin to the fertile plains from Gabes to Bone. The agricultural lands of this region were destroyed by the plundering of the nomads, and industry, so carefully organized since the ninth century, suffered almost equally. As a matter of fact, the end of the elaborate irrigation and agricultural system of this area, established in Punic and Roman times, came in the late eleventh century, not earlier. Tunisia today still shows what nomads are capable of doing to the richest of lands.[75]

This destruction by the nomads did more than destroy the bases of Tunisian agriculture and industry. It cut the two western caravan routes through the Sahara to the Sudan and the Niger—both that passing through Ouargla and that through Gadames. Gold no longer came north to this section of the Magreb. Even the carefully organized post system which linked Ceuta with Alexandria had to be abandoned by 1048, as there ceased to be any possibility of protecting the forts along it from bedouin raids.[76] Only a coastal fringe from Tripoli to Bone and the mountainous domains of the Hammadites remained of the prosperous North Africa, which had supported the strong Aghlabid, early Fatimid, and Ziridite states. Even the nomadic Berber tribes of the interior became deracinated and arabized through their contacts with the Beni Hilal and Beni Solaim.[77]

Under these circumstances, it is not surprising that Magrebi maritime commerce declined, though it certainly did not disappear. What apparently happened was that it fell more and more into the hands of Western Europeans, principally Italians. The treaty between Roger of Sicily and Tamin of Medhia in 1075 shows how soon relations were regularized between African shores and Sicily under its new conquerors. The provision of the agreement between this same ruler and the victorious Italian flotilla, which attacked Medhia in 1087, by which he promised that he would not interfere with their shipping, seems to point to commercial activities of Western merchants in these waters. The rulers of Bougie are known to have traded extensively with the Italians from the early twelfth century on, if not before.[78]

[75] Marçais Berbérie, p. 208-14.
[76] Al Marrakeshi, p. 299. Lombard op. cit., p. 150-51.
[77] On this see Gautier op. cit., p. 385-94.
[78] Lopez "Le facteur économique dans la politique Africaine des Papes" in Rev. Hist. (1947) cxcvii, 178-86.

Spain, particularly after 1086, presented quite another picture. The Berber Almoravids were not destructive in an economic sense. Therefore their domains in both Andalusia and Morocco remained agriculturally and industrially prosperous. Furthermore, they controlled Sidjilmasa, the terminus of the westernmost caravan route to the gold of the Senegal. Over this route gold continued to flow after it had been interrupted further west. The Almoravid's gold dinars, or maraboutins, as they were known, remained for centuries the most important gold coinage in the West.[79] Upon this Almoravid prosperity and that maintained by their successors, the Almohads, the great culture of Moslem Spain in the twelfth century was based.[80]

It seems probable, however, that this period, particularly after 1086, saw an increase of trade between the Almoravid domains and the rest of Latin Western Europe. Despite Italian raiding, trading was not unknown. The *mancusi* coined in Catalonia in this period[81] and in nearby Montpellier suggest an active commerce with Moslem Spain as well as Africa.[82] Certainly by the twelfth century, this commerce, largely in the hands of the Genoese and Pisans, reached sizable proportions.

There is less information about the East than the West in this period. Fatimid Syria and Egypt, after the terrible disorders and convulsions that afflicted them between 1060 and 1073, seem in the last years of the century under Badr to have recovered a large measure of their former prosperity. The devaluation of the Fatimid gold dinar, however, suggests some diminution of the prosperity of this region.[83] Perhaps it was the result of less gold reaching Egypt from North Africa because of the break with the Ziridites and because of the Hilalian nomad cutting of the caravan routes south to the Sudan. The trade of Egypt with the Magreb was probably less important after 1052 than before. But there is no evidence of any diminution in the Red Sea and Nubian commerce. Nor was Syria economically ruined by civil war and Seljuk invasions. When the crusaders and their Italian naval allies captured the coastal cities from Alexandretta to Gaza, they found warehouses filled with

[79] Lopez "Orig. du Cap. Gén.," p. 446-47.
[80] Hitti *History of the Arabs*, p. 557-601.
[81] Bloch "Le problème d'or," p. 20-21.
[82] *Hist. Gén. de Languedoc* new ed. v, 346.
[83] Lane-Poole *Egypt*, p. 147-48.

the spices and precious goods of the East—evidence of a continuing trade with Persia, India and China.[84]

The Byzantine Empire was perhaps less fortunate than Egypt and Syria. The incursions of the Seljuk Turks and of Turkish nomads in South Russia seem to have interfered with old established trade routes leading to Trebizond and Cherson. And the Italian merchants, even before 1081, were already skimming off the economic cream of Constantinople's Western trade. The old governmental economic controls had been already largely abandoned before the time of Alexius Comnenus. The opposition to the establishment of a grain monopoly in the capital in 1073 by Michael VII indicates how things had changed since the time of Liudprand of Cremona.[85] Free trade had become the rule, and the older system could not be enforced.

But even more serious from the standpoint of Byzantium's economic future was another development already noted, the tendency for the international trade routes to bypass Asia Minor and the Black Sea region and flow west directly by way of Syria and Egypt. Even before the Crusades, the appearance of more and more Italian ships from Bari, Amalfi, and Venice in Alexandretta (Antioch's port) and the coastal cities of Moslem Syria and Egypt tended to draw trade south out of the orbit of Constantinople. As long as Byzantine rulers controlled Antioch and had a firm grip with adequate sea power in Crete and Cyprus, they could share in the profits of this commerce. But after the loss of Antioch in 1086 and Venice's commercial privileges granted in 1082, this traffic tended to bypass Byzantine controlled areas. The Crusades represented the final step in the direct trade connection between the Latin West and the Moslem East without Constantinople's participation in the process. To understand this point is to see why the Comneni in the next century were so eager to establish some sort of control over Antioch and had so little interest in expelling the Seljuks from Asia Minor. They were seeking trade revenue, not territory.[86]

It was this major shift of trade routes south, even before cru-

[84] Munro *op. cit.*, p. 77.

[85] Bratianu, G. "Le monopole de blé" in *Byzantion* (1934) IX, 643-62.

[86] This aspect of the policy pursued by the Comneni has long been misunderstood. The Byzantine revenues from Cyprus in the 12th century amounted to 700 lbs. of gold annually, showing the value of this trade. Arnold of Lubeck *Chron. Slav* in *MGH Script.* XXI, 178.

sading conquests in Edessa and Syria assured the channelling of trade to Syria, which explains why Trebizond and Cherson lost so much importance. It explains, even more than nomadic invasions in South Russia, why both the Varangian kingdoms and the Varangian route began to wither from this time on. International trade routes were bypassing the Black Sea-Russian regions.

Even then, of course, Constantinople remained a great metropolis, prosperous and rich, and an important source of industrial and luxury products for the entire Mediterranean, as the testimony of Benjamin of Tudela in the next century makes very clear.[87] But the persistent financial difficulties of the Comneni[88] and the presence of Italian traders who gathered the major middleman's profits show that less and less of Byzantium's wealth from this time on was to remain in the hands of either her emperors or her citizens. Already by 1100 the Byzantine Empire had become, to a large extent, a colonial area economically exploited by Western merchants, as the West had been exploited by the Syrians and Greeks at the time of Justinian.

To some extent the same situation existed in the Moslem East. Even before the Crusades, the attempts of Egypt's government to maintain a merchant fleet in the Mediterranean seem to have been abandoned. The collapse of North Africa under the impetus of the Hilalian Arab invasion and the conquest of Sicily further destroyed the position of the Magrebi and Moslem Sicilian middlemen merchants trading with Syria and the East. The Italians hastened to take their place. The Crusades simply represented the culmination of a process. After 1100 all commerce from Syria and Palestine and most of that from Egypt was carried in Western bottoms.

There remains Latin Europe itself, which of course benefited most from changed conditions. Not only did Italian merchants come to monopolize almost all of the Mediterranean trade of Byzantium, Syria, and Egypt, but the opportunities afforded them by the Norman conquest of the rich industrial and agricultural island of Sicily were not neglected. As already noted, trade with Moslem Africa and Spain was similarly developed, though perhaps not so much in this period as in the next century.

An important change was that Pisa and Genoa gradually came

[87] Benjamin of Tudela *Travels* in *Contemporaries of Marco Polo* ed. Komroff (New York 1928), p. 264-66.
[88] Runciman *Byzantine Civilization*, p. 177.

to replace the Campanian cities of Amalfi, Salerno, Gaeta, and Naples as the great international traders of the Christian West. Not that buccaneering was abandoned by the mariners from these Northern Italian centers.[89] But by 1100 trading, based on capital built up in large measure by means not too scrupulous, replaced raiding as a major economic activity.[90] The turning point was probably the Crusades. Pisa and Genoa began to share with Venice and other centers in the carrying of pilgrims to the Holy Land and in the trade in the spices and Eastern wares available in the cities of the Syrian-Palestinian coast. They became Venice's chief competitors in Eastern waters and remained so during the remainder of the Middle Ages.

The rise of Pisa's and Genoa's maritime and economic strength in both Eastern and Western Mediterranean waters had immense effects upon the path of European trade. Their merchants began to carry Eastern and other wares to the coasts from Barcelona to the Tiber. As they did, they revived the economic life of these regions. A few instances may help to show the results for Western Europe. Barcelona in the tenth century had been largely non-commercial.[91] Between 1054 and 1074 her economic status had so changed that her sea laws were written down.[92] Montpellier and Narbonne's commerce had become important enough so that they negotiated a trade treaty in 1085.[93] The Montpellier area, at the mouth of the Rhone, was, as a matter of fact, immediately affected by the revival of the Rhone Valley route. Montpellier soon became a sizable town, surrounded in 1090 by walls.[94] The Bishop of Maguelone moved from the interior, reunited his chapter, and began the rebuilding of Maguelone, destroyed in the eighth century.[95] Bridges were constructed, agreements on tolls were negotiated and money became important once more for those who had the right to coin it.[96] Marseilles again became an important port, as well.

[89] On 12th century buccaneering at Genoa see Lopez *Dieci Documenti della Guerra di Corso* (Milan 1938).

[90] Lopez "Orig. du Cap. Gén.," p. 446-51.

[91] Dupont *op. cit.*, p. 29-30.

[92] Poumaride *Les Usages de Barcelona*, p. 58-62.

[93] *Cart. des Guillems* ed. Germain (Montpellier 1884-86), p. 169-70.

[94] Guiraud, L. "Recherches topographiques sur Montpellier au Moyen Age" in *Mém. Soc. Arch. Mont.* 2nd ser. I, 92.

[95] Arnaud de Verdale *op. cit.*, pp. 508, 510.

[96] *Cart. des Guillems*, p. 98-99. *Cart. de Gellone*, pp. 23, 267, 293, 332.

an merchants also began to appear in Northern Europe in numbers. Gregory VII in 1074, for instance, remonstrated King Philip I of France for his cheating of a number of Italians in his domains.[97] Nor were Alpine routes to the north from the Po Valley neglected. Italian merchants were carrying northern cloth to Genoa in 1095.[98] Everywhere, along every route, trade with the East by the Rhone, by the Alps, even by the Danube, was increasing. The Hungarians, settled and Christianized, had become at last a part of Western civilization. Crusaders passed through their domains on their way to the Holy Land, and there was also a colony of Hungarians in Constantinople.[99]

An index of these trade connections with the East is to be seen in the increase in gold in the West beyond Italy. A Lorraine abbey was able to loan 500 byzants to the Countess of Hainault in 1071.[100] An abbot of St. Laurent near Narbonne possessed an ounce of gold in 1060.[101] Catalonia coined *mancusi* with the name of a Catalonian prince embossed thereon.[102] So, too, did Melgeuil in 1080.[103] The *Song of Roland*, dating from this period, is filled with references to byzants and mangons (*mancusi*). In Normandy, gold byzants were already known in 1100.[104] These are all indications of the growing absorption of Western Europe into the international trading system of the Mediterranean and its gradual turn from a silver to gold standard.

By 1100, then, the Latin West had begun to come into its own. From a naval standpoint its ships controlled the major areas of the Mediterranean from Spain to Syria, and its peoples held those positions and bases which could make this naval power effective. Its Italian cities had become the great international middlemen carrying the wares of the East to the West and vice versa. They had opened up again to large-scale commerce the old Rhone Valley route, while still maintaining important traffic through the Alpine passes. The whole coast from Barcelona to the Tiber again hummed with economic life, and trade flowing from this region north began again to link France and Belgium and England firmly with the Mediterranean, as had been the case in Roman and Merovingian times. But with this great difference: The East, both Mos-

[97] Jaffé *Registrum* II, 115, 132, 146. [98] Schaube *op. cit.*, pp. 65-66, 89-96.
[99] Heyd *op. cit.*, p. 82-84. [100] Bloch *op. cit.*, p. 14-15.
[101] *ibid.*, p. 12-13. [102] *ibid.*, p. 20-21.
[103] *Hist. Gén. de Languedoc* v, 346.
[104] Deslisle, L. in *Bibl. de l'École des Chartes* (1848-9) v, 207.

lem and Byzantine, had become the passive commercial region, the West the active trade agent. Even Moslem Spain and Africa appear to have begun to pay economic tribute to the Latin West. Western Europe was already in the process of becoming the dominant area of the Mediterranean, Byzantium and Islam the subsidiary ones. The economic groundwork had been laid, not only for the great culture of the twelfth and thirteenth centuries, but for the maritime, economic, industrial and commercial leadership which Western European civilization has maintained ever since.

By 1100 Europe, formed in the eighth and ninth centuries by Latin Church and Carolingians, had at last come of age.

Conclusion

The many changes and shifts in maritime strength and economic development which took place in the Mediterranean-Black Sea world between 500 and 1100 saw Western Europe, the region which throughout had the least strength, emerge the victor over Byzantium and Islam. This was surprising. It was in many ways as startling as Rome's triumph in the Mediterranean more than a millennium earlier. And it marks the beginning of the gradual growth of Western European civilization to its present position of world dominance.

It must not be supposed, however, that by 1100 the victory of Western Europe was complete or conclusive. The next century saw certain rallies in three earlier centers of maritime strength and economic life in the Mediterranean world. The Islamic peoples of the West rallied to form a united Moslem-Spanish and North African kingdom under the Almoravids and Almohads. Under their rule Spain, Morocco, and Algeria rebuilt fleets, retook the Balearics and North Africa, and enjoyed again a high level of economic prosperity. Particularly rich was the culture developed in Moorish Spain in this period. Similarly, Egypt and Syria were reunited under Saladin and were formed into a strongly prosperous and efficient state—militarily powerful enough to drive the Christian crusaders back from the interior to the coastline of Syria and Palestine. Though Saladin's domains were perhaps not so advanced intellectually as Moslem Andalusia, the level of civilization maintained was high. Byzantium under its Comneni rulers also recovered a large measure of political, military, and economic power. Its cultural contributions, and developments, particularly in the artistic sphere, were as remarkable as those produced at the time of Justinian or the Macedonian Emperors.

Not until the thirteenth century did the conquest of all Spain, save Granada, and the destruction of Byzantine power in the Fourth Crusade deal fatal blows to two of these revivals. These two events linked Western European Atlantic coasts with the Mediterranean by way of the Strait of Gibraltar and opened up the Black Sea to Italian merchant fleets. The Crusading states of Syria and Egypt, however, disappeared in the process and fell to Mameluke Egypt, with only Cyprus remaining as a remnant of Latin power in the East.

But it must be emphasized that the naval power and economic strength of Ayyubid Egypt, Comnenian Byzantium, and Almoravid and Almohad Spain were local in nature. Culturally vigorous these centers remained, but they never seriously threatened Western European dominance of the waters and commerce of the Middle Sea. Newer maritime centers in the West, such as Barcelona, Montpellier, and Marseilles were, after 1100, actually far more important rivals to Pisa, Genoa, and Venice than were the Byzantines or Moslems of Spain and Egypt. And even these shores did not displace Italian ships and merchants from their control of the Middle Sea. Up until 1500 they remained what they were in 1100, the chief seamen and masters of commerce of the Mediterranean world. Only in the sixteenth century did they lose out to the Spanish, Portuguese, French, English, and Dutch, as the trade routes and commerce of Europe spread to the four corners of the earth.

Appendix

I. The Mysterious Unknown Factors

The study of naval power and its economic consequences in the Mediterranean world from 500 to 1100 may be important to the historians of this period, but it cannot solve many of the perplexing problems that confront them. Far too many questions are still left unanswered. Perhaps they are the most important questions. To a large extent maritime strength and economic development are actually the results rather than the causes of the changes that took place in the period. They are a reflection of those mysterious inner forces that appear to infuse peoples and cultures with vigor and strength at certain times and to lead them to chaos, decay and collapse at other times. While a study of them assists the historian and thoughtful reader to a balanced judgment of the nature and causes of change, they cannot give him any final answer.

For instance, neither naval and military policies nor economic factors really explain why the Romania, refounded by Justinian, collapsed in the seventh century. Nor do they explain why the Carolingians in the ninth century and the Ottos in the tenth failed to muster sufficient strength to break into a Mediterranean dominated by Byzantium and Islam, while the Italian fleets and feudal adventurers of the eleventh century were able to do so.

Still less does a consideration of such factors give any final answer as to why the Moslem world of North Africa was unable to defend itself in the eleventh century against nomadism. Yet the weaker and less prosperous Islamic society of earlier times triumphed over Kharijism in the eighth century and the rising of Abu Zezid's nomadic bedouins in the tenth. Why did the Ziridites fail, while the Aghlabids and Fatimids proved successful?

Byzantium's waxing and waning presents problems of equal magnitude. Why did this Empire rally under the Isaurians to meet the challenge of the Arab Ommayids, and fail to respond to the weaker threat of the Moslems upon the sea in the ninth and early tenth centuries? And why, after its magnificent comeback under the Macedonian Emperors, did it collapse in the late eleventh century? Certainly the triumph of the West was more closely related to the mysterious weaknesses of Islamic and Byzantine societies in the eleventh century than to any inherent superiority of its own. Yet, why did such weaknesses develop and what exactly were they?

Obviously a full study of all phases of these civilizations is necessary before any conclusive answer can be given to such questions. Perhaps a study of the religious, cultural, and intellectual processes is a more rewarding method of approach than any other, though institutional, agricultural, and political aspects should not be neglected. Only as one gains a fuller understanding of the minds and attitudes of the men who lived in each of these cultures can one grope toward a full understanding of the ebb and flow which each of these societies, Islamic, Western and Byzantine, revealed at varying periods. Naval power and economic life are just two aspects of this process.

Nevertheless, it is the duty of the historian to form judgments, however tentative and ill-advised they may appear to be. And in this respect the collapse of Islamic and Byzantine civilizations in the eleventh century provides a starting point for examining their particular weaknesses, as they developed throughout the years covered by this book.

Byzantium's weakness, which led to her fatal decline in the course of the eleventh century, seems due less to poor leadership or any lack of institutional development in her society, than to something else—her rigid, defensive attitude toward the outside world. She inherited this attitude from the Roman Empire, developed it further at the time of Justinian and in the course of the Isaurian struggle with the Ommayids fastened it firmly upon herself. This attitude was embodied in the cultural and economic barriers she raised against all outsiders. Thus she not only fought her enemies, but she closed her own people defensively within a hard shell. She made herself a fossilized state, rigidly resisting outside pressures. Thus her vital juices were sucked out by Italian and other foreign traders, who were her main economic link with the world beyond her borders, while her culture continued to refine itself into something approaching futility. She became a living triumph of archaism, until the whole dried system collapsed under its own weight.

The Islamic failure was very different. Abbassid Iraq and Syria fell to the Turks, Fatimid Egypt decayed, Ziridite Africa collapsed, and Ommayid Spain disappeared as a result of internal weaknesses, but they were not those of Byzantium. The Moslems had during this period, and kept later, a freedom in economic development and a cultural and intellectual breadth of spirit in inquiry quite the opposite of Byzantine rigidity. The failure in the Islamic world was political. Ibn Khaldun, the wisest of Moslem social philosophers, viewing his people's failure in retrospect, seems to have sensed this quite clearly. He pointed out that the nomadic influence in North Africa was decisive in these words, "a land held by the Arabs [he refers to Arab nomads] is a ruined land." He also noted the insecurity and lack of permanence of Islamic ruling dynasties—a sort of three-generation-shirt-sleeve-to-shirt-sleeve tradition.

But perhaps he did not probe deeply enough. The causes of both nomad inroads and dynastic insecurity lay in the Islamic anarchic individualism of social and particularly political patterns. This meant that the Arab and Moslem aristocracies could never be adequately used in the service of the state, to build a self-perpetuating bureaucracy and army in the interests of the population as a whole. Moslem rulers never had what Rome and Byzantium possessed in the way of political institutions and what England and France were to foster so carefully. Only a very few Islamic potentates of great personal ability such as Moawiyah, al-Moeizz and Abd-ar-Rahman III were ever able to harness Moslem and Arab individualism to the service of the state.

Most other rulers, however able, therefore followed a different system. They entrusted their government departments to social inferiors—to Christians, Jews, and slaves. Thanks to the evil harem system, inherited largely from Sassanian Persia, they even chose their consorts from the same groups. Their armies tended more and more to be recruited from slave or mercenary sources. Such military forces and bureaucracies were completely amenable to the will of the sovereign, as the Arab aristocracy never was. But this political system had terrible consequences for Islamic civilization. When strong dynastic personalities disappeared and weaker ones came upon the throne, the slaves and inferiors who actually governed and defended the state discovered that they were not the servants of the ruler, they were his masters. They then rose in revolt, and chaos ensued. The protectors murdered those they were supposed to protect, and the nomads marched in to destroy the settled economic life upon which these kingdoms depended.

If Byzantine failure was a too rigid, too defensive culture and economic life, Islamic failure lay in the use of a politically dictatorial slave-state system. And to Moslem successor states such as those of the Mamelukes and Ottoman Turks this same evil system was bequeathed to spread its poison through the veins of later Moslem civilizations.

Viewed in this light, the advantage that Western Europe had over its rivals lay in the fact that it lacked the defensive rigidity of Byzantine culture and economic life and the slave-state system of Islam. The Italian mariners and Western feudal adventurers were crude and uncouth in many respects, but they had the flexibility of freedom in their political, economic, and cultural life. The West has it still to a greater degree than any other section of the world.

II. A Parallel with the Ancient World

Obviously a comparison between the Mediterranean world in Roman times and after A.D. 700, when it was divided into three distinct culture areas, is an impossibility. The single World Empire of Rome was quite different from the Mediterranean world which followed its breakup. But if one views the classical world at the time of Greece and Persia, there is a remarkable parallel in events. The Byzantine Empire of A.D. 700 covered almost the identical regions that the classical Greeks did, if one adds the interior of Asia Minor, actually largely under Greek influence since the time of Croesus. Classical Hellas and her colonies were placed around the Aegean. Most of Sicily and Magna Graecia were Greek. So, too, was the south coast of Russia and the Crimea, where Greek colonies were very numerous. Greeks extended as far east as Cyprus, which was divided with the Phoenicians. In 700 Byzantium covered the identical area, even to a division of Cyprus with the Syrian Moslems.

If one joins Semitic Carthage's Western domains with the Persian Empire and adds Greek Cyrene, one discovers that this area, too, is almost identical with that covered by the Ommayid Empire. In each case the Western European region was weak and thoroughly disorganized. The classical Greeks, like Byzantium, were able from their central position and island possessions to separate African naval power and trade from that of Syria. Like Byzantium too, they faced a double attack, from the west a Carthaginian assault on their Sicilian bastion, from the east a combined land and sea campaign. These attacks we know as the Persian Wars. And in defending themselves the classical Greeks, like the Byzantines in 717-718, weathered the storm chiefly because of their superior sea power. Salamis and Mycale bear a startling resemblance to the naval war of 717-718, and Himera is not unlike the great assaults on Sicily between 704 and 752. In each case the victories were followed by Greek control of the Mediterranean, in classical times the age of Cimon and Pericles, in Byzantine times the Mediterranean Sea Empire of 752-827.

In each case the attacking Eastern state fell after its defeat at the hands of the Greeks, the Ommayid Empire being replaced by that of the Abbassids, just as the Persian state was replaced by that of Alexander. In each case, too, the second Empire soon broke up. The Abbassid Empire was divided into a Tulunid, Ikhshid, and Fatimid Egypt much like that of the Ptolemies, and an Abbassid state proper much like the kingdom of the Seleucids in area covered and in weaknesses. Byzantium greatly resembles a combination of Hellenistic Greece and Pergamum. Bulgaria seems very like Macedonia. And the same sort of balance of power which prevailed in these areas in Hellenistic times existed during the ninth and tenth centuries A.D.

Meanwhile in both cases in the West, Africans and Greeks fought it out over Sicily from the same regions in much the same way. Palermo was the African center under the name of Panormus in both periods, and Syracuse was the Greek and Byzantine center. In each period the Greeks gradually lost out to the more aggressive Africans. Only when Greek assistance from the East arrived were the Sicilian Hellenes able to take the offensive. In each case there was a last great expedition west, the classical one being that of Pyrrhus, the Byzantine one that of George Maniaces. Each failed after initial success.

And the final victory was won in each case by a third party coming from Italy in the north and overwhelming both the Greek and the African dominion of Sicily and Southern Italy. In classical times that power was Rome. In medieval times it was the Norman feudal adventurers, encouraged by a spiritual Rome.

In each case, when the new aggressive Westerners had conquered Sicily and Southern Italy and won naval control in the Western Mediterranean, they turned east. In each case they did so partly because of requests for assistance from the Aegean world with which they were closely linked in culture. In classical times the aggressors were Macedonia and the Empire of the Seleucids, in the late eleventh century the aggressors were the Seljuk Turks. The appearance of both the Romans and the crusaders in the Aegean area resulted in the defeat of those attacking the Greek world. Also in both cases friction developed between the Greek inhabitants (suspicious of the help and what it portended) and the Westerners. And both Byzantines and Hellenistic Greeks were quite justified in their suspicions. For in each case, after some years, the Westerners overthrew the Greek governments and destroyed the civilizations they had built up, thus making themselves masters of the Mediterranean.

This close parallel between the two periods cannot be considered mere accident. Obviously political geography, naval power, and the characteristic reactions of peoples and civilizations must be viewed as much more constant than most historians are willing to admit.

III. The Disruptive Role of the Fatimids

The importance of the Fatimids in the disintegration of the Islamic World of the Mediterranean in the eleventh century has never been sufficiently emphasized. Older accounts, such as Wustenfeld's classic history of the dynasty and Quatremère's life of al-Moeizz, the greatest Fatimid ruler, leave much to be desired. So too do later ones. Even Ibn Khaldun does not seem to appreciate their full significance. Yet these Shiah rulers played a part in the weakening of the Dar-es-Islam as vital as that of Monophysitism in ending Justinian's Romania or of Iconoclasm in finally splitting the Greek and Latin Christian worlds.

On the surface the Fatimids do not seem to contribute an unusual chapter in the turbulent rise and fall of Islamic dynasties. Ommayids, Abbassids, Idrissids, Tulunids, Ikhshids, Aghlabids, Saffarids, and many others had appeared before them in many parts of the Mohammedan world. Furthermore, their Empire was in a sense but the political expression of North Africa's naval and economic mastery of the Mediterranean. The spread of their domains west to Ceuta and east to include Egypt, Syria, and the Hijaz was thus simply the result of the control of the trade and waters of the Middle Sea exercised by the merchants and sailors of the Magreb in the tenth century. Justinian's revived Romania was a very similar expression of Graeco-Syrian maritime and economic power four centuries earlier.

In addition, their Empire can be considered in a different light, as a reaction of the Berbers of North Africa against the arabization to which they had been exposed since the eighth century. Kharijism had been a first unsuccessful reaction; the Fatimid movement was a successful one. The Fatimid movement, having overthrown the Arab Aghlabids, then turned east and west, spearheaded by al-Moeizz's loyal Kotamas, to expand over Algeria and Morocco and Arab Egypt, Syria and Arabia. Thus, just as the Caliphate of the Abbassids was in part made possible by a Persian reaction from the East directed against the Arabs of Syria and the Near East, so the Fatimids represented a very similar movement of the Berbers from the West in the tenth and eleventh centuries. In both cases the Arabs at the center of the Islamic world were the victims of newly converted peoples on the periphery.

There is still another point to consider. The period of Fatimid expansion and greatest power was one of real prosperity for Islamic peoples. Not only did their own domains in North Africa, Sicily, Syria, and Egypt prosper mightily under their rule, but so too did those of their rivals, the Ommayids of Spain and the Moslem dynasties of the East. The Age of the Fatimids was equally distinguished by the vigor of intellectual life in Cordova, Cairo, and Bagdad.

Had this been all there was to Fatimid expansion, their Empire might have resulted in only good for the Mohammedan peoples who inhabited the shores of the Mediterranean. It might have had few serious consequences for Islam. But in addition to Berber economic and political dominance and prosperity and intellectual advance, these Shiah rulers brought elements with them not so favorable in their results. These were the religious doctrines which they introduced along with their rule—their own heretical brand of Shiism, which fatally divided the Dar-es-Islam at a crucial time.

They were not the first or the last to profess this Alid faith. Shiism went back to the quarrels between Ali and Moawiyah in the earliest days of Islam. The Shiah movement had long been strong in Persia, where it represented a kind of Persian nationalism which early flamed into serious Alid revolts against Abbassid authority. In Morocco, Idrissid rulers had emphasized their descent from Ali in refusing to recognize the political authority of Bagdad's Caliphs. Other nests of Shiah opinion existed elsewhere in Arabia and the Near East.

But prior to the time of the Fatimids such Alid movements had done little to compromise the cultural and religious oneness of the Islamic world. Despite political differentiation, the Dar-es-Islam had a common religious and cultural unity. The Abbassid Caliphs had lost political power over local dynasties both in the East and in the West, but prior to the Fatimids their religious prestige as Caliphs of all Islam was never challenged, not even by the Spanish Ommayids.

No sooner had the Fatimids come into power in Kairouan, however, then they shattered this religious unity by proclaiming themselves Caliphs in opposition to Bagdad. As they spread their rule eastwards and westwards they increased their religious sway over the larger portion of the Islamic world. In self-defense their Western rival, Abd-ar-Rahman III of Spain, who had a large Berber Moslem population open to the Fatimid fifth column and who feared their political ambitions, followed suit and proclaimed himself Caliph. As a result, by the middle of the tenth century an Islamic world formerly united in religion suddenly found itself divided, with three Caliphs, one in Cordova, one in Kairouan and one in Bagdad, each claiming supreme authority. This impossible situation greatly resembled that faced by late medieval Europe when the Great Schism caused a similar destruction of religious unity. The responsibility for this Islamic religious crisis lies at the door of the Fatimids.

But Fatimid success caused more than a divided Caliphate. Their own particular brand of Shiism emphasized an element heretofore alien and foreign to Orthodox Islam, the divine character of the ruler. The Fatimids claimed a religious and divine mission which no other rulers of the Moslem world had done before them— not even the Abbassid Caliphs, who went much further along these lines than their Ommayid predecessors. The Fatimids merged church and state in a way quite foreign to anything Islam had known previously. Seizing upon the Alid doctrine of Imanship, they proclaimed themselves the source of Divine Revelation. This claim reached its apogee in the person of the mad al-Hakim, but was present in all Fatimid thinking and actions.

Prior to the Fatimids, Islam's most striking characteristic had been its insistence upon the divinity of God and the humanness of Man—even including the prophet Mohammed himself. Islam's quarrel with Christianity lay primarily in its refusal to accept the Graeco-Roman concept of the Word made Flesh or the common divinity and humanness of Christ. In this Islam was closer to Semitic Judaism than it was to Christianity. And it was just this basic tenet of faith that Shiah Fatimid doctrines compromised.

Furthermore up to the tenth century there had always been a separation between the temporal rule of the Caliphs and viceroys of the Moslem world and the religious side of Islam. The Cadis, who interpreted the *Koran* and the religious law which developed out of it, were largely independent of temporal authority and seldom hesitated to rebuke even the strongest Islamic rulers when they infringed upon the customs laid down by Mohammedan tradition. As public consciences their warnings were frequently heeded. But the Fatimids, claiming their divine Imanship, broke with these traditions too and laid down the law to Cadis and laymen alike.

The result was a crisis wherever Fatimid rule penetrated. The Orthodox Cadis and population denied both the doctrine of

Imanship and the pretensions to religious authority which grew out of it. Some Fatimid rulers like al-Moeizz were wise enough not to press their claims too far in the face of this opposition. On the whole, though, most of the dynasty, and particularly al-Hakim, used force on their religious opponents and whipped Orthodox Cadis and subjects into line by use of mercenary and slave Berber, Negro, and Turkish soldiery. Thus religious as opposed to political persecution made its first appearance on a wide scale within Islam, heretofore free of all except occasional repression for intellectual heresies. And this intolerance and persecution was extended to the Christian and Jewish elements of the population. A hostile Orthodox Spanish West and a hostile Abbassid East thus faced a Fatimid Empire which seemed to violate the basic tenets of their faith and imposed heretical views by force upon a largely reluctant and tyrannized population.

As a result, the Islamic world in general turned in upon itself in religious civil conflict and controversy. Just so was Europe split in the sixteenth century, when the Reformation destroyed its older religious unity and left it for a time unable to check the Ottoman Turks, who were overwhelming the Balkans and Central Europe and seizing control of much of the Mediterranean. It is not surprising, then, that Islamic society disintegrated so easily under the blows of nomadic Almoravids, Caramathes, Hilalian Arabs, and Seljuk Turks. Nor should it surprise us that Western adventurers and crusaders and Italian seamen so easily seized control of the Mediterranean from the slipping grasp of Islam. Paralyzed within, the Mohammedan world was in no position to give more than a token, peacemeal resistance to her foreign foes.

It is true that the Shiah Fatimid dominion did not long endure. By the middle of the eleventh century it had retreated from North Africa and Sicily, and a century later Saladin ended its final stand in Egypt. Sunnite Orthodoxy triumphed everywhere in the lands which the Fatimids had formerly controlled. But until the Fatimid Empire disappeared, its effect, lying as it did athwart the Islamic world, was to hopelessly divide and paralyze Islamic peoples and help make possible their failure to hold the water and trade of the Middle Sea. Shiah doctrines have remained since that time, in their later Persian and Anatolian manifestations and in their hold upon the Druzes, the Yemen, and the Mahdi of the Sudan and others, a powerful divisive element within Islam.

Index